Fodor's  SECOND New EDITION

Cuba

The complete guide, thoroughly up-to-date

Packed with details that will make your trip

The must-see sights, off and on the beaten path

What to see, what to skip

City strolls, countryside adventures

Smart lodging and dining options

Essential local do's and taboos

Transportation tips, distances and directions

Key contacts, savvy travel tips

When to go, what to pack

Clear, accurate, easy-to-use maps

Fodor's Travel Publications, Inc.
New York • Toronto • London • Sydney • Auckland
www.fodors.com/

Fodor's Cuba

Editorial Contributors: Rob Andrews, Miguel Barnet, Angel Martinez Bermejo, Heidi Sarna, Helayne Schiff, M. T. Schwartzman, Dinah Spritzer, Steve Veale, Manuel Vincent, Chris Warnasch
Production Editorial: Laura M. Kidder, Linda K. Schmidt
Maps: Carlos y Chema Requejo, *cartographer*; Robert Blake, *map editor*
Design: Fabrizio La Rocca, *creative director*; Guido Caroti, *associate art director*; Jolie Novak, *photo editor*
Production/Manufacturing: Mike Costa
Cover Photograph: Bryan Whitney

Copyright

Second Edition

ISBN 0–679–03404–8

Special Sales

Fodor's Travel Publications are available at special discounts for bulk purchases for sales promotions or premiums. Special editions, including personalized covers, excerpts of existing guides, and corporate imprints, can be created in large quantities for special needs. For more information, contact your local bookseller or write to Special Markets, Fodor's Travel Publications, 201 East 50th Street, New York, NY 10022. Inquiries from Canada should be directed to your local Canadian bookseller or sent to Random House of Canada, Ltd., Marketing Department, 1265 Aerowood Drive, Mississauga, Ontario L4W 1B9. Inquiries from the United Kingdom should be sent to Fodor's Travel Publications, 20 Vauxhall Bridge Road, London SW1V 2SA.

CONTENTS

ON THE ROAD WITH FODOR'S

CUBA, THE LARGEST of the Antilles islands, is unarguably the most controversial and notorious neighbor of the continental United States. Is there anyone who has never dreamed, before and after Ernest Hemingway, of stowing away on this tropical island paradise just 90 miles from Key West? Recent political history notwithstanding, no one can return from Cuba indifferent. No praise seems an exaggeration of Cuba's charms, beginning with Christopher Columbus's description of the island as "The most beautiful thing I have ever seen" 500 years ago. Even today, despite Cuba's embattled economy, the island seems determined to live up to its reputation, and there is little doubt that Cuba will re-emerge as a major tourist attraction in the years to come. In these pages we give detailed information that will help you to enjoy Cuba to the fullest.

How to Use This Guide

Organization

Up front, **Highlights** discusses a number of recent developments in Cuba of interest to travelers. **Fodor's Choice** has our picks for the very best there is to see and do—the sights and activities that make Cuba such a rich, exciting destination.

The first chapter, **Essential Information,** is an easy-to-use section divided alphabetically by topic. Under each listing you'll find tips and information that will help you accomplish what you need to in Cuba. You'll also find addresses and telephone numbers of organizations and companies that offer destination-related services and information and publications.

The **destination chapters** that follow are arranged geographically. Each is broken into city and/or regional sections that have information on exploring, shopping, sports, dining, lodging, and arts and nightlife.

Icons and Symbols

★   Our special recommendations
☞   Sends you to another section of the guide for more information
☎   Telephone number

FAX   Fax number
☉   Opening and closing times
💵   Admission prices

Numbers in black circles that appear on the maps and in the margins correspond to one another.

Dining and Lodging

Restaurants and hotels are chosen with a view to giving you the cream of the crop in each location and in each price range. Dollar signs in the margin denote price ranges.

Unless otherwise noted, restaurant ratings throughout the book follow this price chart:

CATEGORY	COST*
$$$$	over $30
$$$	$25–$30
$$	$20–$25
$	under $20

Prices are per person and do not include wine or service (although they do include two beers or a soft drink).

Unless otherwise noted, lodging ratings throughout the book follow this price chart:

CATEGORY	COST*
$$$$	over $100
$$$	$60–$100
$$	$35–$60
$	under $35

Prices are for two people in a double room in high season (December–April and July–August). Cuban hotels impose no added service charges or local taxes.

New This Year

We're proud to announce that the American Society of Travel Agents has endorsed Fodor's as its guidebook of choice. ASTA is the world's largest and most influential travel trade association, operating in more than 170 countries, with 27,000 members pledged to adhere to a strict code of ethics reflecting the Society's motto, "Integrity in Travel." ASTA shares Fodor's devotion to providing smart, honest travel information and advice to travelers, and we've long recommended that our readers consult ASTA member agents for the experience and professionalism they bring to the table.

On the Web, check out Fodor's site (www.fodors.com/) for information on major destinations around the world and travel-savvy interactive features. The Web site also lists the 85-plus radio stations nationwide that carry the *Fodor's Travel Show*, a live call-in program that airs every weekend. Tune in to hear guests discuss their wonderful adventures—or call for answers to your most pressing travel questions.

Please Write to Us

You can use this book in the confidence that all prices and opening times are based on information supplied to us at press time; Fodor's cannot accept responsibility for any errors. Time inevitably brings changes, so always confirm information when it matters—especially if you're making a detour to visit a specific place. In addition, when making reservations be sure to mention if you have a disability or are traveling with children, if you prefer a private bath or a certain type of bed, or if you have specific dietary needs or other concerns.

Were the restaurants we recommended as described? Did our hotel picks exceed your expectations? Did you find a museum we recommended a waste of time? If you have complaints, we'll look into them and revise our entries when the facts warrant it. If you've discovered a special place that we haven't included, we'll pass the information along to our correspondents and have them check it out. So send us your feedback, positive *and* negative: E-mail us at editors@fodors.com (specifying the name of the book on the subject line) or write the Cuba editor at Fodor's, 201 East 50th Street, New York, New York 10022. Have a wonderful trip!

Karen Cure
Editorial Director

CUBA: A LATIN COCKTAIL

DELICIOUS, ROMANTIC, so near and yet so far, Cuba is the perfect impossible love—beautiful and forbidden, hermetically sealed, vacuum-packed in a steamy past of nostalgia and desire. That this lovely damsel in distress should languish as both captive and exile just 90 miles from Key West seems the ultimate tease, the final irony in North America's ongoing tug of war with itself.

Throughout history, falling in love with Cuba has been a syndrome of all but epidemic proportions, beginning with the discoverer's open-mouthed, *"Nunca tan fermosa cosa vido"* ("Never such lovely thing I see" [sic]) and continuing through passionate affairs with the likes of Ernest Hemingway, Winston Churchill, Ava Gardner, Buster Keaton, Graham Green, Edward VIII, and a lengthy list of other famous Cubanophiles. Havana (the word even sounds like a libidinous sigh) was always the closest place to the United States where everything from cockfights to gambling to unchecked and rum-abetted sensuality was allowed to run wild just beyond the jurisdiction of church, state, or much of anything else.

Cuba is at once the most Spanish country in America and the most American of the Hispanic countries in the New World. Liberated from Spanish imperial rule in 1898 only to fall under the aegis of an even greater local power, Cuba has, nevertheless, always admired the colossus to the north. Baseball, basketball, and boxing are the national sports; jazz, blues, and African rhythms permeate Cuban music and dance; rangy American *carros* circulate on whatever scarce fuel trickles through the 30-year blockade.

Spain, Africa, North America, and the Caribbean all contribute to this powerful cocktail: 400 years of Spanish imperial rule, a half million African slaves, the indigenous Taina and Arawak Caribbean cultures . . . all of this less than an hour from the United States. Stuck on the cusp of everything, wedged between the Atlantic, the Gulf of Mexico, and the Caribbean, the once splendid "Pearl of the Antilles" is an exciting blend of peoples and forces that has fiercely maintained its identity through hard times and brutal leadership, especially during this century.

On the eve of a new era, Cuba is grooming tourism as the basis of its future economy. New hotel complexes are springing up everywhere and offering a wide range of activities, from world-class scuba diving to spelunking to bird-watching, sport fishing, shooting, and equestrian tours of the Sierra Maestra. Golf courses in Havana and Varadero will soon be accompanied by several new links. The extraordinarily well-preserved colonial architecture of Havana, Trinidad, Camagüey, and Santiago de Cuba ranks among the best in the world, much of it declared Patrimony of Humanity by UNESCO. Salsa, lambada: Cuban music and nightlife, the tavern and restaurant circuit from Bodeguita del Medio to La Floridita, the Tropicana and an endless lineup of dusk-to-dawn favorites, will soon again make Havana famous as the hottest town in the hemisphere.

After nearly half a century of acute political and economic woes, Cuba will almost certainly become more and more a part of North American life: an exciting resource—both familiar and exotic—our closest and most distant neighbor.

— George Semler

Longtime Fodor's contributor George Semler writes frequently about Spain and its neighbors from his home in Barcelona.

HIGHLIGHTS

Since early 1995 Cuba has experienced the effects of the initial economic changes introduced by the Castro regime. The fall of the socialist bloc provoked an acute scarcity of goods on the island—perhaps the worst crisis of its history—and obliged the Cuban regime to begin a process of economic opening that quickly transformed the country's economy. The legalization of the possession of dollars, the authorization of certain forms of private initiative, and the 1994 reimplantation of agricultural markets governed by the law of supply and demand have liberalized the regime and brought about social changes that have affected tourism. Today the streets of Cuba abound with crafts and popular markets, Cubans are permitted to buy in stores that accept dollars and to use hotels and facilities once reserved for foreign visitors only. Phenomena such as begging and prostitution have, on the other hand, been exacerbated.

The opening sui generis of Cuba has had direct effects on travelers visiting the island, above all in Havana. During recent years, private supply of goods and services has increased considerably. Now in Cuba it is possible to eat in a privately owned restaurant, rent an apartment, or take a taxi without dealing with the state superstructure, all at a lower cost and with a reasonable amount of warmth. In 1997, there were 1,500 privately owned restaurants in Cuba, called *paladares,* half of which were in Havana. Some are genuinely luxurious. In spite of diverse limitations imposed on these restaurants by the state, such as prohibiting them from offering beef- or seafood-based dishes or reducing their seating capacity to 12, the majority overcomes these problems with imagination. In this new edition we have included a short list of privately owned restaurants on which you can expand simply by arriving on the island and speaking with Cubans.

To overcome the crisis and serious supply problem currently asphyxiating the Cuban people, the authorities have prioritized the tourist sector. Thus, over recent years the construction of hotels, restaurants, and recreational centers has been accelerated. At the end of 1994 the Ministry of Tourism was created. Several capitalist corporations were founded with the goal of fully developing the tourist industry, destined to become the country's most important source of revenue. Thus, whereas in 1993 500,000 tourists traveled to Cuba, the number of visitors in 1996 approached one million. However, along with the profits generated by this tourist development— fundamentally, an increased range of opportunities and improved services—the tourist arriving in Cuba today will encounter problems such as elevated prices, growing differences among Cubans, and, especially, differences between Cubans and foreigners. The Cuban economic opening features foreign investment as one of its pillars. Up to the present time tourism has been one of the areas that has sparked the greatest interest in the business community. Spanish companies and groups have been the pioneers. Chains such as the Sol-Meliá have already built three hotels on Varadero beach, bringing to seven the total number of hotels across Cuba run by the chain. By 1997, the management of more than 15% of Cuban hotel capacity was in the hands of foreign companies. Although the prices of these hotels are usually higher, the quality of their service is superior.

By the end of 1997 Sol-Meliá will complete a new five star hotel in Havana. The chain has expanded its operations in Cuba with a ship, the *Meliá Don Juan,* which cruises between three days and one week around the Cuban coast and the Caribbean. Other hotel groups will complete new facilities this year in Cayo Coco, while Cuban authorities modernize and expand the tourism infrastructure in Havana, Varadero, Santa Lucía, Marea del Portillo and Santiago de Cuba. Destinations such as Cayo Levisa or Cayo Coco that until recently offered no lodging and were exclusively day trips now have exceptional facilities. Cayo Coco, for example, is an island just under half the size of Rhode Island with more than 20 km (12 mi) of virgin beaches on its northern coast.

In Havana, although the general tendency has been to restore the old glories such as the Hotel Nacional, the Plaza, the Copacabana, or the Château Miramar, new construction also continues to appear. In 1995 the Sol chain opened the luxurious **Hotel Meliá Cohiba** in the Vedado neighborhood. This modern 462-room establishment is ideal for conventions and for people on business trips.

Around Havana, new restaurants, cafés, and banquet halls appear every day, while others change their character or prices— or even disappear. For this reason it is difficult to establish an accurate and complete list. El Floridita, Tropicana, and La Bodeguita del Medio continue to be the indispensable triangle for first-time visitors to Cuba.

Havana's historic quarter was declared a World Heritage Site by UNESCO in 1982, and many buildings, squares, and structures have been restored by the city historian's office. Plaza Vieja, the Plaza de San Francisco, the Plaza de las Armas, and the Plaza de la Catedral are all gems that you can enjoy for relatively little money. Many museums also have low admission fees.

The Office of the City Historian has opened numerous cafeterias and bars in Old Havana and, in 1997, will inaugurate three splendid hotels. The first, the Ambos Mundos, is on Calle Obispo and is famous because Ernest Hemingway stayed here during the '40s. The second is the Hotel Santa Isabel, a palace of the 18th century situated on the Plaza de las Armas. The third is the Conde de Villanueva boarding-house, a residence constructed in 1714 and located on Calle Mercaderes; it will have nine very exclusive rooms.

In 1988 UNESCO also declared the colonial city of **Trinidad** a World Heritage Site and included the nearby valley of San Luis, also known as the Valle de los Ingenios (Valley of the Sugar Mills), in its proposal. The conversion of this valley into a gigantic Museum of Slavery is being planned. It is easy to reach the valley by train. The itinerary includes a visit to the old sugar mill at El Guarisco, the stockpile or collection center of Magua (where, during the sugar harvest, you can observe modern methods of sugarcane processing), the Guachinango country estate, and the Manacas-Iznaga tower, where lunch is served before the return trip.

Ecological tourism is gaining importance in Cuba. One of the most interesting projects is the **Parque Nacional de la Cienaga de Zapata** (Zapata Marshland National Park) in the province of Matanzas. The complete tour lasts six days and visits, among other sites, the breeding grounds of birds and other wild fauna, the protected area of Las Salinas and its deep natural pools and inlets, the animal sanctuary at Santo Tomas, and the crocodile breeding grounds. Other eco-tourism opportunities in the Zapata Marshlands (where 80% of Cuba's fauna is concentrated) include a week of bird-watching or spelunking through submarine caves and grottoes.

As for cultural events, the one that draws the widest range of participants is the **Caribbean Culture Festival,** which takes place each June in Santiago de Cuba. The annual **Cinema Festival of Havana,** held the first two weeks of December, is also popular. Since 1996 the carnivals of Havana have been celebrated once again during the month of February.

FODOR'S CHOICE

Although no two people will agree on what makes a perfect vacation, it can be useful and interesting to know what others think. We hope that during your trip to Cuba you will have the opportunity to experience some of Fodor's choices for yourself. For detailed information on individual entries, see the relevant sections of this guidebook.

Beaches

★ Cayo Largo (Isla de la Juventud)

★ Varadero (Matanzas)

★ Playas del Este (Havana)

★ Cayo Levisa (Pinar del Río)

★ Santa Lucía (Camagüey)

★ Marea del Portillo (Granma)

★ Guardalavaca (Holguín)

★ Any of the sites near Baracoa (Guantánamo)

★ Playa Larga (Matanzas)

★ Beaches in Baconao Park (Santiago de Cuba)

Hotels

★ Nacional (Havana)

★ Inglaterra (Havana)

★ Plaza (Havana)

★ Santiago (Santiago de Cuba)

★ Villa Gaviota Santiago (Santiago de Cuba)

★ La Ermita (Vinales)

★ El Castillo (Baracoa)

★ Plaza (Camagüey)

★ Meliá Las Américas (Varadero)

★ Pullman (Varadero)

Restaurants

★ La Bodeguita del Medio (Havana)

★ El Aljibe (Havana)

★ Tocororo (Havana)

★ Casa de Don Tomás (Viñales, Pinar del Río)

★ Palacio del Valle (Cienfuegos)

★ El Ovejito (Camagüey)

★ Las Acacias (Santiago de Cuba)

★ Fuerteventura (Varadero)

Privately Owned Restaurants (Paladares)

★ La Cocina de Lillian (Havana)

★ La Kakatúa (Havana)

★ Doña Eutimia (Havana)

★ Claro de Luna (Cojímar)

Nightlife

★ Tropicana (Havana)

★ El Palacio de la Salsa (Hotel Riviera de La Habana)

★ Tropicana (Santiago de Cuba)

★ Hotel Tuxpan (Varadero)

Special Foods and Beverages

★ Crocodile meat at La Boca (Guama)

★ A daiquiri at El Floridita (Havana)

★ A *mojito* at La Bodeguita (Havana)

★ A *canchánchara* at La Canchánchara (Trinidad)

★ Prawns at La Casa del Marisco (Viñales, Pinar del Río)

Best Views

★ The Viñales Valley from La Ermita and Los Jazmines hotels (Pinar del Río)

★ The Valle de los Ingenios, near Trinidad

★ The mouth of the Yumuri River, the Cuchillas del Toa, and El Yunque around Baracoa

★ The Baconao coast from the Gran Piedra heights, near Santiago de Cuba

★ The Soroa Valley from the Castillo de las Nubes restaurant

★ The Escambray Mountains from any point on the road that crosses them

Diving

★ Isla de la Juventud

★ María la Gorda (Pinar del Río)

Fiestas

★ Carnaval in Santiago de Cuba (July)

★ Parrandas de Remedios (December)

★ Parrandas de Bejucal (December)

★ Carnaval in Havana (July)

★ Carnaval in Varadero (January and February)

To Get Away from It All

★ Cayo Levisa

★ Maguana beach (near Baracoa)

★ Remedios

★ Baracoa

★ Botanical garden at Cienfuegos

★ Bird-watching on the Zapata peninsula

★ Spelunking in the caves of Pinar del Río

★ Equestrian tours of the Sierra Maestra from Marea del Portillo

Museums

★ City Museum, Old Palace of the Commanders-in-Chief (Havana)

★ Romantic (Trinidad)

★ Indocubano (Holguín)

★ Parrandas (Remedios)

Small Details

★ Visiting the Peasant House at Mayaba (Holguín)

★ Listening to the traditional music at the Casa de la Trova in Trinidad

★ A boat tour through the underground river in the Indio cave (Viñales, Pinar del Río)

★ The nonpareil color of the water at María la Gorda (Pinar del Río)

★ A tour in a horse-drawn carriage through the historic center of Bayamo

★ An evening walk through San Juan de Dios Square in Camagüey

★ The journey between Guantánamo and Baracoa on the road known as La Farola

★ A performance of the Camagüey Ballet

Eternal Favorites

★ A few days in Old Havana

★ Walking slowly through the cobblestone streets of Trinidad

★ Listening to the folk music at the Casa de la Trova in Santiago de Cuba

★ Spending time at a Varadero beach

The Caribbean

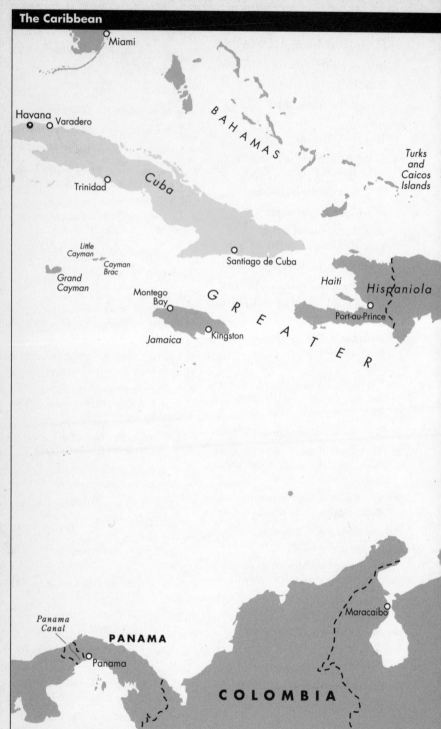

Miami

Havana Varadero

Cuba

Trinidad

BAHAMAS

Turks
and
Caicos
Islands

Little
Cayman

Cayman
Brac

Grand
Cayman

Santiago de Cuba

Haiti

Hispaniola

Port-au-Prince

Montego
Bay

G R E A T E R

Jamaica Kingston

Panama
Canal

PANAMA

Panama

Maracaibo

COLOMBIA

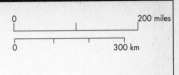

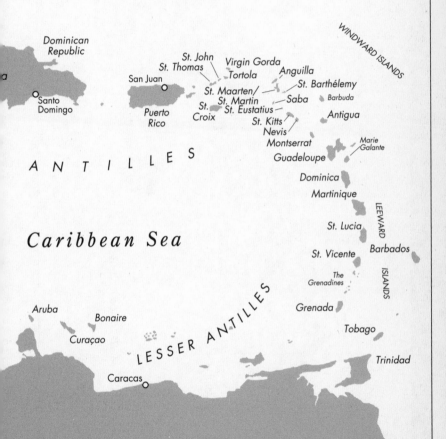

ATLANTIC OCEAN

WINDWARD ISLANDS

Dominican
Republic

St. John
St. Thomas   Virgin Gorda
                    Tortola   Anguilla
San Juan   St. Barthélemy
                St. Maarten/   Saba   Barbuda
        St.   St. Martin
Santo   Croix   St. Eustatius   Antigua
Domingo   St. Kitts
Puerto   Nevis
Rico   Montserrat   Marie
                Guadeloupe   Galante

A N T I L L E S

                Dominica
                Martinique

Caribbean Sea   LEEWARD

                St. Lucia
                St. Vicente   Barbados
                The
                Grenadines   ISLANDS

Aruba   Grenada
        Bonaire
Curaçao   Tobago
                LESSER ANTILLES

                                            Trinidad
Caracas

V E N E Z U E L A

0   200 miles
0   300 km

N

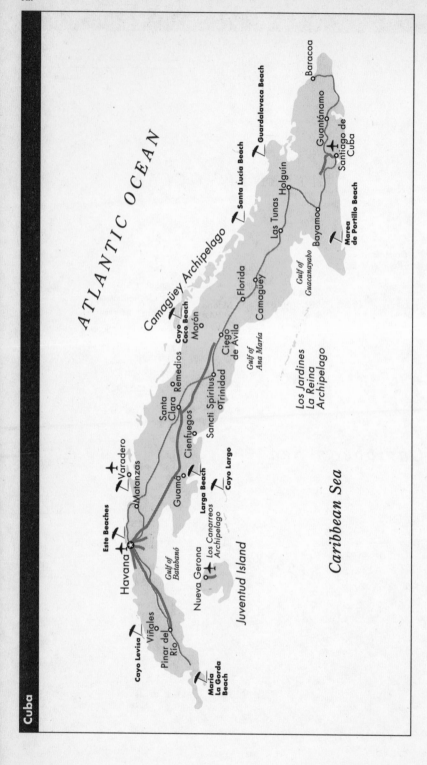

The Gold Guide

SMART TRAVEL TIPS A TO Z

Basic Information on Traveling in Cuba,
Savvy Tips to Make Your Trip a Breeze,
and Companies and Organizations to Contact

American travelers should note that although individual American citizens are allowed to visit Cuba—the warning on the passport states that going to Cuba is "not recommended" for U.S. citizens—American companies cannot legally do business with Cuba owing to the U.S. trade embargo. Therefore, trips must be booked through a Canadian or Mexican tour operator or travel agent. Further, if there are problems with transportation or during the trip, U.S. citizens will not be able to file complaints with any U.S. agency. If you encounter problems, we suggest that you take your complaint directly to your travel agent, tour operator, or airline.

A

ADDRESSES

In Cuba, addresses are given as locations. For example, the address of the National Museum of Fine Arts is Trocadero e/Zulueta y Monserrate, La Habana Vieja, Cuidad Habana, which means that the museum is between (e/ = *entre* = between) the other two streets in the municipal district of La Habana Vieja (Old Havana) in Ciudad Havana (Havana City). The address of the Hotel Habana Libre is 23 y L, Vedado, La Habana, that is, it occupies one of the corners at the crossing of 23rd and L streets in the municipal district of Vedado in Havana. The streets of Vedado are geometrically laid out. Paseo is the axis, running from Plaza de la Revolución to Malecón (at the intersection are the Juventud Fountain and the Habana Riviera and Cohiba hotels). Parallel to the Paseo, on one side, the streets are successively named for the letters A to O (toward the Hotel Nacional). On the other side, the streets are numbered, starting from two and continuing in even numbers. Perpendicular streets have odd numbers. Thus, using these coordinates, it is easy to find the Hotel Habana Libre or any other address in Vedado.

Many streets whose names have changed continue to be popularly known by their old names. In Havana, the Avenida de Belgica continues to be Monserrate, and Simón Bolívar is universally known as Reina. This double-naming of streets is common in many cities. When both names appear, the new name is usually placed first with the old name placed in parentheses afterward.

AIR TRAVEL

Travelers originating in the U.S. cannot fly nonstop to Cuba. Connections must first be made in Canada, Mexico, or the Caribbean. As noted above, arrangements must be made through a non-U.S. airline, travel agency, or tour operator. American companies cannot make these bookings for you.

From Canada, the two major gateways to Cuba are **Pearson International Airport** in Toronto and **Mirabel International Airport** in Montreal. Cuba's main airports are **José Martí International Airport** in Havana and **Juan Gualberto Gomez International Airport** in the vacation area of Varadero, about 1½ hours from the capital. Secondary gateways (all international) include **Antonio Maceo** in the country's "second city," Santiago de Cuba, **Ignacio Agramonte** (Camagüey), and **Frank Pais** (Holguín); smaller air terminals can be found in the towns of Manzanillo, Cayo Largo, Cienfuegos, and Ciego de Ávila. Flying time is approximately four hours direct from either Toronto or Montreal to Havana or Varadero.

From Mexico, the major gateway to Cuba is the main airport in Mexico City, **Benito Juarez International Airport.** Flying time to Havana is 2 hours and 20 minutes.

From the United Kingdom, the most direct route is from London to Paris, where you can pick up a Saturday flight aboard Cubana to Santiago. Total flying time is just over 11 hours. Also from London, you can fly to Mexico City and connect to a Friday or Sunday flight aboard Mexicana to Havana. Total flying time is 14 hours, 20 minutes.

Service to Cuba is also available from various Caribbean islands: Cubana flies from Kingston (Jamaica), Barbados and Santo Domingo; Iberia and Viasa fly from Santo Domingo (Dominican Republic); and ALM flies from Curaçao.

➤ CARRIERS: **Cubana Airlines** (☎ 514/871–1222) operates the only regular scheduled flights (Sunday only) from Canada (Toronto and Montreal departures). **Mexicana Airlines** (☎ 52/5/325–0990) provides regular service from Mexico City.

CHARTERS

➤ TO BOOK DIRECT: **Air Transat** (☎ 905/678–1011 in Toronto or ☎ 514/476–1011 in Montreal), **Canada 3000** (☎ 416/674–0257), **Canadian Airlines International** (☎ 905/612–2100), **Cubana Airlines** (☎ 514/871–1222), **Royal Airlines** (☎ 514/828–9000), and **SkyService** (☎ 888/599–0789 in Toronto, 514/636–3300 in Montreal); **Mexicana Airlines** (☎ 52/5/325–0990).

➤ THROUGH TRAVEL AGENTS: **Magna Tours** (☎ 905/761–1380) in Toronto or **Vera Playa** (☎ 514/861–2897) in Montreal.

WITHIN CUBA

Cuba's domestic aviation system, like its bus and rail system, is designed primarily for the needs of its citizens. Tourists who want to travel around the island would be better advised to rent a car or hire a driver. (☞ Cars for Hire *and* Long-Distance Taxis, *below*.)

Cars for Hire *and* Long-Distance Taxis, *below*.

AIRPORT TRANSFERS

Transfers between the airport and the hotel are included in all prearranged packages and tours. For independent travelers, cabs are always available at the airport; you will have to pay in dollars.

B

BEACHES

Beaches are among Cuba's greatest attractions. There are all types of beaches, ranging from large sandy stretches covered with bathers, such as the Playas del Este, to remote coves where you're unlikely to encounter another soul. You can choose between white sand and black. Varadero is Cuba's best known beach, but Cayo Largo has become the favorite destination for those who want to get away from it all for sun, sand, and good food. Many of the island's other fine beaches are hardly known outside of Cuba, as tour operators do not market them. Guardalavaca, Santa Lucia, and Marea del Portillo are a few examples.

Even where resort hotels have been constructed, facilities vary, so always **check to see what beach services are available** before booking. Inquire about the availability of refreshments, beach chairs, and if you're interested, nude beaches. These are not the norm in Cuba, but topless bathing is not unusual in areas frequented by foreigners.

BUS TRAVEL

Bus travel in Cuba is a very practical mode of transportation. However, it is designed primarily for use by locals, many of whom need to get to a nearby town for work or to visit family on a Sunday outing. In fact, drivers will sometimes prevent tourists from boarding buses—which are always overcrowded—because the visitors will be taking the seats of locals who need the transportation.

Cuban buses are not the deluxe, glistening chrome vehicles of North American sightseeing tours. The buses here have definitely seen better days. Often, they are gifts from a Cuban trading partner (the donating country simply gives the buses to Cuba rather than scrapping them).

The bus station in Havana is always chaotic; **be prepared to wait three days for the next available bus.** Also **be prepared to pay in U.S. currency.** Smoking is allowed on Cuban buses, and there are no designated no-smoking sections.

➤ TICKETS: **Oficina Reservaciones Pasajes** (Calle 21, Esq. 4, Vededo, Havana).

BUSINESS HOURS

Public offices and banks are usually open weekdays from 8:30 AM to 12:30 PM, then in the afternoon from 1:30 to 5:30. Service in the post office is from 8 AM to 6 PM. Restaurants close around 11:30 PM or until you decide to stop spending your U.S. dollars. Drugstores or "chemists" stay open only until 5 PM; if you need emergency service, ask the people at your hotel to help you find a 24-hour shop (although, owing to the shortages in Cuba, you may not find the medicine you need).

C

CAMERAS, CAMCORDERS, & COMPUTERS

Always **keep your film, tape, or computer disks out of the sun.** Carry an extra supply of batteries, and **be prepared to turn on your camera, camcorder, or laptop** to prove to security personnel that the device is real. Always **ask for hand inspection of film,** which becomes clouded after successive exposure to airport x-ray machines, and **keep videotapes and computer disks away from metal detectors.**

Cuba is a photographer's paradise. Very rarely will anyone refuse to be photographed. Remember that, for the moment, photography is a hobby beyond the means of the average Cuban citizen, and for this reason, a portrait makes a good gift. You can be sure that your subject will eagerly await the photograph that you offer to send; if you promise them one, keep your word.

Don't forget to **bring more film than you think you will need.** The selection of film in Cuba is limited, and there is little guarantee that it has been stored properly.

➤ PHOTO HELP: **Kodak Information Center** (☎ 800/242–2424). *Kodak Guide to Shooting Great Travel Pictures,* available in bookstores or from **Fodor's Travel Publications** (☎ 800/533–6478; $16.50 plus $4 shipping).

CAR RENTAL

Although most private vehicles in Cuba are prerevolution makes and models dating from 1959 or earlier, rental cars are late-model vehicles. Travelers should also consider hiring a car and driver as an alternative to renting a car. (☞ Long-Distance Taxis, *below.*)

Rates in Havana begin at about $45–$50 per day for basic transportation. This price includes the first 100 km; any additional mileage costs about 30₽ per km.

➤ CAR-RENTAL AGENCIES: **Havanautos** (Calle 36, No. 505, Av. 5e, Miramar, Havana, ☎ 33–0648). **Cubacar** (Av. 146 e/11 y 13, Playa, Havana, ☎ 33–2104).

CUTTING COSTS

To get the best deal, **book through a travel agent** while arranging your trip. Always **find out what equipment is standard** at your destination before specifying what you want; **do without automatic transmission or air-conditioning** if they're optional. Cuba is a big island, and mileage can add up quickly, so **ask if unlimited mileage rates are available** if you intend to do some serious driving. Always **remember that gasoline is expensive** at about $1 per liter—when you can find it. There is a definite gasoline shortage in the country, so **never let your tank get too empty** or you could find yourself stranded between gas stations.

NEED INSURANCE?

When driving a rented car you are generally responsible for any damage to or loss of the vehicle. You also are liable for any property damage or personal injury that you may cause while driving. Before you rent, **see what coverage you already have** under the terms of your personal auto-insurance policy and credit cards, **and check whether you will be covered while driving in Cuba.**

If you are uncovered or unsure, your best bet is to **eliminate your liability by purchasing a collision damage waiver (CDW)** from the car-rental company.

MEET THE REQUIREMENTS

In Cuba you must be 21 years of age and possess a valid driver's license from your country of origin. An International Driver's Permit is a good idea; it's available from the American or Canadian automobile association, or, in the United Kingdom, from the Automobile Association or Royal Automobile Club.

CARS FOR HIRE

➤ CAR & DRIVER: **Tourist Taxis** (Hotel Nacional, Vedado, Havana, ☎ 33–3564).

CHILDREN & TRAVEL

BABY-SITTING

Baby-sitting is still a fairly foreign concept to Cubans; as in most Latin countries, babies and children are an integral part of the family unit and just naturally go everywhere with their parents. Certain hotels may provide baby-sitting services; it's wise to **inquire about children's programs before you leave home, and make arrangements in advance.** Delta Hotels & Resorts (☞ Lodging, *below*) is one company with programs and special facilities.

CHILDREN IN CUBA

Generally, children traveling with their parents in Cuba are eligible for discounted lodging. However, this is mainly true only of the major hotels. Children under 2 can often stay for free, and children between the ages of 2 and 12 get a 25% to 30% discount. When booking, **always check with the individual property regarding its policy on accommodations for children.**

Travelers planning to rent or hire a car should **be aware that car seats are not available.**

CUSTOMS & DUTIES

When shopping, **keep receipts** for all of your purchases. Upon reentering the country, **be ready to show customs officials what you've bought.** If you feel a duty is incorrect, appeal the assessment. If you object to the way your clearance was handled, get the inspector's badge number. In either case, first ask to see a supervisor, then write to the port director at the address listed on your receipt. Send a copy of the receipt and other appropriate documentation. If you still don't get satisfaction, you can take your case to customs headquarters in Washington.

ENTERING CUBA

Visitors may enter Cuba with two bottles of liquor, a carton of cigarettes, and 50 cigars (although why anyone would bring cigars to Cuba is a complete mystery). Personal items (cameras, video equipment, radios, typewriters, etc.) should be noted before you leave your country of origin and declared again when leaving Cuba. Firearms are not allowed, and drugs are totally forbidden unless they are in the original bottle or package and are accompanied by a prescription from a doctor.

Although the Cuban government is cracking down on the importation of gifts by tourists, visitors often bring everyday household items for friends or even for tipping. Many things that we take for granted are rationed in Cuba; for instance, a household—not just one person, but an entire household—is only allowed one bar of soap per month! Common items such as chocolate bars, chewing gum (small children will always ask you for "cheeklets"), toiletries—especially shampoo—pens, T-shirts, and the like are highly sought after. People appreciate these items more than a few pesos' tip.

ENTERING THE U.S.

Normally, U.S. citizens may bring home $400 worth of foreign goods duty-free if they have been out of the country for at least 48 hours and haven't already used the $400 exemption, or any part of it, in the past 30 days. Bringing back goods from Cuba, however, is generally prohibited. If you travel to Cuba without a license from the State Department, **be prepared for U.S. customs officials to confiscate any souvenirs** you bring back with you. Licensed travelers may bring back $100 worth of goods including cigars, but they must return directly from Cuba.

➤ INFORMATION: **U.S. Customs Service** (Box 7407, Washington, DC 20044, ☎ 202/927–6724; complaints, Commissioner's Office, 1301 Constitution Ave. NW, Washington, DC 20229; registration of equipment,

Resource Management, 1301 Constitution Ave. NW, Washington DC, 20229, ☎ 202/927–0540).

➤ LICENSES: **U.S. Treasury Deparment,** Licensing Division, Office of Foreign Assets Control, ☎ 202/622–2480.

ENTERING CANADA

If you've been out of Canada for at least seven days, you may bring in C$500 worth of goods duty-free. If you've been away for fewer than seven days but more than 48 hours, the duty-free allowance drops to C$200; if your trip lasts 24–48 hours, the allowance is C$50. You may not pool allowances with family members. Goods claimed under the C$500 exemption may follow you by mail; those claimed under the lesser exemptions must accompany you.

Alcohol and tobacco products may be included in the seven-day and 48-hour exemptions but not in the 24-hour exemption. If you meet the age requirements of the province or territory through which you reenter Canada, you may bring in, duty-free, 1.14 liters (40 imperial ounces) of wine or liquor *or* 24 12-ounce cans or bottles of beer or ale. If you are 16 or older, you may bring in, duty-free, 200 cigarettes and 50 cigars; these items must accompany you.

You may send an unlimited number of gifts worth up to C$60 each duty-free to Canada. Label the package UNSOLICITED GIFT—VALUE UNDER $60. Alcohol and tobacco are excluded.

➤ INFORMATION: **Revenue Canada** (2265 St. Laurent Blvd. S, Ottawa, Ontario K1G 4K3, ☎ 613/993–0534, 800/461–9999 in Canada).

ENTERING THE U.K.

From countries outside the EU, including Cuba, you may import, duty-free, 200 cigarettes or 50 cigars; 1 liter of spirits or 2 liters of fortified or sparkling wine or liqueurs; 2 liters of still table wine; 60 milliliters of perfume; 250 milliliters of toilet water; plus £136 worth of other goods, including gifts and souvenirs.

➤ INFORMATION: **HM Customs and Excise** (Dorset House, Stamford St., London SE1 9NG, ☎ 0171/202–4227).

D

DINING

Cuban cuisine is somewhat different than the famed hot-and-spicy Cuban concoctions found in the Miami area; strangely enough, for a Caribbean country, the food here is very bland. Many tourists returning for their second visit even **bring salt, pepper, and spicy seasoning.**

The staple of Cuban cooking is meat—not fish, for, strangely enough, there is no fishing industry on this island country—with roast pork, barbecued chicken, and fried beefsteak as staples. Local specialties include black beans, *moros y cristianos* (rice and beans), tamales, *ayacas* (made from corn), and *tachinos* (fried bananas), with roast potatoes and cooked vegetables rounding out the table. And, although it all looks good, it is basically bland; sometimes you aren't sure whether you are eating the pork or the chicken. Travelers on special diets should **remember that vegetarian menus are difficult to find.**

The kitchens in tourist restaurants are usually well supplied. In local restaurants, try to arrive as early as possible. Fruits and vegetables are usually scarce, and the best dishes sell out quickly.

DRINKS

As if to make up for their lack of tempting tastes in food, the Cubans have put the taste into their drinks. Cuban rum is some of the finest in the world; aficionados should savor seven-year-old Havana Club straight. Refreshing local creations include *cuba libre* (light, dry rum mixed with cola and a splash of lemon juice served on ice with a slice of lemon); Havana *especial* (light, dry rum, pineapple juice, lemon juice, and a maraschino cherry); Isla de Pinos (light, dry rum mixed with grapefruit juice and red vermouth); *cubanito* (as you would make a Bloody Mary but with rum instead of vodka); and, Hemingway's favorite, the *mojito* (light, dry rum mixed with sugar and lemon and served with crushed mint leaves).

For an incredible nonalcoholic sugar hit, **find a little corner café that makes** a *guapa*—pure sugarcane juice made by running a cane stalk through a grinder. Then, of course, there is Cuban coffee: hot, thick, and rich. And, if you are Cuban, each cup has at least six spoonfuls of sugar.

ACCESS IN CUBA

During the last few years, Cuba has been upgrading its facilities and services for tourists. Such upgrades are beginning to include facilities for travelers with disabilities, but Havana remains inaccessible by North American standards. For instance, there are no curb cuts in the sidewalks. Bathrooms present another problem: The doors are generally accessible if the building was built with accessibility in mind, but don't count on a toilet seat. You may want to buy your own in advance of your trip and take it along. Check in medical supply stores.

TIPS & HINTS

When discussing accessibility with an operator or reservationist, **ask hard questions.** Are there any stairs, inside *or* out? Are there grab bars next to the toilet *and* in the shower/tub? How wide is the doorway to the room? To the bathroom? For the most extensive facilities meeting the latest legal specifications, **opt for newer accommodations,** which are more likely to have been designed with access in mind. Older buildings or ships may offer more limited facilities. Be sure to **discuss your needs before booking.**

E

ELECTRICITY

Cuba is on the North American system of 110 volts, 60 cycles AC. Travelers from the United Kingdom should pack an adapter if they intend to bring an electric razor, hair dryer, or other electrical appliances.

EMBASSIES

Canadian Embassy (Calle 30, Esq. 4, Miramar, Havana, ☎ 33–2516); **U.K. Embassy** (Calle 34, No. 708 e/7 y 17, Miramar, ☎ 33–1717). **Swiss Embassy** (Calle Calzada e/L y M, Vedado, Havana, ☎ 30–0551), which represents U.S. citizens in Cuba.

H

HEALTH

In Cuba, there is very little health risk, and you should experience no problems with the food or water if you are dining at a resort, a hotel, or a good tourist restaurant. You may have minor stomach irregularities if you buy any food or drink water from a street vendor or local side-street restaurant (☞ Staying Well, *below*).

If you do get sick, **check with your tour leader or at your hotel for any necessary medical assistance.** If you need specific medicine, **brush up on your Spanish and visit the local pharmacist.** Medical treatment in Cuba is of relatively high quality—more advanced than in many Caribbean countries. Although the country has produced an impressive number of doctors and well-equipped hospitals, medical supplies are often difficult to find. However, neighborhood health clinics (known as Poly-clinics) are numerous. The cost to see a doctor is $25.

Perhaps the most common health problem travelers to Cuba experience comes from overexposure to the sun. If you are heading to a beach resort, be sure to bring the necessary gear (☞ Packing for Cuba, *below*), and **limit your time in the sun**—especially during the first few days.

A word of caution to all visitors: With the breakup of the former Soviet Union, the island of Cuba was suddenly cut off from its central funding, and many citizens are facing financial difficulties. As a result, many girls have taken to working the streets just to put food on the table. The risk of AIDS is very high in Cuba, and the lonely tourist would be well advised to abstain during a vacation here.

➤ FINDING A DOCTOR: **Servimed** (☎ 24–2658 or 24–2023).

STAYING WELL

In Cuba the major health risk is Montezuma's Revenge, or traveler's diarrhea, caused by eating contaminated fruit or vegetables or drinking contaminated water. So **watch what you eat.** Stay away from ice, uncooked food, and unpasteurized milk and milk products, and **drink only**

bottled water or water that has been boiled for at least 20 minutes. Mild cases may respond to Imodium (known generically as loperamide) or Pepto-Bismol (not as strong), both of which can be purchased over the counter. Drink plenty of purified water or tea—chamomile is a good folk remedy. In severe cases, rehydrate yourself with a salt-sugar solution (½ teaspoon salt and 4 tablespoons sugar per quart of water).

According to the National Centers for Disease Control (CDC), there is a limited risk of Hepatitis A, Hepatitis B, and dengue fever. In most urban or easily accessible areas you need not worry. However, if you plan to visit remote regions or stay for more than six weeks, **check with the CDC's International Travelers Hotline.** In areas where dengue, which is carried by mosquitoes, are prevalent, use mosquito nets, wear clothing that covers the body, apply repellent containing DEET, and use spray for flying insects in living and sleeping areas. There is no vaccine that combats dengue.

➤ HEALTH WARNINGS: **National Centers for Disease Control** (CDC, National Center for Infectious Diseases, Division of Quarantine, Traveler's Health Section, 1600 Clifton Rd., M/S E-03, Atlanta, GA 30333, ☎ 404/332–4559, FAX 404/332–4565).

MEDICAL PLANS

No one plans to get sick while traveling, but it happens, so **consider signing up with a medical-assistance company.** Members get doctor referrals, emergency evacuation or repatriation, 24-hour telephone hot lines for medical consultation, cash for emergencies, and other personal and legal assistance. Coverage varies by plan, so **review the benefits carefully.**

Travelers are insured of immediate evacuation to the closest medical facility and repatriation in an emergency. Fees range from $55 per person for a two-week trip to $98 for a month of coverage.

➤ MEDICAL-ASSISTANCE COMPANIES: **International SOS Assistance** (Box 11568, Philadelphia, PA 19116, ☎ 215/244–1500 or 800/523–8930; Box 466, pl. Bonaventure, Montréal,

Québec H5A 1C1, ☎ 514/874–7674 or 800/363–0263; 7 Old Lodge Pl., St. Margarets, Twickenham TW1 1RQ, England, ☎ 0181/744–0033).

I

INSURANCE

Travel insurance is the best way to **protect yourself against financial loss.** The most useful policies are trip-cancellation-and-interruption, default, medical, and comprehensive insurance.

Citizens of the United Kingdom can buy an annual travel-insurance policy valid for most vacations during the year in which it's purchased. If you are pregnant or have a preexisting medical condition, make sure you're covered.

Travelers originating in the U.S. should **double-check any insurance to make sure it covers travel in Cuba.**

➤ TRAVEL INSURERS: In Canada, **Mutual of Omaha** (Travel Division, 500 University Ave., Toronto, Ontario M5G 1V8, ☎ 416/598–4083, 800/268–8825 in Canada). In the U.K., **Association of British Insurers** (51 Gresham St., London EC2V 7HQ, ☎ 0171/600–3333).

L

LANGUAGE

The official language in Cuba is Spanish although English (plus French and German) is spoken in the main tourist areas such as Havana and the resorts of Varadero. Best to pick up a phrase book before you go.

LODGING

In Cuba, you have a choice of a hotel or a resort. All are operated under some degree of state control, and there are no bed-and-breakfasts, farm holidays, campgrounds, or home-exchange programs. A few years ago, you had to mentally lower your standards for the accommodations in this country: A five-star hotel in Cuba might have rated only two stars elsewhere. This, however, has rapidly changed with the increased emphasis on tourism and the drive to build an infrastructure for visitors.

Travelers to Cuba must **arrange accommodations in advance,** at least for the first few nights. If you arrive without paid reservations, you will have to make arrangements at the airport, where your choices will probably be limited to the most expensive hotels. Although you can make reservations on your own, it is best to **consult a travel agent.** If you plan to go to Cuba during the winter (☞ When to Go, *below*), be sure to **make your hotel reservations as far ahead as possible.**

HOTELS

You'll find few well-known hotel brand names in Cuba. Spanish-based Meliá and Canadian SuperClubs are both represented by Cubanacán (☞ Visitor Information, *below*). Both Spanish and Canadian hotel companies operate resort properties in Cuba. Delta Hotels & Resorts, another Canadian company, has two properties around the Holguín area: Las Brisas Club Resort and the "eco-lodge" Pinares de Mayari.

Cuban-run hotels include Cubanacán's six resorts near the popular Santiago de Cuba area: Sierra Mar; Los Galeones; Balneario de Sol; and three "eco" resorts (El Salton, El Colibri, and La Gran Piedra). The eco-lodges are smaller specialty lodges—with from 12 to 28 rooms—that feature historical sites and eco-tourism themes. Gaviota S.A. Hotels has smaller properties in main tourist areas throughout the country. Gran Caribe Grupo Hotel has 30 hotels and resorts throughout Cuba in different architectural styles ranging from classic to modern; most of them are quite luxurious. The group also offers exclusive arrangements for their guests at the spectacular Tropicana nightclub and two of Hemingway's favorite restaurants, La Floridita and La Bodeguita del Medio. Still another Cuban hotel group, Horizontes Hotels, operates properties in resort areas as well as urban hotels. These are not quite as luxurious as the Gran Caribe, perhaps, but they are much more casual and affordable.

➤ HOTELS: **Delta Hotels & Resorts** (350 Bloor St. E, Toronto, Ontario M4W 1H4, ☎ 416/926–7800) **Gaviota S.A. Hotels** (Calle 16, No. 504 e/5 y 7, Miramar, Havana, ☎ 22–7670). **Gran Caribe Grupo Hotel** (Av. 7ma, No. 4210 e/42 y 44, Miramar, Havana, ☎ 33–0259). **Horizontes Hotels** (Calle 23, 156 e/N y O, Vedado, Havana 4, ☎ 33–7818).

M

MONEY

The monetary unit in Cuba is the Cuban peso; it is found only on this island nation and is immediately worthless once you leave. The peso comes in bills of 1, 3, 5, 10, 20, and 50 pesos (as well as 1- and 3-peso coins), and the coins—100 centavos to 1 peso—are in denominations of 1, 2, 5, 20, and 40 centavos. The official exchange rate is U.S. $1 to 1 peso.

However, as a tourist, you really cannot spend pesos. Hotels, restaurants, bars, taxis, bus and train services, wait staff, and the "strictly tourist" shops accept only U.S. dollars. In fact, although there is a large Canadian tourist trade to Cuba, Cubans rarely accept Canadian funds. You only need to exchange a few dollars into pesos for the occasional coffee in a little café or as a souvenir from your trip; again, once you leave Cuba, your pesos will be worthless.

There is also a special currency known as "B certificates" or tourist money because only tourists are allowed to use it as currency; locals must use pesos. These bills look like Monopoly money but they spend like U.S. dollars. Sometimes you receive it as change after you've paid in hard currency. But don't worry, unlike pesos, you can exchange these certificates for dollars at the airport before leaving the country.

ATMS

There are no automatic teller machines (ATMs) in Cuba.

COSTS

Cuba is the best financial bargain of the Caribbean; airfares, tour packages, hotels, and resorts are less expensive here than on any of the other islands.

CREDIT CARDS

American Express and Optima cards are not accepted in Cuba. You may use Visa, MasterCard, Access, or Diner's Club as long the card has not been issued by a U.S. bank. In other words, Canadians and U.K. travelers can use their credit cards but U.S. citizens generally cannot.

TRAVELER'S CHECKS

Only certain kinds of travelers checks—those issued by a non-U.S. bank—are accepted at international hotels. These include Access, Banamex, Bancomer, Carnet, Diner's Club, JCB, MasterCard, and Visa. They are often a hassle, however, to exchange, and it may be more convenient to bring only hard currency. American Express traveler's checks are never accepted in Cuba.

WIRING FUNDS

Funds cannot be wired by an American agency to Cuba for anyone other than military personnel. For other foreign travelers, it is best to have money wired directly to your hotel or resort.

➤ WIRING FUNDS: **Western Union** (☎ 800/321–2923 in Canada; ☎ 0800/833–833 or visit the Western Union location at your nearest major post office in the U.K.).

P

PACKING FOR CUBA

Remember you are packing for the Caribbean heat, so **bring casual and lightweight-cotton clothing.** If you are going to a resort, you may want to bring various colored bathing suits. Shorts and T-shirts are fine for resort wear, but most men wear slacks for city sightseeing tours. (Cuban men, instead of a jacket, wear the *guayabera*, a light pleated shirt worn outside the trousers). For an evening at the famed Tropicana nightclub, a lightweight jacket for men and a dress for women will be required. When visiting churches, women should remember to carry a scarf or shawl to cover their shoulders. Don't forget to **pack cool and comfortable shoes** for walking over cobblestone streets. You'll need a sweater or light windbreaker if you plan to spend any time in the mountains. Resort-bound travelers should pack sunblock, sunglasses, a hat, and of course, bathing suits.

Given the scarcity of some consumer items in Cuba, it is best to **bring all the personal care products that you** will need, such as soap, toilet paper, deodorant, shampoo, and perfume.

Bring an extra pair of eyeglasses or contact lenses in your carry-on luggage, and if you have a health problem, **pack enough medication** to last the entire trip or have your doctor write you a prescription using the drug's generic name, because brand names vary from country to country. It's important that you **don't put prescription drugs or valuables in luggage to be checked**: it might go astray. To avoid problems with customs officials, carry medications in the original packaging, and bring your doctor's written prescription. Also, don't forget the addresses of offices that handle refunds of lost traveler's checks.

LUGGAGE

In general, you are entitled to check two bags on flights within the United States and on international flights leaving the United States. A third piece may be brought on board, but it must fit easily under the seat in front of you or in the overhead compartment.

If you are flying between two foreign destinations, note that baggage allowances may be determined not by piece but by weight—generally 88 pounds (40 kilograms) in first class, 66 pounds (30 kilograms) in business class, and 44 pounds (20 kilograms) in economy. If your flight between two cities abroad *connects* with your flight, the piece method still applies.

Airline liability for baggage is limited to $1,250 per person on flights within the United States. On international flights it amounts to $9.07 per pound or $20 per kilogram for checked baggage (roughly $640 per 70-pound bag) and $400 per passenger for unchecked baggage. Insurance for losses exceeding these amounts can be bought from the airline at check-in for about $10 per $1,000 of coverage; note that this coverage excludes a rather extensive list of items, which is shown on your airline ticket.

Before departure, **itemize your bags' contents** and their worth, and label the bags with your name, address, and phone number. (If you use your home address, cover it so that potential thieves can't see it readily.) Inside each bag, **pack a copy of your itinerary.** At check-in, **make sure that each bag is correctly tagged** with the destination airport's three-letter code. If your bags arrive damaged or fail to arrive at all, file a written report with the airline before leaving the airport.

PASSPORTS & VISAS

Once your travel plans are confirmed, **check the expiration date of your passport.** It's also a good idea to **make photocopies of the data page;** leave one copy with someone at home and keep another with you, separated from your passport. If you lose your passport, promptly call the nearest embassy or consulate and the local police; having a copy of the data page can speed replacement.

All visitors to Cuba are required to **buy a tourist card** ($20) in addition to a passport. This can be obtained from the travel agent or tour operator who booked your trip or from the Cuban Consulate. Students planning to live with a family for an extended period of time must obtain a visa from the Cuban Consulate.

U.S. CITIZENS

U.S. citizens are free to visit Cuba, even though they must fly there from a third country. Upon entry, they can request that Cuban passport control not stamp their passport. Officials will put the official stamp on a separate sheet of paper, which the visitor will then carry with a valid passport; the official stamp also makes a good souvenir upon returning home.

All U.S. citizens, even infants, need only a valid passport to enter Cuba for stays of up to 90 days.

➤ INFORMATION: **Office of Passport Services** (☎ 202/647–0518).

CANADIANS

You need only a valid passport to enter Cuba for stays of up to 90 days.

➤ INFORMATION: **Passport Office** (☎ 819/994–3500 or 800/567–6868).

U.K. CITIZENS

Citizens of the United Kingdom need only a valid passport to enter Cuba for stays of up to 30 days.

➤ INFORMATION: **London Passport Office** (☎ 0990/21010) for fees and documentation requirements and to request an emergency passport.

S

SAFETY

Street safety will not be a problem in Cuba as the crime rate is much lower than in any other Caribbean country—even walking at night in Cuban cities isn't really a safety risk. The ample police presence in the streets helps to reinforce this impression. Even so, it is better not to ask for trouble and to **take some simple safety precautions.** Try to keep objects of value in the hotel safe, if there is one. Street robberies and purse snatchings have increased in recent years, mainly in La Habana Vieja and in the downtown areas of Cuba's major cities, so it is a good idea to be careful.

Lock up baggage by key or combination lock in your hotel room. In hotel establishments and restaurants dedicated exclusively to tourists, examine bills carefully, as there tend to be "mistakes."

SHOPPING

For Canadians and citizens of the United Kingdom, Cuban cigars are prized souvenirs. These, of course, cannot be legally imported into the United States. Other good gifts and keepsakes from Cuba include rum and folk art. Pottery, paintings, and wood carvings can be found in Havana or the tourist resorts, but best buys can be found in the less-visited villages in the countryside.

SPORTS & THE OUTDOORS

BICYCLING

Cycling enthusiasts can do short itineraries or circumnavigate the island. Bicycles can often be rented in tourist centers.

DIVING

Cuba has over 5,700 km (3,500 mi) of coastline, which is surrounded by more than 4,000 small islands and keys with abundant coral formations. Water temperature and visibility are well suited to diving. There are international diving centers at Maria La Gorda (Pinar del Río), Hotel Colony (Isla de la Juventud), the Jardines de la Reina Archipelago (Ciego de

Ávila), Santa Lucia (Camagüey), and Los Galeones (Santiago de Cuba). In addition, there are many other spots where you can dive in marked areas: Marina Veneciana, Guanabo, and Playas del Este (Havana); Marina Acqua (Varadero); the hotels Ancón and Costasur (Trinidad); Hotel Rancho Luna (Cienfuegos); Giron tourist village (Playa Giron) and Cayo Largo. It will soon be possible to go diving in Cayo Levisa.

Scuba divers take note: **Do not fly within 24 hours of scuba diving.**

ECOTOURISM

In the last few years, environmentally sensitive tourism has caught on in Cuba. Good destinations are the national parks of Sierra Maestra, La Guira, and Boconao. For bird-watching the best spot is the Zapata Peninsula (Matanzas).

FISHING

There are three types of fishing in Cuba: (1) deep-sea fishing with heavy equipment; (2) ocean fishing with light gear; and (3) freshwater fishing. Deep-sea fishing is for very experienced anglers and is practiced mainly in spring and summer, when the swordfish migrate through the Caribbean. Various international competitions are organized around this migration. The annual fishing tournaments are Currican, Hemingway, and Castero—all from the Hemingway Marina in Havana; the Torneo de Primavera (Spring Tournament) in Playas del Este; the Cayo Largo International Tournament I in Cayo Largo; and the Torneo de Jardines de la Reina (Queen's Gardens Tournament) on the keys south of Ciego de Ávila. The Hemingway Tournament was founded by the novelist-adventurer himself and has survived for nearly 40 years.

Ocean fishing with light tackle is common only around Cayo Guillermo, where palometa and robalo (sea bass) abound, and at Jardines de la Reina, where the quarry is the macabi. Everything the angler needs is available (marinas, boats, tackle, and guides), although fishermen should bring their own artificial lures.

Cuba's most popular freshwater fish is the largemouth bass. Good fishing spots include Tesoro Lagoon (Matanzas); Lake Hanabanilla (Villa Clara); La Redonda Lagoon (near Moron in Ciego de Ávila); the preserves in Maspotón and Virama, Lake Cuyaguateje, and Laguna Grande (all in Pinar del Río); and Lake Zaza (Sancti Spíritus).

GOLF

The only golf courses in Cuba are in Havana and Varadero. The Varadero course is between the Meliá and Tuxpan hotels near the Las Americas restaurant. The Havana course is in the Diploclub on the Vento Road (Boyeros district).

MARATHON RUNNING

It is possible to participate in the marathon organized each November in Varadero. Information can be obtained at the Cuban Tourist Office or on arrival.

SPELUNKING

Cuba has one of the best cave systems in the Americas. The most interesting and most visited caves are at Pinar del Río.

T

TAXES

AIRPORT

There is an airport departure tax of U.S. $12 that must be paid—they stamp your ticket—before you leave. This is not included in the price of your ticket.

TAXIS

Taxis in Cuba are plentiful—although they seem to be constantly in use in busier cities such as Havana. Fares are reasonable; a taxi from the airport to Old Havana is about $15. The "peso taxis" are for citizens only; foreigners must ride in the taxis marked "dollar tourist taxi" and pay in U.S. dollars.

LONG-DISTANCE TAXIS

As an alternative to renting a car, **consider hiring a driver to take you sightseeing around the island.** This is not uncommon for tourists, especially those staying at resorts. It may seem expensive, but if you share the cost, the price can be quite reasonable. For example, if you are staying at a resort in Varadero and wish to see Havana for the day (about a two-hour drive) without signing up for one of the many day-trip bus tours, the 300-km (186-mi) round-trip costs $120. ☞ Car Rental, *above.*

☞ Car Rental, *above.*

TELEPHONES

The country code for Cuba is 53. It is fairly straightforward to get telephone information from Canada or the United Kingdom (although if you don't speak Spanish, it may be somewhat frustrating). To call Cuba from points in North America, first dial 011 then the country code, the provincial number (☞ *above*), and then the number. It is wise to get all the telephone numbers you require in advance from your travel agent and keep a record of them safely at home with a family member or friend.

What follows is a list of provincial numbers for several Cuban cities and resort areas: Boconao, 226; Camagüey, 322; Cienfuegos, 432; Guardalavaca, 24; Havana, 7; Isla de la Juventud, 61; Sancti Spíritus, 41; Santiago de Cuba, 226; Trinidad, 419; and Varadero, 5.

LONG-DISTANCE

When placing an international call to anywhere except the United States from Cuba, first **dial 88, and then the country code, the area code, and the number.** If you do not have the number, it would be helpful if you can speak some Spanish, or you can hope to find a patient operator to help you at your hotel. To call the United States, dial 119 to reach the international operator. For further assistance while in Cuba, dial 113 during the day and 60–7110 at night. You can **place your long-distance call from your hotel or go to an international telephone center.** Keep in mind, however, that calls placed from a hotel will be subject to a surcharge of 10% to 20%. Telephone centers can be found in Havana and Varadero; there are two types: one for international calls and one for domestic calls. Telephone calls must be paid for in cash (U.S. dollars); there are no collect or credit-card calls. The average cost to the United States and Canada is $2 to $2.50 a minute.

TIPPING

Gratuities are only included in resort packages and in "tourist" restaurants. In all other establishments and for all other services, tipping is voluntary. U.S. currency is preferred over Cuban pesos. A good rule is $1 per night's stay at a resort for the chambermaid, $1 for a doorman who gets you a cab, and $1 a bag for a bellhop. You may also want to tip the concierge $5 if he or she makes special arrangements for you. In restaurants, tip 10% of the bill for good service.

TOUR OPERATORS

As with air travel, U.S. citizens interested in booking a tour or package to Cuba must generally go through a non-U.S. operator. However, there is one tour operator, New Jersey–based Marazul Tours, that has been operating tours to Cuba for the past 18 years—although only to U.S. citizens who satisfy all requirements established by the U.S. government. Such travelers must have written permission from the Treasury Department. U.S. citizens who can apply include members of the United Nations or U.S. government officials; reporters on assignment; professors and teachers on research/writing assignments; and those traveling for humanitarian reasons, such as visiting sick relatives or attending a funeral.

Buying a prepackaged tour or independent vacation can make your trip to Cuba less expensive and more hassle-free. Because everything is prearranged you'll spend less time planning.

Operators that handle several hundred thousand travelers per year can use their purchasing power to give you a good price. Their high volume may also indicate financial stability. But some small companies provide more personalized service; because they tend to specialize, they may also be more knowledgeable about a given area.

A GOOD DEAL?

The more your package or tour includes, the better you can predict the ultimate cost of your vacation. Make sure you know exactly what is covered, and **beware of hidden costs.** Are taxes, tips, and service charges included? Transfers and baggage handling? Entertainment and excursions? These can add up.

THE GOLD GUIDE / SMART TRAVEL TIPS

SMART TRAVEL TIPS / THE GOLD GUIDE

If the package or tour you are considering is priced lower than in your wildest dreams, **be skeptical.** Also, **make sure your travel agent knows the accommodations** and other services. Ask about the hotel's location, room size, beds, and whether it has a pool, room service, or programs for children, if you care about these. Has your agent been there in person or sent others you can contact?

BUYER BEWARE

Each year consumers are stranded or lose their money when tour operators—even very large ones with excellent reputations—go out of business. So **check out the operator.** Find out how long the company has been in business, and ask several agents about its reputation. All operators in Canada and the United Kingdom who sell packages to Cuba are required by law to cover your payments and travel arrangements in case of default.

Although the Department of Transportation watches over charter-flight operators, no regulatory body prevents tour operators from raiding the till. You may want to protect yourself by buying travel insurance that includes a tour-operator default provision.

It's also a good idea to choose a company that participates in the American Society of Travel Agents Tour Operator Program (TOP; ☞ Travel Agencies, *below*). This gives you a forum if there are any disputes between you and your tour operator; ASTA will act as mediator.

USING AN AGENT

Travel agents are excellent resources. In fact, large operators accept bookings made only through travel agents. But it's a good idea to **collect brochures from several agencies,** because some agents' suggestions may be influenced by relationships with tour and package firms that reward them for volume sales. If you have a special interest, **find an agent with expertise in that area;** ASTA (☞ Travel Agencies, *below*) has a database of specialists worldwide. Do some homework on your own, too: Local tourism boards can provide information about lesser-known and

small-niche operators, some of which may sell only direct.

SINGLE TRAVELERS

Prices for packages and tours are usually quoted per person, based on two sharing a room. If traveling solo, you may be required to pay the full double-occupancy rate. Some operators eliminate this surcharge if you agree to be matched with a roommate of the same sex, even if one is not found by departure time.

GROUP TOURS & PACKAGES

Among companies that sell tours to Cuba, the following are nationally known, have proven reputations, and offer plenty of options. The classifications used below represent different price categories, and you'll probably encounter these terms when talking to a travel agent or tour operator. The key difference is usually in accommodations, which run from budget to better, and better-yet to best.

➤ U.S. OPERATORS: **Marazul Tours Inc.** (Tower Plaza, 4100 Park Ave., Weehawken, NJ 07087, ☎ 201/319–9670) operates a daily charter service from Miami to Havana.

➤ CANADIAN OPERATORS: **Canadian Holidays** (191 The West Mall, 6th floor, Etobicoke, Ontario M9C 5K8, ☎ 416/620–8687). **Canada Cuba Sports and Cultural Festivals** (7171 Torbram Rd., Unit 51, Mississauga, Ontario L4T 3W4, ☎ 905/678–0426) for study programs as well as beach packages. **Conquest Tours** (85 Brisbane Rd., Downsview, Ontario M3J 2K3, ☎ 416/665–9222). **Enroute Holidays** (554 Gordon Baker Rd., Willowdale, Ontario M2H 3B4, ☎ 416/495–9779; winter packages only). **Magna Holidays** (163 Buttermill Ave., Unit 3, Concord, Ontario L4K 3X8, ☎ 905/761–7330).

➤ CUBAN OPERATORS: **Cubamar Specialized Tourism** (Calle 15, No. 752, Esq. A, Paseo, Vedado, Havana 4, ☎ 30–5536 or 30–0662) for eco-tours and youth tours. **Cubanacán** (Calle 9na y 146, Playa, Havana, ☎ 33–6247). **Cubatur** (Calle 23 y L, Vedado, Havana, ☎ 32–6507). **Gaviota S.A.** (Calle 16, No. 504 e/5 y 7, Miramar, Havana, ☎ 23–6977 or 29–1059). **Gran Caribe Hotel Group** (Av. 7ma, e/42 y 44, Miramar Havana, ☎ 24–0575). **Havanatur** (Calle 2, No. 17 e/1 y 3, Miramar, Havana, ☎ 33–2273). **Horizontes Hotels** (Calle L, No. 456 e/25 y 27, Vedado, Havana, ☎ 33–4042). **Islazul Tourist Chain** (Calle G y Malecón, Vedado, Havana, ☎ 33–0571). **Marinas Puertosol Matrix House** (Villa Marina Tarara, Cabre No. 34404 e/2da y 4ta, Havana, ☎ 33–3510). **Sol y Son/Cubana Airlines Travel Agency** (Calle 23, No. 64 e/Infanta y P, La Rampa, Vedado, Havana, ☎ 33–5169).

➤ Mexican Operators: **Mexicana Airlines** (☎ 52/5/325–0990).

➤ U.K. Operators: **Bike Tours** (Box 75, Bath, Avon BA1 1BX, ☎ 01225/310859). **Cox and King** (45 Buckingham Gate, London SW1E 6AF, ☎ 0171/873–5001). **Journey Latin America** (16 Devonshire Rd., London W4 2HD, ☎ 0181/747–3108). **Kinetic Travel** (55 Old Church St., London SW3 5BS, ☎ 0171/352–4984). **Progressive Tours** (12 Porchester Pl., Marble Arch, London W2 1NR, ☎ 0171/262–1676). **Regent Holidays** (15 John St., Bristol BS1 2HR, ☎ 0117/921–1711). **South American Experience** (47 Causton St., London SW1P 4AT, ☎ 0171/976–5511). **Sunworld/Iberotravel Ltd.** (71 Hough Side Rd., Pudsey LS28 9BR, ☎ 0113/239–3020).

TRAIN TRAVEL

If you're not going to rent a car or hire a car and driver (☞ Taxis, *above*), **take the train rather than the bus.** It is a good way to see the countryside and perhaps converse in broken Spanish with your seatmate, but a prolonged journey may leave you stiff and sore; these trains are designed for very practical transportation and not passenger comfort.

Tourists must pay in U.S. dollars and must **buy rail tickets in person in advance** from the main terminal. The cost of train travel is fairly reasonable; for example, a return ticket to Santiago de Cuba from Havana, a terrific sightseeing tour about 800 km (496 mi) to the opposite end of the island, is $120 round-trip. Smoking is allowed on Cuban trains, and there are no designated no-smoking sections.

➤ Tickets: **Oficina Reservaciones Pasajes** (Calle 21, Esq. 4, Vedado, Havana); from **Ferrotour** (Calles Arsenal y Egido, Havana, ☎ 62–1770). **Hotel Habana Libre tourist desk** (Calle L & 23, Vededo, Havana, ☎ 30–5011).

TRANSPORTATION

Whether you travel by bus, train, hired car, or a rented vehicle, it is important to **plan your transportation carefully.** The only means of transportation that can be arranged before you go to Cuba is a car rental; all others must be reserved locally. For more information on your options within Cuba, *see* the individual headings for Air Travel, Bus Travel, Renting a Car, Train Travel, and Taxis, *above.*

TRAVEL AGENCIES

A good travel agent puts your needs first. Look for an agency that has been in business at least five years, emphasizes customer service, and has someone on staff who specializes in your destination. In addition, **make sure the agency belongs to the American Society of Travel Agents** (ASTA). If your travel agency is also acting as your tour operator, *see* Tour Operators, *above*).

➤ Local Agent Referrals: **American Society of Travel Agents** (ASTA, ☎ 800/965–2782 24-hr hot line, ℻ 703/684–8319). **Alliance of Canadian Travel Associations** (Suite 201, 1729 Bank St., Ottawa, Ontario K1V 7Z5, ☎ 613/521–0474, ℻ 613/521–0805). **Association of British Travel Agents** (55–57 Newman St., London W1P 4AH, ☎ 0171/637–2444, ℻ 0171/637–0713).

U

U.S. GOVERNMENT

The U.S. government can be an excellent source of inexpensive travel information. When planning your trip, **find out what government materials are available.** The U.S. State Department has a comprehensive consular information sheet outlining current conditions in Cuba and U.S. government policy regarding travel to Cuba.

➤ ADVISORIES: **U.S. Department of State American Citizens Services Office** (Room 4811, Washington, DC 20520); enclose a self-addressed, stamped envelope. **Interactive hot line** (☎ 202/647–5225, FAX 202/647–3000). **Computer bulletin board** (☎ 202/647–9225).

V
VISITOR INFORMATION

Although the Cuban government maintains no official tourism office in the United States, American travelers can still get information from the Center for Cuban Studies (be sure to request a copy of the bimonthly magazine *Cuba Update*) or from Cuban tourism offices in Canada. Canadians can contact the Cuban Tourism board in Toronto or Montreal. Cubanacán, a Cuban-based travel company, also maintains an office in Toronto.

Once in Cuba, the main tourist office is your best source for general information and maps as well as specific advice on the various tours, hotel-room availability, and travel fares. There are offices throughout the country as well as a counter at José Martí Airport. Questions about tours can also be directed to Havanatur, the largest international tour operator with hotel properties as well, or Cubatur, which also runs many tour-related programs and owns most of the tourist hotels. Travelers looking to establish tourism-related business contacts in Cuba should contact Cubanacán.

➤ IN THE U.S.: **Center for Cuban Studies** (124 West 23rd St., New York, NY, 10011, ☎ 212/242–0559).

➤ IN CANADA: CUBA TOURIST BOARD (55 QUEEN ST. E, SUITE 705, TORONTO, ONTARIO M5C 1R6, ☎ 416/362–0700). BUREAU DE TOURISME DE CUBA (440 BLVD. RENE LEVESQUE WEST, BUREAU 1105, MONTREAL, QUÉBEC H2Z 1V7, ☎ 514/875–8004). CUBANACÁN (375 BAY ST., SUITE 1902, TORONTO, ONTARIO, CANADA M5H 2W9, ☎ 416/601–0343).

➤ IN THE U.K.: **Cuban Consulate** (15 Grape St., London WC1V 6PA, ☎ 0171/240–2488).

➤ IN CUBA: PALACIO DEL TURISMO (OBISPO 252, HABANA VIEJA, ☎ 61–1544). CUBANACÁN (AV. 146 E/11 Y 13, PLAYA, HAVANA, ☎ 33–6043), CUBATUR (CASA CENTRAL, CALLE F, NO. 157 E/9 Y CALZADO, VEDADO, HAVANA, ☎ 32–7075), AND HAVANATUR (CALLE 2, NO. 7 E/1 Y 3, MIRAMAR, MUNICIPO PLAYA, HAVANA, ☎ 33–2273).

W
WHEN TO GO

The best time to visit Cuba is between November and April. Although prices are a little higher, this season is slightly cooler and drier than summer. Hotels fill up quickly during this period, especially at Christmastime, so don't delay in making your reservations (☞ Lodging, *above*).

Prices in hotels drop 15% to 20% from May through October, but this is the rainy season. (The heaviest rains fall in September and October.) Hurricanes are also a concern during this period. In summer, the temperature and humidity rise, sometimes to uncomfortable levels, discouraging midday activity. This is more noticeable in the eastern provinces. The temperature of the sea, however, is pleasant for swimming year-round.

CLIMATE

Cuba is hot anytime; the annual average is about 25.5°C (78°F), but it reaches well over 30°C (90°F) in the summer shade. In general, the eastern provinces are somewhat warmer than the western ones.

➤ FORECASTS: **Weather Channel Connection** (☎ 900/932–8437), 95þ per minute from a touch-tone phone.

1 Havana

MYSTERIOUS HAVANA

By Miguel
Barnet

Anthropologist
and novelist,
author of
Gallego,
Barnet is one
of the great
Cuban writers,
heir to the
literary tradition
of José Lezama
Lima and Alejo
Carpentier.

Behind the columns described in the works of novelist Alejo Carpentier, those eclectic and mysterious colonnades that provide cover from the rain and sun, there are *orishas*, African deities brought to Cuba from the Yoruba civilization.

The columns, a hundred years old, offsprings of the Spanish Baroque or the French neoclassical period, stand there, cracked but solid, so that the orishas can perform their magic.

This is what Havana is all about. The winking orisha behind an ancient column. The European columns and the African orishas are a perfect expression of the fusion of the two cultures, two worlds that shaped Cuba in a dramatic nuptial embrace.

Havana is the concave mirror, the artistic distortion, of this transcultural process. In its streets, its corners and squares, and its neighborhoods there is a magic that some, the luckiest, discover. And that others never see.

This is Havana. An elusive and enigmatic city. A city with many different faces. Everything in it can confuse us. Its light can blind us, its streets can lead to nowhere. And sometimes they simply sink into the earth. That's when we're only looking at what appears on the surface. But under that white and dazzling light there is the ancient soil. The true Havana. Mistress of time and memory, with places no one has ever seen.

Havana is not merely its historic Old Quarter, perhaps its most beautiful section and the one most envied in America, with its official monuments, its fortresses, and its grandiose town houses once inhabited by the hemisphere's most ostentatious bourgeoisie, what historians call, in rich hyperbole, the *zacarocracia*, or "pasturocracy."

Havana is its barrios, its neighborhoods, its outskirts and its inner city, its inside-the-walls and its outside-the-walls. It is also its stone houses and Catalan tiled roofs, its Creole patios decorated with ceramic tiles from Seville, its surrounding hills where the rough gourd and the *bata*, or double-skinned drum—the king of drums—hold sway. Havana is its Baroque churches with naves that reach up to touch the sky. Its Catholic churches and its syncretic temples strewn all across the city.

The Church of the Virgin de Regla across the bay, where the creation of man is depicted with four randomly scattered coconut shells. The church, once built of wood, stands in a village far across the sea, and its Virgin de Regla, originally from Andalusia, has become Yemayá, mother of all the orishas, mistress of intelligence and of the salt sea.

Yemayá, who goes to the river in a procession every September 7, carried on a platform by worshippers who see in her the Black Virgin, charred in a faraway fire and brought to Cuba in a galleon that set sail from the Guadalquivir River in southern Spain.

Or the sanctuary of San Lázaro, saint of crutches, who does not appear in the hagiographies and is not a sainted bishop but simply San Lázaro, the leper of the miracles, syncretized as Babalú Ayé, the Arará god; San Lázaro with his sores, purulent, iconoclastic. San Lázaro of the processions, the most popular of all the gods of Santería.

Every December 17, as in Sevilla during Easter Week or in Santiago de Compostela on feast days in honor of St. James, the people of Havana show their devotion to Babalú Ayé. The chapel overflows with the faithful, and all along the pilgrimage route men, women, and children make their way to Rincón, either dragging stones or with stones hanging from their necks, on one foot or on their knees, to give thanks to Babalú, to Baba Soroso, for his miracles. There are few Cubans who fail to note the occasion. And Rincón is just outside the city.

Havana has places no one has ever seen.

In Guanabacoa, one of the oldest districts, the aroma of fresh bread from the bakeries blends with the smell of fish, and the sound of the beating of drums is a dominating ancestral presence. There Palo Mayombe and Santería exist side by side, spiritualism and the men-only Abakuá Society—the only organization of its kind in America.

Guanabacoa is also, like Regla, part of Havana. Its African and Spanish roots have become intertwined in the creation of a world that is quintessentially Caribbean, one that has little in common with the rest of America.

Havana is the mythological bridge between the real and the unreal. It is a crossroads. It is the Caribbean.

In Guanabacoa a rooster is sacrificed every five minutes.

The *iyawó*, all dressed in white, newly initiated into the spiritualist cult, struts around streets filled with balding half-breeds. You have to fold your arms and say "Okú Awó" as he passes by. The flesh-and-blood iyawó, covered with necklaces and with a white handkerchief on his head, and La Giraldilla, erect in her tower commanding the four points of the compass—these are the two emblems of the city.

Spacious squares, tiny ones, squares with green parks and wrought-iron benches. Entrances with rows of columns where the orishas lurk.

Havana has places no one has ever seen.

The shuttered windows lend an air of desolation. At times Havana seems like a ghost town. The very patina of its buildings contributes to its air of mystery.

And the Havana *solar,* or town house, that ancient mansion that has now become a multifamily dwelling? It is still there. As is the classic rumba played on a wooden box, never supplanted by the salsa, with its shrill metallic and electronic sound.

The Havana town house, even today, is an institution.

With its narrow patio and wooden water trough—a box to beat a rhythm on. Sticks striking each other, spoons, anything at all to make the box resound. And the rumba thunders out of the windows and doors in search of space. This is Havana. It is also a pointed arch filled with gaudy stained glass. At night the heat and the silence create an all-pervasive sensuality, and the stained glass takes on gentler colors.

At night the streets of Havana sink into the earth. This is how travelers and novelists used to see Havana. This is how René Portocarrero painted her and the way Alejo Carpentier described her, the way Nicolás Guillén perceived her.

In Havana, Federico García Lorca wrote: "If I get lost, look for me in Cuba or in Granada."

This is Havana. The winking orisha behind the column. The forgotten silence in some park that no longer exists. Havana is uproar and tumult, scandal and revelry.

It is also hard-working people. And children with kerchiefs around their necks. People with no children and not much to do. People who keep living for something that doesn't seem to happen, either during the day or at night.

You can see the bay from the Colina del Cristo. The Cristo of Havana is not the same Cristo you see in Rio. But he's Havana's Cristo and he has endured there, unscathed, with his offerings of rotten fruit and colored ribbons.

He's the Cristo who watched a people undergo a revolution.

He's also a syncretic Cristo. One for all the people.

This is Havana. A hybrid city, mysterious, a city for everyone.

HAVANA HISTORY

Declared the capital of Cuba in 1607—after having been the de facto capital since 1553—Havana is the island's principal city and unquestionably its main tourist attraction. The traditional point of entry for visitors, Havana presents you with your first impressions of the country as it is now: streets nearly empty, buildings desperately in need of much more than simply a coat of paint, posters with revolutionary slogans, lines of potential shoppers in the stores. Yet once you begin to explore, you will discover one of the friendliest cities on the planet, a city bravely struggling to survive the country's dire economic troubles. A few days in Cuba will leave you with conflicting impressions and unforgettable memories.

The exact date of the city's founding is not recorded, however it is believed that it was established in its first location, on the island's south coast, in 1514. A short time later it was moved to the north coast, to the mouth of the Almendares River. Then in 1519 it was once again relocated to the spot on the bay now occupied by the Plaza de Armas. There is also some debate about the origin of the city's name, although it is probable that it derives from the name of a local dignitary mentioned in various chronicles, a certain Habaguanix. From the very beginning, Havana was important primarily because of its strategic position on the Straits of Florida. The Bay of Havana, one of America's safest ports, became a stopping point for ships plying the Atlantic between Seville and America. The riches from Mexico and Peru passed through Havana, as did those of the Far East, carried by galleon from Manila in the Philippines by way of Acapulco. Havana became the third most populous city in the New World, and its port certainly had the best defenses. Reflecting all this, as early as the 17th century Havana was known as "the Key to the New World." A heterogeneous population of sailors, clerics, merchants, slaves, and soldiers collected in Havana, waiting months for the arrival of the last ship needed to form a convoy capable of fighting off pirates while crossing the Atlantic. The city continued to grow during the 19th century, but now not so much owing to the goods passing through it as because of the wealth of the island itself. Sugar, tobacco, coffee, and rum were the chief exports shipped out of Havana's harbor. The primitive huts of wood and palm leaves from the early 16th century had gradually been replaced by splendid mansions, great convents and cathedrals, and a formidable system of walls and ramparts.

Havana preserves more of its historic colonial legacy than any other city in the Americas. In 1982, UNESCO declared La Habana Vieja, or Old Havana, a World Heritage Site, a veritable living museum. A popular couplet compares the tiny enclave to the city of Cadiz, in southern Spain, and in it no fewer than 144 buildings from the 16th and 17th centuries are preserved.

The modern city stretches outward from this core. Modern Havana is a city of 2 million inhabitants and has undergone a significant transformation since the 1959 revolution.

HAVANA ESSENTIALS

Arriving and Departing

By Boat

Yachts and cruise ships dock at the **Marina Hemingway** or **Varadero Beach,** where they pass through immigration and customs. Owners or captains are required to contact the nautical branch of the National Institute of Tourism by VHF radio.

By Plane

José Martí Airport, in Rancho Boyeros, is 15 km (9 mi) from the center of Havana. For information on arrivals and departures, call 33 51 77/79, 70 77 01, or 45 32 75.

Staying in Havana

Emergencies

Ambulance (☎ 30 75 20 or 40 50 93). **Fire** (☎ 79 85 61/69). **Police** (☎ 32 35 20 or 32 10 60).

HOSPITALS AND PHARMACIES

Hospital Cira Garcia (Playa, Calle 20, No. 4101, ☎ 33 28 11/14, FAX 537 33 16 33) provides emergency services and has a 24-hour pharmacy. Another possibility is the **Hospital Hermanos Almeijeiras** (Centro Habana, San Lazaro and Belascoaín, ☎ 70 77 21).

Money Matters

TRAVELER'S CHECKS

Most hotels and shops accept traveler's checks unless they were issued in the United States. Hotels also cash traveler's checks—although, sometimes you'll encounter difficulties—as does the **Banco Financiero Internacional** (Vedado, Calle Linea 1, ☎ 33 34 23 or 33 34 24).

Visitor Information

Cuba's tourist agencies can help you customize your plans—before and during your trip. **Cubanacán** (✉ Av. 146 e/11 y 13, Playa, Havana, ☎ 33–6043). **Cubatur** (Calle F, No. 157, e/9 y Calzada, Vedado, ☎ 33 41 11, 33 41 22, 33 41 04, or 33 30 30); **Fantástico** (Calle 148A, No. 1107, Siboney, ☎ 33 60 31/31 or 33 60 41/45); **Gaviotatours** (Calle 16, No. 511, e/5 y 7, Miramar, ☎ 33 88 08 or 29 45 28); **Havanatur** (Calle 2, No. 17, e/1 y 3, Miramar, ☎ 33 21 21, 33 21 61, or 33 22 48; Calle 6, No. 117, e/1 y 3, Miramar, ☎ 33 27 12 or 33 27 14); and **Tryp Habana Libre** (☎ 33 41 35).

Upon your arrival, the **tourist office at José Martí Airport** can find you a room. You must book it for a minimum of three nights, and there is no guarantee of a stay in the hotel of your choice.

Almost every hotel in Havana has a **buró de turismo** (tourist office), where you can coordinate your daily activities, reserve a table at a restaurant or cabaret, charter a yacht, sign up for a city tour, or book a hotel room anywhere in the country.

Asistur (La Habana Vieja, Calle Prado 254, ☎ 63 82 84) offers financial assistance in case you lose or misplace your money or credit cards. The same organization sells travel insurance. **Assist Card, Europe Assistance,** and **Gessa Assistance** also assist tourists. **Esicuba** (☎ 62 50 51) is another international company that offers insurance.

The people of Havana are friendly, kind, and talkative. Do not hesitate to ask for directions from a stranger or even to strike up a conversation. You are almost certain to be told, promptly and cheerfully, whatever it is you wish to know.

Getting Around

From the Airport to Downtown

If you come as an independent traveler, you must either take a taxi or rent a car (☞ *below*). A taxi to a hotel in the central Vedado district (the Habana Libre or the Riviera, for example) costs $15–$20 depending on the type of cab. The trip, which is a straight shot down the Avenida de Boyeros, takes about a half hour.

If you book your trip through one of Cuba's travel agencies (☞ Visitor Information, *above*), you can save money by having them arrange your transportation to and from the airport.

Within Havana

GETTING ORIENTED

An extremely spread-out city, Havana is divided into 15 districts or municipalities, six of which—Playa, Plaza, Centro Habana, La Habana Vieja, Regla, and La Habana del Este—are on the ocean. The others, Boyeros, La Lisa, 10 de Octubre, Marianao, Arroyo de Naranjo, Cerro, Guanabacoa, Cotorro, and San Miguel del Padron, are far from the city center.

In La Habana Vieja and Centro Habana the streets are named—Prado, San Joaquin, Obispo, San Rafael, or Virtudes, for example. In Vedado (Plaza) and Miramar (Playa) the streets are identified by letters and numbers. Streets that run parallel to the shore in these major districts bear odd numbers, 1st being closest to the bay, 3rd, 5th, and 7th lying progressively farther inland to the south.

In Vedado, streets that run perpendicular to the coastal Avenida Malecón are known by the letters A through O toward the east and the even numbers 2 through 28 toward the west. Next to Vedado, which ends at the Almendares River, is the diplomatic district of Miramar, where the streets that run perpendicular to the coast are also labeled with even numbers (from 0 to 100 east to west). Finding your way in these two neighborhoods is very simple, but it is essential that you know which district you want; a given address—Calle 4 and Avenida 3, for example—could be either in Vedado or in Miramar.

Most restaurants, cabarets, nightclubs, museums, and historical sites are clustered in La Habana Vieja, Centro Habana, Plaza (mainly Vedado), and Playa. They are all well known to taxi drivers. Many hotels and some restaurants and nightclubs are in Vedado and Miramar, far from the historic heart of La Habana Vieja. If your destination is off the beaten track, confirm the address and the district before you set out.

PRECAUTIONS

Havana is a relaxed city, with little traffic and even less delinquency—although it appears to be on the rise over the last few years. Nevertheless, stay alert when you're in Centro Habana and La Habana Vieja. You will encounter dozens of young people offering to sell you something. It's best to avoid these street hustlers, as they will trick you if they can. Muggings are rare, but thievery is not uncommon, especially from rental cars. Purse-snatching is also a problem in these areas.

PUBLIC TRANSPORTATION

As a tourist, public transportation (specifically, buses) is not an option. Current fuel shortages mean that it may be hours between buses, and they are always packed.

RENTING A BICYCLE

Ask at the tourist office in your hotel.

RENTING A CAR

Reserve a vehicle at least a week in advance, especially in high season; there are often not enough cars to meet the demand. Despite the island's fuel shortage, there are plenty of stations and as a tourist paying in dollars you should have no trouble getting gasoline. Overall, traffic is not heavy, and parking is not difficult.

For the cheapest rates on cars, Jeeps, or vans try **Havanautos.** *José Martí Airport, Terminal 1 (Cubana de Aviación), ☎ 45 21 75, and Terminal 2 (Iberia and other carriers), ☎ 54 24 13; Vedado, Hotel Capri, 21 y N, ☎ 33 34 84; Playas del Este, Hotel Marazul, ☎ 0 (687) 30 93 and 23 51; Miramar, Complejo Ibero Star Tritón-Neptuno, Calle 3 y 72, ☎ 33 29 21; and Vedado, Hotel Habana Riviera, Paseo and Malecón, ☎ 33 37 33.*

Cubacar charges more, but its cars are in better condition. *José Martí Airport, Terminal 2, ☎ 33 55 46; Hotel Comodoro, ☎ 33 17 06; Hotel Biocaribe, Calle 158 y Ave. 31, ☎ 33 60 32; Residencial Marina Hemingway, ☎ 33 17 07.*

Also try **Transautos.** *Miramar, Hotel Copacabana, Calle 1, e/44 y 46, ☎ 33 06 21; Vedado, Hotel Capri, Calle 21 y N, ☎ 33 40 38 or 33 55 32.*

TAXIS

The meter starts at $1. A ride to the Plaza de Armas from the central Hotel Habana Libre costs about $5, from the Hotel Comodoro in Miramar $10. Four or five cab rides a day can easily add up to $50. If you plan to make many trips around the city, renting a car may be more economical.

WALKING

Havana is so spread out that you will probably find cars the only reasonable way to travel from district to district. However, if you stick to one district for the day—La Habana Vieja, for example—distances between sights will be manageable.

Organized Tours

Bus Tours

Check with your hotel's tourist office. **Cubanacán** and **Cubatur** (☞ Visitor Information, *above*) offer panoramic tours of the city. **Havanatur's** (☞ Visitor Information, *above*) four-hour **city tours** feature transportation around town in air-conditioned buses and walks through Old Havana, which UNESCO has declared a World Heritage Site. Sights include the Plaza de Armas, the Plaza de la Catedral, and other parts of Old Havana as well as a brief stop in the Plaza de la Revolución. ▧ $13. ☯ *Departures daily at 9 AM from your hotel.*

Boat Tours

Another delightful way to see Havana is from the water. The **Marina Hemingway** (Santa Fe, Av. 5 y 248, ☎ 33 16 89 or 22 55 90, ext. 701; or speak with your hotel's tourist office) offers two-hour tours on a 31-foot yacht that can carry from four (minimum) to six passengers and three-hour tours on a 46-foot yacht (8–25 passengers). Both trips cost $30 per person and include transportation from your hotel to the marina, a cocktail, and an ocean swim. If you have more time (seven hours), book a trip that includes a meal; the cost is $45 per person.

Private Guides
Arrange a guide for a day or for the duration of your stay through **Cubatur** (☞ *above*). Rates range from $22 for 12 hours ($28 for tours outside the city) to $170 for 1 week or $300 for 2 weeks.

Walking Tours
The Office of the City Historian recently opened its San Cristóbal agency, which offers art and history tours of Old Havana. Itineraries include visits to artists' workshops and tours of churches, convents, and Spanish fortresses. The folks at San Cristóbal can also update you on the cultural and artistic happenings in this part of town. *Oficios 110, between Lamparilla and Amargura, Old Havana,* ☎ *33 86 93/94,* FAX *33 86 97.*

EXPLORING HAVANA

The first two walking itineraries suggested here are confined to La Habana Vieja (Old Havana). The third covers the avenues created when the old walls were torn down, and it passes some of the most important monuments of recent centuries. The fourth concentrates on the fortresses built to protect the bay, and the fifth offers a tour of the bay across to the Regla district and a different view of the city. Tour 6 explores modern Havana, and Tour 7 follows in the steps of Ernest Hemingway through the city and beyond to the Playas del Este.

Numbers in the margin correspond to points of interest on the Havana and Old Havana maps.

Tour 1: La Habana Vieja—Plaza de Armas and Plaza de la Catedral

➊ Start at the **Plaza de Armas,** the city's oldest square and for centuries its political and military center. This is one of the finest and most beautifully restored architectural ensembles in Havana. The last major renovation of the square was accomplished in 1935, based on engravings showing what it looked like much earlier. Beginning in 1577 the square was known as the Plaza de la Iglesia, as this was the site of Havana's parish church. For many years this was the city's civic center, but the construction of military buildings radically changed its character. At midday you can rest on benches in the welcome shade of the trees.

Most of the structures near the square are of historic interest, but the
➋ most impressive of all is the **Palacio de los Capitanes-Generales** (Palace of the Commanders-in-Chief), which takes up one whole side. The palace is the culmination of Cuban Baroque architecture, much imitated by other buildings of the epoch. Its facade, dominated by 10 immense columns, is one of the finest in Cuba. Construction began in 1776, by order of the governor and captain-general Marquess de la Torre, but the building was not ready for use until 1790. Initially, it was the seat of the island's government, housing both the *cabildo* (town council), entered from Calle Obispo, and a jail, entered from Calle de Mercaderes. In the 108 years following Cuba's independence, the palace served as the residence of 65 successive commanding generals. Later it became the presidential palace and ultimately the town hall. It now houses the **Museo de la Ciudad de La Habana** (City Museum). Beside the main entrance, in front of the portico, are bells from the churches of several sugar mills. As you pass through the huge mahogany doorway, on your

right is a statue of the Spanish king Fernando VII, which originally adorned the courtyard. The courtyard is filled with a lush garden of medicinal and aromatic plants and examples of the royal palm, Cuba's national tree. A statue of Christopher Columbus by Italian sculptor Cucchiari now stands in the center. Here you also see the cannons that once announced the opening and closing of the city gates and a tombstone dating from 1557, Cuba's oldest monument. You may witness an ancient Cuban custom while visiting the palace: When girls turn 15 they are given something like a debutante party, the *quince*. Photographing the celebrant in her most elegant dress in front of a major monument is an important part of the festivities, and the palacio is a favored backdrop.

The City Museum contains a good collection of paintings, furniture, uniforms, and documents relating to the history of Havana. One of the best known pieces on display is *La Giraldilla*, a small bronze statue representing Doña Inés de Bobadilla, Cuba's only woman governor, who replaced her husband Hernando de Soto when he set off to conquer Florida in 1539. Tradition has it that Doña Inés spent long hours scanning the horizon while waiting for her husband's return, and it was for that reason that her statue was placed on the highest point of the nearby Real Fuerza fortress, facing the entrance to the harbor. It was later toppled by a hurricane and replaced by a copy. La Giraldilla has become the emblem of Havana, one readily recognized by rum fanciers, as her image appears on the Havana Club label. *La Habana Vieja, Museo de la Ciudad de La Habana, Tacón e/Obispo and O'Reilly,* ☎ 61 28 76. 🖼 $3, $4 with guide. ⊙ *Mon.–Sun. 10:30–6:30.*

❸ On your left as you leave the museum is the **Palacio del Segundo Cabo.** Built shortly before the Palace of the Commanders-in-Chief, this is another of the city's important Baroque structures. It originally housed the *casa de correos* (post office), but in 1853 it became the residence of the Segundo Cabo (Second Corporal), the island's political authority during the colonial era. The building's facade features a row of columns fronting a portico. The entryway, with its five-lobed arch, leads to an Andalusianlike courtyard. Visitors are not allowed inside, as the building now contains the offices of two publishing houses.

❹ Next door is the **Castillo de la Real Fuerza** (Castle of the Royal Forces), ringed by a water-filled moat. Spain's first fortress in Cuba, it is the second-oldest in America, but it is not the original structure. The fortress built by Hernando de Soto in 1538 was poorly sited—some 350 yards from the present location—and highly vulnerable to enemy attack. It was easily destroyed by the French pirate Jacques de Sores in 1555. Construction of the building you see today was begun in 1558, following the plans favored in Renaissance Europe: a square box with bastions at the corners, ringed by a moat, and accessible by means of a drawbridge. In time, much larger fortresses were built to defend the city and the port in more strategic spots. This one then served in turn as the treasury, the home of the public archives, and the National Library Archives. Since 1977 it has been the **Museo do las Armas** (Arms Museum), with exhibits that trace the development of armaments technology through the end of the 19th century. A copy of *La Giraldilla* stands in one of the corner towers. *La Habana Vieja, Castillo de la Real Fuerza, O'Reilly y Av. del Puerto,* ☎ 61 50 10. ⊙ *Thurs.–Mon. 9:15– 4:45.*

❺ On the corner of the third side of the square is **El Templete,** Havana's first civic building constructed in the neoclassical style. According to tradition, it was here, in the shade of a ceiba, or kapok tree, that the first Mass was celebrated in Havana. It was also here that the first ca-

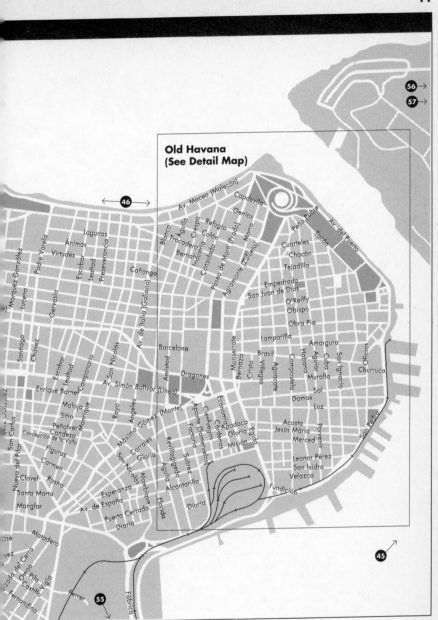

**Old Havana
(See Detail Map)**

Av. Maceo (Malecón)
Capdevila
Genios
Peña Pobre
Blanco
Aguila
Crespo
Refugio
Colón
Morro
Av. del Puerto
Trocadero
Industria
Cuarteles
Tacón
Bernal
Consulado
Paseo de Martí (Prado)
Chacón
Agramonte (Zulueta)
Tejadillo
Lagunas
Ánimas
Virtudes
Cañongo
Empedrado
San Juan de Dios
Marqués González
Padre Varela
Escobar
Lealtad
Perseverancia
O'Reilly
Lucena
Gervasio
Av. de Italia (Galiano)
Obispo
Obra Pía
Santiago
Chávez
Escobar
Lealtad
Campanario
San Nicolás
Barcelona
Lamparilla
Amargura
Monserrate
Bernaza
Cristo
Brasil
Villegas
Aguacate
Habana
Aguiar
Cuba
San Ignacio
Oficios
Enrique Barnet
Amistad
Dragones
Compostela
Muralla
Churruca
Maloja
Manrique
Rayo
Angeles
Av. Simón Bolívar (Línea)
Sol
Damas
Luz
Sitio
Peñalver
Condesa
Concepción de la Valla
Máximo Gómez (Monte)
Economía
Acosta
Jesús María
Merced
San Pedro
Figuras
Carmen
Rostro
San Nicolás
Alambique
Gloria
Corrales
Cienfuegos
Cárdenas
Aponte (Someruelos)
Factoría
Apodaca
Gloria
Misión
Egido
Porvenir
Nueva del Pilar
Clavel
Santa Marta
Manglar
Esperanza
Av. de España
Puerta Cerrada
Aguila
Suárez
Revillagigedo
Leonor Pérez
San Isidro
Velazco
Alcantarilla
Florida
Diaria
Fundición
Diaria
Matadero
José
vez
Nueva del Cerro
Omoa
Pila
Castillo
Fernandina
Ferrer
Fábrica

Old Havana

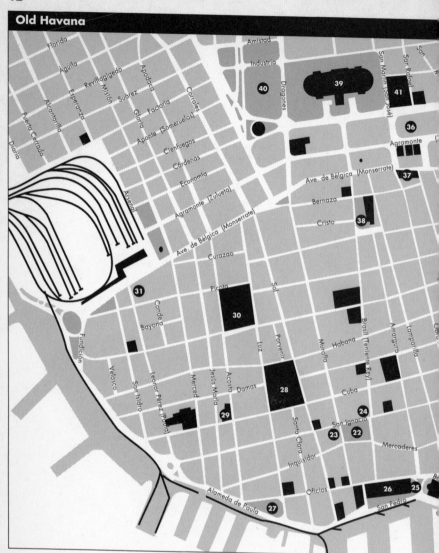

La Bodeguita del Medio, **19**
Capitolio, **39**
Casa de África, **11**
Casa de Chacón, **18**
Casa de Gaspar de Rivero de Vasconcelos, **12**
Casa de la Comedia, **7**
Casa de la Obrapía, **10**

Casa de las Hermanas Cárdenas, **24**
Casa de Lombillo, **16**
Casa de los Condes de Jaruco, **23**
Casa del Árabe, **8**
Casa del Marqués de Arcos, **17**
Casa del Obispo Peñalver, **20**
Casa Natal de José Martí, **31**

Castillo de la Real Fuerza, **4**
Castillo de los Tres Santos Reyes Magos del Morro, **43**
Castillo de San Salvador de la Punta, **42**
Cathedral, **15**
Convento de Nuestra Señora de Belén, **30**
Convento de Santa Clara, **28**

El Floridita, **37**
Gran Teatro de la Habana, **41**
Granma Memorial, **34**
Iglesia del Espíritu Santo, **29**
Museo de la Revolución, **33**
Museo Nacional de Bellas Artes, **35**

Palacio de
los Capitanes-
Generales, **2**

Palacio de los Condes
de Santovenia, **6**

Palacio de los
Marqueses de Aguas
Claras, **14**

Palacio del Segundo
Cabo, **3**

Palacio Pedroso, **21**

Parque Central, **36**

Parque de la
Fraternidad, **40**

Plaza de Armas, **1**

Plaza de la
Catedral, **13**

Plaza de San
Francisco, **25**

Plaza del Cristo, **38**

Plaza Vieja, **22**

Plazuela de la Luz, **27**

Restored shops, **9**

Saint Francis of
Assisi church and
convent, **26**

San Carlos de la
Cabaña Fortress, **44**

El Templete, **5**

Trece de Marzo
Park, **32**

bildo was held after Havana was established in its present location. The original monument commemorating the event was erected in 1754; it was a three-sided column representing the three provinces into which the island was divided at that time. El Templete was built in 1828. It houses three canvases by the French painter, Jean-Baptiste Vermay, as well as a bust of Christopher Columbus. The present ceiba tree was planted in 1959; it is held sacred, as are all others of its kind in Cuba. Folklore has it that the spirit of the ceiba will grant the wishes of those who circle the trunk of the tree three times in silence. To many, the neo-classical Templete in the shade of the sacred ceiba is reminiscent of the one in Guernica beneath an oak.

6 Next comes the **Palacio de los Condes de Santovenia** (Palace of the Counts of Santovenia), built in the late 18th and early 19th centuries and famous in its time for the splendid fiestas held here. The most lavish of these by far was the celebration of Isabel II's accession to the throne (which went so far as to have a balloon liftoff from the palace's roof). The structure was later converted into the Santa Isabel, perhaps the most important hotel in Havana in the second half of the 19th century.

Leaving aside for now the fourth side of the square, turn into Calle Baratillo, a narrow alley that apparently takes its name from the *barato* (inexpensive) shops once found on it. At the intersection with Jústiz is **7** the **Casa de la Comedia,** one of the oldest buildings in Havana. The name, meaning theater or playhouse, goes back to the 18th century. The building was used for theatrical performances up until 1776, when the new Teatro Principal was erected. A theater company has its offices in the building even today. Continue along Jústiz to the intersection with Oficios, where you will see the **Museo de Autos Antiguos** (Old Car Museum). The museum houses a small collection of automobiles that once belonged to noted show-business or political figures, from Benny Moré to Che Guevara.

Oficios was one of the first four streets in Havana and owes its name to the *oficios de escribanos,* or scribes' offices, set up along it. In them the early settlers could have documents prepared, from wills to love **8** letters. In front of the Old Car Museum is the **Casa del Árabe** (Arab's House), another of the oldest structures in the city. It is known that the house was bought by Bishop Diego de Compostela in 1688 for use as Havana's first school. To appreciate the building's architecture, pass through the doorway to the interior courtyard. Artifacts discovered in the building's cellar are displayed inside, along with gifts from various Arab countries. On the upper floor there is a restaurant. *La Habana Vieja, Casa del Árabe, Oficios, e/Obispo and Obrapia,* ☎ 61 58 68. ☺ *Tues.–Sun. 9–6.*

Next door, in what was until the 17th century the **Casa del Obispo** (Bishop's House) is the **Museo Numismatico** (Currency Museum). The building has undergone numerous renovations; the present facade is neoclassical. Portions of the original structure can be seen on the right side of the inner courtyard. On the upper floor is an exhibit of Cuban coins from the 16th century to the present. Continuing toward the Plaza de Armas, you pass a **butcher shop** that appears to be a relic from another era; in fact, cabildo documents confirm that there has been such a shop at this spot since 1550. Until the first shop specializing in seafood was opened, it also sold fish and tortoise. The building on the **9** corner of Calle Obispo, across from the square, houses a series of **restored shops:** the ice-cream parlor El Anon, the Casa del Café con Leche, the restaurant La Mina, and the so-called water house La Tinaja. Centuries ago, water houses were where people bought water that was safe to drink, unlike that provided by the public fountains. In the 19th century, they came to be called *fuentes de soda,* or soda fountains, and bars in many American countries continue to go by that name today. The present one, opened in 1981, is a reminder of the earlier water houses and offers refreshment to the many sightseers in this part of the city. The next building, Obispo 113, houses a traditional barber shop and the Casa de la Natilla (Custard House). The barber shop is another re-creation of the sort of establishment found here centuries ago. A signboard reproduces a decree from the Spanish governor that the owner of the shop is the only person in Havana qualified to perform the functions of both barber and surgeon.

Calle Obispo is one of the most interesting streets in La Habana Vieja. Some say it got its name from the fact that Bishop Morell de Santa Cruz habitually traversed it on his tours of the city. Others claim that the name is even older and refers to Bishop Jerónimo de Lara, who lived here in 1641. Another of the street's famous regulars was Ernest Hemingway, who often walked this way when he lived at the Hotel Ambos Mundos, whether on his way to the harbor or in the other direction toward El Floridita, his favorite bar.

As you continue along Obispo, you will see two English cavalry cannons next to the Palace of the Commanders in Chief. The cannons are marked with the emblem of the British Crown and the monogram of King George III, who ordered the capture of Havana in 1762. On this street you will also find a veritable anthology of 16th- to 19th-century architecture. The oldest building you pass is the one with obvious Moorish features on the corner of Mercaderes. It has the best-preserved Mudejar-style roof in Havana. The **pharmacy** and *casa de infusiones* (herbal tea shop) that occupy the building reproduce the look of such establishments in centuries past. Across the street is the **Hotel Ambos Mundos** (Both Worlds). One of the most modern buildings in La Habana Vieja, the hotel has become famous for the fact that Ernest Hemingway lived here for a time. His room is preserved as a museum. On the opposite corner is the modern **Ministerio de Educacion,** with a monument to Havana's first university. The bronze bell was used to call the students to class.

To continue your tour of colonial palaces, take **Calle Mercaderes,** between the hotel and the Casa de Infusiones. As the name suggests, this street was once home to the city's chief merchants and commercial establishments. The first block was also known as La Tesorería, because the treasurer of the Real Hacienda (Royal Revenue Service), Marquess de Arcos, lived here. On the left is the restaurant La Torre de Marfil and across the way is the **Casa de Puerto Rico,** home of the **Academia Cubana de la Lengua** (Cuban Language Academy). At the corner of Obrapía are the **Casa Benito Juárez,** which has exhibits relating to Mexican history and culture; the **Casa de la Obrapía,** a huge 17th-century mansion whose massive doorway was made in Spain; and the **Casa de África,** an immense 19th-century structure that houses a permanent exhibition of African cultures, including the Afro-Cuban collection of the ethnologist Fernando Ortiz. The latter is especially interesting, as it highlights the impact on Cuban history of African peoples, especially the Yoruba. *La Habana Vieja, Casa de África, Obrapía, e/Mercaderes and San Ignacio,* ☎ *61 57 98.* ☉ *Tues.–Sat. 10:30–12:30 and 2–4, Sun. 10–noon.*

Continue to the right along Obrapía to the intersection with San Ignacio, where you will see a 17th-century mansion known as the **Casa de Gaspar de Rivero de Vasconcelos.** The structure now houses a center for women's arts and crafts, a bar, and a banquet hall that presents shows several days a week. Take the opportunity to see the mansion's inner courtyards and admire its architecture while you treat yourself to some refreshment.

⓭ Turn right on San Ignacio and walk three blocks down, crossing Obispo and O'Reilly, to the **Plaza de la Catedral.** Just before the square, a few meters to the left of the intersection with O'Reilly, is the O'Reilly Café, which has changed very little since the beginning of the century. Note the unusual cast-iron staircase that leads to the upper floor.

The Plaza del la Catedral is Havana's most harmonious architectural unit. As you enter from San Ignacio, the cathedral is framed by some of Havana's most impressive and best preserved palaces. All of these buildings are from the 18th century, and the square has been called by its present name since that time. Prior to that, it was known as the Plaza de la Cienaga, or swamp, and was where visitors and residents alike collected rainwater. As you enter the square, the street on your left is the **Callejón del Chorro,** which follows the course of the Zanja Real (Royal Aqueduct) that once supplied water to Havana. This conduit led from the Chorrera River 11 km (7 mi) away, and once it reached Havana it branched in two, with one channel leading to the Quai de la Luz, the other to this square, where the citizenry came for drinking water. This was easily the most ambitious engineering project in the city during the 16th century.

The first building to the left as you advance toward the cathedral has recently been rebuilt in keeping with the design of the rest of the square but with an added third floor. This was the site of Havana's first public baths; a plaque on the facade commemorates the Zanja Real. The building now houses an **arts and crafts gallery.** Farther along is the **⓮ Palacio de los Marqueses de Aguas Claras,** occupied by El Patio restaurant. This establishment has one of the Havana's best locations; the tables on its upper floor overlook the terrace, from which you can view the entire square. The interior courtyard is used as a bar, as is the portico. Performances of folkloric and traditional Cuban dancing are presented. This is not the first time the palace has been used for such a purpose; earlier in the century the restaurant El Siglo occupied these same privileged quarters. From the terrace you can study the details **⓯** of the upper part of the facade of the **cathedral.**

The Jesuits were the first to build a church on what was then called the Plaza de la Cienaga. At that time La Parroquial Mayor (main parish church), documented to 1555, stood on the Plaza de Armas. That structure was almost completely destroyed when the magazine of the *Invencible,* a ship anchored in port next to the church, exploded. Religious objects and other salvageable artifacts were moved to the Jesuits' chapel. Later, when the island was divided into two provinces and the Jesuits were expelled, this church was elevated to cathedral rank. Its carved facade is one of the loveliest in Cuba, perfectly described by the great Havana writer Alejo Carpentier as "music transformed into stone." One of its most unusual features is its asymmetry: The tower on the left is more slender than the other, as the builders did not want to close off the side street. The facade presents a number of features typical of Jesuit churches in the Americas. The interior, however, is executed in various styles, the result of repeated renovations over the years. When you enter, you see that the church is divided into three aisles with eight lateral chapels. Most of the paintings, sculptures, and objects in precious metals are the work of Italian artists. To the left of the main altar you can see where the tomb monument to Christopher Columbus once stood. When the island of Hispaniola was divided in two, with France occupying the part that is now Haiti, Columbus's remains were brought from Santo Domingo to Havana, where they were kept for a century in the cathedral before being sent back to Seville in 1898. Some claim that the remains sent to Spain were not his at all, that his actual remains are still in Santo Domingo, where they were recently removed from the Dominican cathedral to the lighthouse (El Faro) built to commemorate the quincentenary of the discovery of America.

16 The palace on your left as you leave the cathedral is the **Casa de Lombillo,** for centuries the residence of some of the wealthiest families in Havana and later a commercial establishment. On the corner there was once a tavern. The building now houses the Education Museum. The main focus of the museum's displays is the literacy campaign under-
17 taken in 1961. To one side, sharing the same porticoes, is the **Casa del Marqués de Arcos,** to many the most perfect example of a colonial mansion in Havana. The house was built in 1741 for the treasurer of the Real Hacienda. Later, it served as the post office, among other things. It is presently occupied by the Experimental Graphics Workshop, which produces engravings and posters. On the ground floor, you can buy samples of the works printed here.

The fourth side of the square, directly opposite the cathedral, is occu-
18 pied by the so-called **Casa de Chacón,** now home to the Museo de Arte Colonial (Museum of Colonial Art). The structure was commissioned in 1720 by the island's governor, Luis Chacón, and like all of the other buildings on the square had various owners and had been used for different purposes. It was once the seat of the College of Notaries, where the newspaper *La Discusion* was published. Before it became a museum it had been used by a rum manufacturer. It now houses exhibits of furniture, lamps, and porcelains from the colonial era. One of the museum's distinctive features is its collection of stained glass decorating the interior walls. *La Habana Vieja, Museum of Colonial Art, Plaza de la Catedral, San Ignacio 61,* ☎ *62 64 40.* 🎫 *$2.* ☉ *Wed.–Sat. and Mon. 10:15–4:45, Sun. 9:15–12:45.*

Cross the square again and take a left up Calle Empedrado. You will
19 soon see the sign for **La Bodeguita del Medio,** one of the finest restaurants in Cuba. Originally a grocery store in what was once a carriage house, or stable, the establishment later became an eatery frequented by the journalists and writers who worked for a nearby publishing firm. Its name, the Little Bar in the Middle, refers to the restaurant's location halfway down the block. Traditionally, bars and taverns occupied corner sites. The renovation was the work of the *gallego* (Peninsular Spanish national) Ángel Martinez, who succeeded in making the spot one of the most famous places on the island. Nicolás Guillén dedicated poems to the Bodeguita and Ernest Hemingway swore that in this tavern he had the best *mojitos* (drinks made of rum, lemon, and ice and garnished with mint leaves) in Cuba. No one who samples the cocktail here is likely to question his judgment. It has become all but obligatory for every visitor to Havana to drop in. The Bodeguita's walls are covered with paintings by satisfied patrons—one of the distinguishing features of the "B del M," as it is more familiarly called. If you're dining here, try one of the Creole specialties, and whatever you do, don't leave without tasting a mojito.

Calle Empedrado takes its name from the fact that it was the first of Havana's thoroughfares to be paved with stone. Leaving La Bodeguita, you will see to the left the **Centro de Promoción Cultural Alejo Carpentier,** dedicated to the study and distribution of the famous author's works. The center occupies an early 19th-century house, a fine example of the final evolution of the Cuban Baroque style. In his novel *El siglo de las luces,* Carpentier spoke of this house as the embodiment of Havana's

㉚ spirit. Coming out into the street, retrace your steps toward the cathedral, turning left along San Ignacio. On the corner is the **Casa del Obispo Peñalver,** a lovely Baroque palace. Proceed along the side of the cathedral, and behind it you come to the **Seminario de San Carlos y San Ambrosio,** another building erected by the Jesuits. This one predates the church that would become the cathedral. Farther along you'll see an archaeological park, where the remains of the **Maestranza de Artillería** (armory) are being excavated. This was the site of the original Castillo de la Real Fuerza, destroyed by Jacques de Sores in 1555. Years later, the first foundry for artillery pieces was established here. You can see the Maestranza sentry box, a relic of the 18th-century city wall. The wall was torn down, beginning in 1863, to allow for the city's ex-

㉑ pansion. Opposite is the **Palacio Pedroso,** better known as the Palacio de la Artesanía (Palace of the Artisans), which now houses a number of tourist shops. Here, you can buy silver rings, coral earrings, and recordings of Cuban music, or have a refreshing drink at one of the tables in the courtyard.

Tour 2: La Habana Vieja—From the Plaza Vieja to the Casa de Martí

The first tour will have given you a good look at La Habana Vieja, and if your time is short you may not wish to explore it further. If you do, this itinerary will take slightly off the beaten track. The monuments are less spectacular and not as well restored, but you will explore streets that enable you to better appreciate the real Havana and those who live here.

㉒ Begin your tour at the **Plaza Vieja,** which is, after the Plaza de Armas and the Plaza de la Catedral, the third most interesting space in La Habana Vieja. In contrast to the other two, this square is surrounded by surprisingly heterogeneous buildings. Intense restoration work is under way here as well, but it will be a long time yet before it is finished. When the Plaza de Armas lost its more civic character as it became the center of political and military power, social and commercial activity moved to this square. Many of these houses, with their great columns and galleries, date from the 18th century and are occupied by official

㉓ agencies. The most luxurious and best preserved of them is the **Casa de los Condes de Jaruco** (House of the Counts of Jaruco) seat of the Cuban National Endowment for the Arts. Enter through the great wooden door and you come into a patio. To the left a splendid stairway leads to the upper floor, where there are exhibits and a broad terrace decorated with stained-glass windows that offers a perfect view of the square. A ground-floor gallery sells Cuban art; this is a good place for anyone interested in purchasing works by contemporary

㉔ Cuban painters. On another corner is the **Casa de las Hermanas Cárdenas** (Home of the Cárdenas Sisters), housing the Center for the Development of the Visual Arts, and on the other side of the square, in the **Casa de Esteban José Portier,** is the Cuban *fototeca* (photo library). The building at the corner of Muralla and Inquisidor is the old **Hotel-Palacio Cueto,** now an apartment house. Although the building is in serious disrepair, it is still possible to appreciate its once-sumptuous decor.

㉕ Leave the square by way of Calle Mercaderes and when you come to Amargura, at the Casa de los Basabe y Aguileras, turn right into the **Plaza de San Francisco,** a lovely spot adorned by a lion fountain. The building on the left is the **Antigua Lonja del Comercio** (Old Trade Exchange), from the early part of this century. Next to it, the customs buildings completely block the view of the bay that opens out just be-

㉖ hind. To the right of the square is the old **Saint Francis of Assisi church and convent.** Continue to the right through Calle Oficios to Calle Luz, where you'll see another 18th-century palace, this one the Casa del Conde

㉗ de Barreto. On the opposite corner is the **Plazuela de la Luz,** behind which is the beginning of the Alameda de Paula, Havana's first promenade, now hidden by the docks and port facilities. From the Barreto

㉘ house turn right onto Calle Luz to come to the **Convento de Santa Clara,** an imposing walled enclave that dates from the 17th century. This is the oldest convent from the early village of San Cristóbal and is now the home of the **National Center for Preservation, Restoration, and Museum Studies.** *La Habana Vieja, Convento de Santa Clara, Calle Cuba, e/Sol y Luz,* ☎ *61 50 43. Guided tour $2.* ☉ *Weekdays 9–4.*

㉙ Continue left on Cuba and at the next corner you find the tiny **Iglesia del Espíritu Santo.** Built in 1632, this is the oldest church on the island and the only one with catacombs. Turn right on Calle Acosta toward

㉚ the immense **Convento de Nuestra Señora de Belén,** which occupies a complete block. Pass through the archway and when you reach Picota, turn left and head to Calle Leonor Pérez. There, across from the cen-

㉛ tral railway station, you will find the tiny **Casa Natal de José Martí,** where the Cuban hero was born in 1853. The building is now a museum devoted to the life and work of the great Cuban poet, essayist, and patriot. *La Habana Vieja, Casa Natal de José Martí, Leonor Pérez 314, e/Picota y Egido,* ☎ *61 37 78. Temporarily closed for repairs.*

Tour 3: Central Havana

This itinerary essentially follows the avenues that border La Habana Vieja, promenades laid out in the last century to open up the city for development after the defense walls were demolished.

㉜ Begin your tour in **Trece de Marzo Park,** at the end of **Calle Monserrate**—also known as the Avenida de las Misiones—behind the Palacio de la Artesanía and near the Castillo de la Punta. From here you can see the monument to Máximo Gómez, another of Cuba's heroes. A corner of the park is occupied by the Spanish embassy. Proceeding up the avenue you come to the **Baluarte del Ángel,** another of the few remaining fragments of the city wall. Here you pass close to a tank used in the fighting at Giron beach after the landing of anti-Castro forces intent on overthrowing the new regime at the Bay of Pigs in 1961. To the left you see the **Iglesia del Santo Ángel Custodio** (Church of the Holy Angel Savior), one of the settings used by Cirilo Valverde in his portrayal of 19th-century Cuban society in the novel *Cecilia Valdes.*

㉝ Next, you come to the Presidential Palace, now the **Museo de la Revolución** (Museum of the Revolution). Inside, various aspects of recent Cuban history are explained in photographs, documents, and personal mementos. There is also a model of the Moncada de Santiago military barracks, the attack on which was one of the key elements in the struggle against the Batista regime. *La Habana Vieja, Museum of the Revolution, Refugio 1, e/Misiones y Zulueta,* ☎ *62 40 91.* ▭ *$3.* ☉ *Tues.–Sun. 10–5.*

㉞ Behind the museum is the **Granma Memorial,** where you can see the yacht that brought Fidel Castro and his staff from Mexico in 1953 to begin guerrilla fighting in the Sierra Maestra. Around it are aircraft,

㉟ tanks, and other vehicles used in the war. The next building is the **Museo Nacional de Bellas Artes** (National Fine Arts Museum) in which, in addition to a fine collection of European paintings and antiques, the most outstanding objects are Cuban works that provide a survey of Cuban art from the 17th century to the present. *La Habana Vieja, Tro-*

cadero, e/Zulueta y Monserrate, ☎ *62 01 40. Closed for repairs until
1998.*

On the opposite corner, at the intersection of Zulueta and Trocadero,
is the Hotel Sevilla, reopened in 1993 after nearly three years of renovations. It served as the setting for various episodes in Graham
Greene's novel *Our Man in Havana.* If you continue along Zulueta you
㊱ come to the **Parque Central,** passing the entrance to the **Hotel Plaza**
on the corner. The Plaza was once one of the great Havana hotels, a
veritable palace that has, fortunately, been restored. The park is one
of Havana's loveliest, with leafy shade trees surrounding a statue of
José Martí. Havana natives congregate here in the evening, and the park
is a favorite venue for sellers of cut-rate tobacco. However, not all of
the conversations that take place in the square are designed to separate you from your dollars.

From the Martí statue, turn left onto O'Reilly until you come to a small
square with a monument to Francisco Albear. On one corner you will
㊲ find one of Cuba's most famous spots: **El Floridita.** This was another
of Hemingway's favorite hangouts; one that he immortalized in his writ-
ings because of its daiquiris. The international renown of the El Floridita
daiquiri is credited to the bartender, Constante, whose real name was
Constantí Ribalaigua and who was originally from Gerona, Spain. Although El Floridita has recently been refurbished and redecorated, step-
ping through its door is like leaping backward in time. The marvelous
mahogany bar, the mural with its romantic depiction of a galleon entering Havana harbor, and the waiters with their old-fashioned red uniforms create a tableau in which the only jarring note is the computer
used to print out the checks. The restaurant, one of the most elegant
and expensive in Havana, is behind the bar.

From El Floridita, walk along Monserrate. You will pass La Zaragozana,
another great Havana restaurant. Farther along, on the right, behind
the Antiguo Instituto de la Habana, Havana's oldest high school, is a
section of the old ramparts. Turn left onto Calle Brasil and you will
see the Hanoi Restaurant, which is in a restored 17th-century house
㊳ on a corner of the **Plaza del Cristo,** in front of the 18th-century church
of Santo Cristo del Buen Viaje. Retrace your steps along Brasil and con-
㊴ tinue until you come to the **Capitolio** (capital building). This is one of
Havana's most impressive buildings, with a cupola nearly 300 feet tall,
inspired by the United States Capitol building in Washington, DC.
Opened in 1929, it housed both the Chamber of Representatives and
the Senate. It has now been given to the Academy of Sciences and the
Museum of Natural Sciences. In front of the main facade is a massive
granite staircase adorned with statues representing Work (on the left)
and Virtue. Beneath the cupola there is another statue, 45 feet tall, sym-
bolizing the Republic of Cuba.

㊵ To the left of the Capitolio is the **Parque de la Fraternidad** in the spot
once occupied by the Campo del Marte, the largest square in colonial
Havana. The ceiba tree in the center of the square was planted in 1928,
using soil from the 21 countries that participated in the sixth Pan-American Convention. In spots throughout the park are busts of important
figures in the history of the Americas, including Bolívar, San Martín,
Juárez, and Lincoln. On one side is La India fountain, also known as
the La Noble Habana, a symbol of the city. At the other end is the **Palacio Aldama,** a splendid example of neoclassical Havana architecture
and now the home of the Instituto de Historia del Movimiento Obrero
de Cuba (Institute of the History of the Cuban Workers' Movement).

From the Parque de la Fraternidad return toward the Capitolio along the **Paseo de Martí** and continue to the Parque Central. On the left is ④ the **Gran Teatro de La Habana,** in a building that was once the Centro Gallego (Galician Center). In terms of its capacity, this is one of the world's great opera houses, comparable to those of Vienna or Paris—which gives you some idea of the importance of the Galician community in 19th-century Cuba. Crossing San Rafael, a pedestrian street that was once an important commercial area, you come to the **Hotel Inglaterra,** another of the recently renovated classics. At the time it was built, more than 100 years ago, the Inglaterra was the city's most elegant hotel, and it is now the oldest one still in use. The interior has been perfectly restored, and the bar is well worth a visit. The section of the Paseo in front of the hotel is known as "La Acera del Louvre" (the Louvre Sidewalk), after a noted café that once welcomed passersby.

Continue along Paseo de Martí (also called the Prado in honor of the Madrid's Paseo del Prado) toward the Castillo de la Punta and Malecón. This paseo was laid out in 1772, but it now looks the way it did in 1928, when it was restored and adorned with benches and street lights. Trees provide shade all the way to the water's edge, making this a pleasant place to stroll (indeed, Habaneros promenade up one side and down the other in the early evening). The street also has many fine examples of late-19th and early 20th century architecture, including theaters, cafés, commercial buildings, and the old Spanish Casino. At the end you cross the Parque de los Enamorados (Lovers' Park), where you can still see the remains of the Tacón prison. Across the way is the Castillo de San Salvador de la Punta and to the left the start of the Malecón.

Tour 4: Havana's Fortresses

From its founding, the town of San Cristóbal de La Havana owed its importance to its harbor, the safest in all of the West Indies. A narrow and easily defensible channel led into a roomy bay that attracted commercial and military fleets from the beginning. In time it became the most heavily fortified harbor in the Americas. Having seen the Castillo de la Real Fuerza (☞ Tour 1, *above*), you ought to tour the other fortresses.

To complete this tour rent a car or hire a taxi for a few hours. The ④ brief itinerary begins at the **Castillo de San Salvador de la Punta,** on the far end of one of the banks of the channel that flows to the bay. It was commissioned by Felipe II, and construction began in 1590 under the direction of the Italian architect Battista Antonelli. The fortress is an irregular quadrilateral with corner bulwarks. Its walls may strike you as surprisingly low, but the fort was designed to complement El Morro, just across the channel. A chain made of logs and iron links extended between the two fortifications. Thus it was possible to seal off the harbor when closing the city gates.

Next to the nearby statue of Máximo Gómez is the entrance to the tunnel that leads to La Habana del Este (East Havana) across the bay. Shortly after you come out of the tunnel you will see signs guiding you to the ④ **Castillo de los Tres Santos Reyes Magos del Morro** (El Morro). Construction began in 1590 and lasted for more than 40 years. For decades the fort, whose irregular base was adapted to the existing terrain, stood firm against attacks by Dutch, French, and English fleets. The English finally took El Morro after a 44-day siege in 1762, and the subsequent English occupation of Havana lasted nearly a year. Under the Treaty of Versailles, Spain recovered her sovereignty over Cuba in exchange for Florida and Louisiana. El Morro now provides one of the finest views of Havana and houses an impressively situated restaurant. The lighthouse, erected in the 19th century, continues to sweep the harbor entrance with its beam every 15 seconds. *Castillo de los Tres Santos Reyes Magos del Morro, Carretera de La Cabaña,* ☎ *62 06 17.* ☉ *Daily 10–6.*

㊹ Once Spain had recovered Havana, Carlos III ordered the construction of yet another fortress, **San Carlos de la Cabaña,** a short distance from El Morro. This is by far the city's largest, and the largest fortress built by the Spanish in America. Its name commemorates both the Spanish King and the fact that the site was previously occupied by *bohíos,* typical dwellings of Cuban peasants. The fortress has recently been restored and you can tour its batteries, magazines, and moats. Each evening at nine a cannon is fired—with all hands decked out in colonial dress—to announce the closing of the gates and of the port. *Carretera de la Cabaña,* ☎ *62 06 17.* ☞ *$2.* ☉ *Daily 10–10.*

Tour 5: Regla

㊺ For a different view of the city, take a boat across the bay to **Regla.** Launches depart for this tiny sailors' village from the Muelle de la Luz across from the intersection of San Pedro and Santa Clara. The docks in Regla are very near the **Iglesia de Nuestra Señora de Regla,** one of Cuba's most frequented pilgrimage churches. The most remarkable feature of the Virgin at Regla is that she is black, although the infant she cradles in her arms is white. Patron and protector of sailors, the Virgin of Regla is considered the equivalent of Yemayá, the goddess of the sea in the Yoruba religion. The Virgin's feast day (September 8) is celebrated with both a Catholic Mass and special rituals of Santería, the religion brought to Cuba by African slaves. The village of Regla seems untouched by time and unacquainted with haste or urgency. A quiet stroll (there are few cars on the streets) reveals this special spirit. If you like to hike, climb **Lenin Hill,** where you'll find the **Museo Municipal de Regla** and enjoy a panoramic view of the bay and Havana.

Tour 6: Modern Havana

㊻ To see Havana by car, drive the length of the **Malecón** and continue on along Avenida 5 to the luxurious Miramar district. If your hotel is in Miramar or you attend one of the shows at the Tropicana (another must on any trip to Havana) or visit sights along the Hemingway Marina, you will become familiar with at least a part of this itinerary. The Malecón is a 7-km (4-mi) sweep along the sea between the La Punta fortress and the mouth of the Almendares River. On it are some of the city's finest hotels as well as monuments, fortresses, and parks. It is the fastest route from La Habana Vieja to Miramar and a favorite place for the natives to congregate. By day it attracts swimmers, sun worshippers, and fishermen. In the evening, it offers a place to promenade while enjoying the sea breeze. At the end of the Malecón you pass through a tunnel under the Almendares River and emerge on **Avenida 5,** a wide boulevard that crosses Miramar. This district was where the wealthiest Cubans once erected their splendid mansions; now it is dotted with embassies and hotels, shops, and restaurants that cater to tourists.

The Malecón borders the district known as **Vedado,** Havana's economic center. For centuries, the area between the San Lázaro Tower and the Almendares River was covered by an impenetrable forest. It was illegal to cut any sort of track through this dense jungle, which was considered a natural defense against pirates. Early in this century the forest was breached and homes were built here in a break with the colonial past represented by La Habana Vieja. To start a small tour of the

④ Vedado on foot, take a taxi to the **Hotel Nacional,** the most imposing structure along the Malecón and one of Cuba's greatest hotels. It stands atop a small hill and represents a part of the city's history. It opened its doors on New Year's Eve of 1930, and soon became a favorite haunt of famous artists and political leaders. Closed for four years, the hotel reopened in May 1992, resuming its place in the front rank of Cuba's hotel offerings. Stroll through its gardens and some of its salons. The terrace bar is a delightful place for a drink at dusk.

The Nacional is on the corner of Malecón and Avenida 23, which crosses
④ the Vedado to the **Cementerio de Cristóbal Colón.** This area is well worth a visit, especially if you hire a guide to tell you some of the secrets and legends relating to the tombs. The first five blocks of Avenida 23 are
④ known as **La Rampa** and constitute the nerve center of Havana. Either on the avenue or just off it are hotels, restaurants, stores, cinemas, min-
⑤ istries, the International Press Center, and the **Heladería Coppelia,** an ice cream parlor that is another quintessentially Cuban institution. You must walk up this street to get the feel of it. In any other city a principal artery such as this would be a crush of humanity, but even here the Cubans manage to preserve their leisurely tempo. At the corner of
⑤ Calle L is the **Hotel Habana Libre.** It once was one of the most modern hotels in the New World, but the passage of time has taken its toll. Renovations, which began in 1994, are being completed a floor at a time so that the hotel may remain open.

⑤ Turn left on L and continue on two blocks until you come to the **Universidad.** The first thing you will see, at the foot of a great staircase, is the monument to **Julio Antonio Mella,** founder of Cuba's first Communist Party. Next door is the **Museo Antropológico Montané,** which exhibits some of Cuba's most interesting pre-Columbian archaeological finds. Although these buildings are still used for classes, there are now branches of the university throughout the city.

⑤ Any tour of present-day Havana ought to include the **Plaza de la Revolución.** Hail a taxi at the university or retrace your steps along Calle L to the stand in front of the Habana Libre. If you enter the Plaza de la Revolución from Avenida Rancho Boyeros, you will see the **Biblioteca Nacional** (National Library) to the left. On the right is the **Ministry of Communications,** along with the **Postal Museum** and the central post
⑤ office. The square is dominated by the **José Martí monument**—a marble statue nearly 60 feet tall in front of a 450-foot-tall obelisk. You can climb the 567 steps or take the elevator to an observation platform at the top. This broad esplanade has been the center of Havana's political life since 1959, site of parades and massive crowds on important holidays.

Tour 7: Hemingway and the Playas del Este

From 1939 until 1960, shortly before his death, Ernest Hemingway called Cuba his home. The places he frequented, especially in La Habana Vieja, have been marked with plaques. One such is the Hotel Ambos Mundos (☞ Tour 1, *above*), where Hemingway's room has been preserved untouched. Others are his favorite bars. Posted behind the bar at the Bodeguita (☞ Tour 1, *above*) is a Hemingway quotation: MY DAIQUIRI AT EL FLORIDITA AND MY MOJITO AT THE BODEGUITA. If you are interested in Hemingway, you will want to visit at least two other spots.

⑤ The **Casa–Museo de Ernest Hemingway** at La Vigía (15 km/9 mi from Havana) was Hemingway's residence for many years. To reach this sight, take a taxi, or, if you plan to continue on to Cojímar, rent a car. The house is in the tiny village of San Francisco de Paula (take the Primer

Anillo del Puerto—Havana's first beltway—then follow the road to Güines). The museum consists of four buildings: Hemingway's house, a three-story tower, a guest bungalow, and a garage. The exhibits communicate the flavor of Hemingway's life; the furnishings, hunting trophies, paintings, and books all suggest something of his personality. *San Francisco de Paula, municipio de San Miguel de Padrón, Finca La Vigía, Carretera Central, Km 2.5,* ☎ *91 08 09.* ⌨ *$2.* ☉ *Mon.–Sat. 9–4, Sun. 9–noon. Closed Tues. and rainy days.*

56 The Primer Anillo de la Habana skirts the city and leads along the Via Monumental directly to **Cojímar,** a tiny fishing village where Hemingway kept his yacht, the *Pilar.* Cojímar is famous as the setting for *The Old Man and the Sea,* the novel for which Hemingway was awarded the Nobel Prize. There is a bust of the writer in the town's central square.

57 Cojímar is on the east side of the bay. The quickest way to get there if you are not visiting the Hemingway Museum is to follow the coast after you emerge from the tunnel between the fortresses of La Punta and El Morro. Once in Cojímar, you are nearly halfway to the **Playas del Este,** the long stretch of beaches where Habaneros come to escape from the city and enjoy the sun and the sea. Bacuranao is the closest, no more than 20 minutes from Havana. Then come the towns of El Mégano, Santa María del Mar, Boca Ciega, Guanabo, Jibacoa, and El Trópico. All of these present the best features of a tropical beach paradise, with white sands bordering a turquoise-blue sea. When the temperature rises, thousands of people flock here. You will have a hard time spending a few hours here without ending up in conversation with other bathers.

Each of these beaches has its share of hotels, villas, restaurants (try the seafood place, Mi Casita de Coral, next to the Hotel Marazul in Santa María del Mar), and bars. Fuel shortages mean that buses from Havana are infrequent, so many people arrive on bicycles (though you can hire a taxi or rent a car).

Checklist of Sights and Activities

Galleries

Centro de Desarrollo de las Artes Visuales (Center for the Development of Visual Arts). This gallery is in the Plaza Vieja, Havana's true commercial center in the 17th and 18th centuries. *San Ignacio 352, at Teniente Rey,* ☎ *62 35 33.* ☉ *Tues.–Sat. 10–6.*

Galería de Arte La Acacia (Acacia Art Gallery). *Centro Habana, San José e/Industria y Consulado,* ☎ *63 93 64.* ☉ *Mon.–Sat. 10–4.*

Galería de Arte Latinoamericano Haydeé Santamaría (Haydeé Santamaria Gallery of Latin American Art). *Vedado, Calle G e/3 y 5, 2nd floor,* ☎ *32 46 53.* ☉ *Weekdays 10–5.*

Galería Domingo Ravenet. *La Lisa, Calle 51 e/160 y 161.* ⌨ *$1.* ☉ *Mon. 2–6, Tues.–Sat. 2–10.*

Galería "Forma" ("Shape" Gallery). *La Habana Vieja, Obispo 255e, at Cuba y Aguiar,* ☎ *62 21 03.* ☉ *Mon.–Sat. 10–5.*

Galería Galiano. *Centro Habana, Galiano 258, at Concordia.* ⌨ *$1.* ☉ *Tues.–Sat. 2–9.*

Galería Habana. *Vedado, Pl. de la Revolución, Línea y F,* ☎ *32 71 01.* ☉ *Mon.–Sat. 10–6.*

Galería Horacio Ruiz. *La Habana Vieja, Tacón 4.* ☉ *Mon.–Sat 10–4.*

Galería Imago. *La Habana Vieja, Gran Teatro de La Habana, Prado y San José,* ☎ *61 23 60.*

Galería Luz y Oficios. *La Habana Vieja, Oficios 362, at Luz,* ☎ *62 32 95.* ⌨ *$1.* ☉ *Tues.–Sat. 10–6, Sun. 9–1.*

Galería Roberto Diago. *La Habana Vieja, Pl. Vieja, Muralla 107, at San Ignacio,* ☎ *33 80 05.* ☉ *Weekdays 10–5.*

Galería Servando Cabrera Moreno. *Miramar, Playa, Av. 5 at 68.* ☎ *$1.* ✆ *Mon.–Sat. 2–9.*

Galería 23 y 12. *Vedado, Pl. de la Revolución, Calle 23 y 12.* ✆ *Tues.–Sat. 10–5.*

Galería Víctor Manuel. *La Habana Vieja, Pl. de la Catedral.* ✆ *Mon.– Sat. 10–5.*

La Casa de la Miniatura de Cuba (House of Miniatures of Cuba). For sale here are pieces certified by the city historian and recognized by the National Heritage Office. *La Habana Vieja, Tacón 4.*

La Casona. *La Habana Vieja, Pl. Vieja, Muralla 107, at San Ignacio,* ☎ *62 26 33.* ✆ *Weekdays 10–5.*

Salón de los Vitrales (Salon of Glass Showcases). Fondo Cubano de Bienes Culturales (Cuban Cultural Assets Fund). *La Habana Vieja, Muralla 107, at San Ignacio.*

Taller de la Serigrafía René Portocarrero (René Portocarrero Workshop of Silkscreen Printing). *La Habana Vieja, Cuba 513, e/Teniente Rey y Muralla,* ☎ *62 32 76.* ✆ *Weekdays 9–4.*

Taller Experimental de Gráfica de La Habana (Havana Experimental Workshop of Graphic Design). *La Habana Vieja, Pl. de la Catedral,* ☎ *62 09 79.* ✆ *Mon.–Sat. 10–4.*

Libraries

Biblioteca del Instituto de Literatura y Lingüística. *Av. Salvador Allende 710, e/Castillejo y Soledad,* ☎ *75405.* ✆ *Weekdays 8–5, Sat. 8–2.*

Biblioteca José Antonio Echevarría. *Vedado, Casa de las Americas, Av. 3 y G,* ☎ *32358.* ✆ *Weekdays 8:15–5:45.*

Biblioteca Memorial Juan Marinello. *Nuevo Vedado, Loma 684, e/Colón y Lombillo,* ☎ *34912.*

Biblioteca Nacional de Ciencia y Tecnología. *Academy of Sciences (former Capitolio Nacional), Prado y Teniente Rey,* ☎ *60 34 11, ext.1329.* ✆ *Weekdays 8:30–5, Sat. 8:30–4.*

Biblioteca Nacional José Martí. *Vedado, Pl. de la Revolución, Av. Independencia y 20 de Mayo,* ☎ *79 60 91.* ✆ *Mon.–Sat. 8–6.*

Museums

Artes Decorativas (Decorative Arts). This collection is in the former mansion of the countess Revilla y Camargo, considered one of the finest examples of Cuban architecture from the first half of the 20th century. On display are important European and Oriental decorative arts from the 18th to the 20th centuries. *Vedado, Pl. de la Revolución, Calle 17 y E,* ☎ *32 09 24.* ☎ *$2.* ✆ *Wed.–Sat. 9:30–4:30, Sun 9–1.*

Casa de la Obrapía. *See* Tour 1. *La Habana Vieja, Obrapía y Mercaderes,* ☎ *61 30 97.* ✆ *Tues.–Sat. 10:30–5:30, Sun. 9:30–12:30.*

Casa–Museo Ernest Hemingway. *See* Tour 7. *San Francisco de Paula, San Miguel del Padrón, Finca La Vigía,* ☎ *91 08 09.* ☎ *$2.* ✆ *Mon.– Sat. 9–4, Sun. 9–noon. Closed Tues. and rainy days.*

Castillo de la Real Fuerza. *See* Tour 1. *La Habana Vieja, Pl. de Armas, O'Reilly e/Av. del Puerto y Tacón,* ☎ *61 50 10.* ☎ *$2.* ✆ *Thurs.–Mon. 9:30–6.*

Convento de Santa Clara. *See* Tour 2. *La Habana Vieja, Calle Cuba, e/Sol y Luz,* ☎ *61 50 43.* ✆ *Weekdays 9–4.* ☎ *$2 for guided tour.*

Museo Casa Natal de José Martí. *See* Tour 2. *La Habana Vieja, Leonor Pérez 314,* ☎ *61 37 78. Closed for restoration.*

Museo de Arte Colonial. *See* Tour 1. *La Habana Vieja, Plaza de la Catedral, San Ignacio 61,* ☎ *62 64 40.* ☎ *$2.* ✆ *Wed.–Mon. 10:15–5:45, Sun. 9:15–12:45.*

Museo de la Ciudad de La Habana. *See* Tour 1. *La Habana Vieja, Pl. de Armas, Tacón e/Obispo y O'Reilly,* ☎ *61 28 76.* ☎ *$3, $4 with guide.* ✆ *Daily 10:30–6:30.*

Museo de la Revolución. *See* Tour 3. *La Habana Vieja, Refugio 1, e/Misiones y Zulueta,* ☎ *62 40 91.* ✉ *$2.* ☉ *Tues.–Sun. 10–5.*

Museo Municipal de Guanabacoa (Municipal Museum of Guanabacoa). The museum has exhibits on Santería, the Afro-Cuban amalgam of Catholicism and African religions. *Guanabacoa, Martí 108, e/Versalles y San Antonio,* ☎ *97 91 17. Closed for restoration.*

Museo Municipal de Regla (Municipal Museum of Regla). *See* Tour 5. *Regla, Martí 158, e/Facciolo y La Piedra,* ☎ *90 69 89.* ✉ *$1.* ☉ *Tues.– Fri. 9–6, Sat. 9–7, Sun. 9–1.*

Museo Nacional de Bellas Artes (National Museum of Fine Arts). This museum houses the most extensive collection of Greek and Roman ceramics in Latin America, as well as one of the best collections of Egyptian art. The permanent collection also has Cuban and European rooms. *La Habana Vieja, Trocadero, e/Zulueta y Monserrate,* ☎ *62 01 40.*

Museo Nacional de la Música (National Museum of Music). *Cárcel 1, e/Habana y Aguiar,* ☎ *61 98 46.* ✉ *$2.* ☉ *Mon.–Sat. 9–4, Sun. 8– noon.*

Museo Napoleónico. *Vedado, Pl. de la Revolución, San Miguel 1159, at Ronda,* ☎ *79 14 60.* ✉ *$2 with guide.* ☉ *Mon.–Sat. 10–5:30, Sun. 9–noon.*

Parque Historico Militar El Morro-La Cabaña. *Habana del Este, Carretera de La Cabaña,* ☎ *62 06 17.* ☉ *Daily 9–6.*

Other Cultural Institutions

Casa del Joven Creador (Young Artists' Club). *La Habana Vieja, San Pedro y Sol.*

Centro de Estudios Martiano (Center of Studies of José Martí). *Vedado, Calzada y 4,* ☎ *31 17 89.* ☉ *Mon.–Thurs. 8:30–4, Fri. 8:30–2:30.*

Centro de Promoción Cultural Alejo Carpentier (Alejo Carpentier Center for Cultural Advancement). *Empedrado 215, e/Cuba y San Ignacio,* ☎ *61 69 87 or 61 37 76.*

Centro Wilfredo Lam. *La Habana Vieja, Oficios 420, at Acosta,* ☉ *Weekdays 8:30–4.*

Palacio del Segundo Cabo (Palace of the Second Corporal). This is the home of the Instituto Cubano del Libro (Cuban Book Institute). *La Habana Vieja, O'Reilly 4, at Tacón,* ☎ *62 80 91/95.*

Union de Escritores y Artistas de Cuba (Writers' and Artists' Union of Cuba). *Vedado, Calle 17 y H,* ☎ *32 45 51.*

SHOPPING

At one time supplies of goods were limited, but now you can find anything—from Benetton outfits to deluxe jewelry—in the shopping centers and malls of such hotels as the Comodoro and the Meliá Cohiba. Although there is still a dearth of quality Cuban products, you'll find unique handicrafts at the city's flourishing street markets, where haggling is always an option. Also, check out stores in the network known as the **Fondo de Bienes Culturales** (Cultural Goods Fund) for antiques, ceramics, crafts with Afro-Cuban motifs, and colorful textiles woven by Cuban artists.

Bookstores

Bookstores are generally open weekdays from 11:30 to 6. On Saturday they open only in the morning.

Ateneo. *Vedado, Línea 1057, e/12 y 14,* ☎ *36 90 09.*
El Siglo de las Luces. *Centro Habana, Neptuno 521, at Aguila.*
Fernando Ortiz. *Vedado, Calle L y 27th,* ☎ *32 96 53.*

La Moderna Poesía. *La Habana Vieja, Obispo 526, at Bernaza,* ☎ *62 21 89. Closed for repairs.*

Librería Alma Mater. *Infanta, at San Lázaro, Vedado.*

Librería Internacional. *Obispo, at Bernaza,* ☎ *61 32 83.*

Luis Rogelio Nogueras. *Centro Habana, Galiano 467, e/Barcelona y San José,* ☎ *63 81 10.*

Palacio del Segundo Cabo. *La Habana Vieja, O'Reilly 4, at Tacón,* ☎ *62 80 91/95.*

Rubén Martínez Villena. *La Habana Vieja, Prado and Teniente Rey.*

Viet Nam. *Centro Habana, San Rafael 256, at Galiano.*

Calle Obispo

Some of the stores on this street in the historic district are amusing, others are intriguing. All are open Monday through Saturday 10:30–6:30 and Sunday 9–1.

Al Capricho. Clothing for men, perfumery. *Obispo 458, e/Aguacate y Villegas.*

Clubman. Clothing for men, perfumery, furrier. *Obispo 514.*

El Clip. Watch and jewelry store. *Obispo 501, e/Villegas y Bernaza.*

Humada. Electronics and hardware. *Obispo 502.*

La Francia. A variety of merchandise. *Obispo 452, at Aguacate.*

La Inesita. Clothing for men, women, and children, and toys. *Obispo 508.*

Salón Crusellas. Perfumery and silk shop. *Obispo 522, e/Villegas y Bernaza.*

Fondo de Bienes Culturales

La Acacia. Here you'll find antiques that are certified by the National Heritage Office. *Centro Habana, San José e/Consulado y Industria,* ☎ *63 93 64.* ◷ *Mon.–Sat. 9–4:30.*

La Casona. This is one of the best Fondo stores. *La Habana Vieja, San Ignacio y Muralla,* ☎ *62 26 33.* ◷ *Weekdays 10–5.*

La Flora. Lamps, furbelows, and quality decorative pieces abound. *Miramar, Puente de Hierro.*

Palacio de la Artesanía. *La Habana Vieja, Cuba 64,* ☎ *62 44 07.* ◷ *Daily 9:15–7.*

Tienda de Arte Castillo de la Fuerza. *La Habana Vieja, Pl. de Armas.*

Tienda de Arte Diago (and Galerí Plaza Vieja). *La Habana Vieja, Muralla 107, at San Ignacio,* ☎ *61 28 75.*

Tienda de Arte del Museo Nacional de Bellas Artes. *La Habana Vieja, Animas y Trocadero.*

Tienda de Arte del Palacio de las Convenciones. *Ciudad Habana, Cubanacán, Calle 146 e/11 y 13,* ☎ *22 55 11.*

Tienda de Arte La Bella Habana. *La Habana Vieja, Pl. de Armas, Palacio del Segundo Cabo.*

Mixed Bag

Antiques

La Maison is truly a mixed bag with antiques, silver, clothes, and the occasional evening fashion show thrown in for good measure. *Miramar, Av. 7 y 16,* ☎ *33 15 43,* ℻ *33 15 85.* ◷ *11–10.*

Cigars

These days, some of the best cigar stores are in the Fábrica Partagás (Partagás Factory) in central Havana and in the lobby of the Hotel Meliá Cohiba (Vedado, Av. Paseo e/1 y 3). **La Casa del Habano** is also an excellent shop. *Miramar, Av. 5 y 16,* ☎ *29 40 40.* ☉ *Mon.–Sat. 10:30–6:30.*

Rum
La Casa del Ron sells rum from Santiago de Cuba—the best and the rarest. *La Habana Vieja, Obispo y Bernaza,* ☎ *63 12 42.* ☉ *Daily 10–8.*

La Taberna del Galcón is similar to the Casa del Ron, though here you can taste before you buy. *La Habana Vieja, Obispo y Baratillo,* ☎ *33 80 61.*

Street Markets

Parque H y 21. Vedado. Formerly on Calle G, it was forced to relocate due to a loss of clientele. Good artisans still continue to attend. ☉ *Weekends only.*

Malecón y Calle D. At this market in Vedado, the wares are similar to those at Plaza de la Catedral (☞ *below*). ☉ *Open daily.*

Mercado de Libros Antiguos do le Plaza de Armas (Old Book Market of the Plaza de Armas). Open almost every weekday, this is a good place to get antique books, magazines of the 1940s, and rare editions. Sometimes the prices are elevated, so haggling is essential.

Plaza de la Catedral. There are handicrafts of all types here, and things may be ordered. ☉ *Daily.*

SPORTS

Participant Sports

For **golf,** there's only one game in town: the course at the Diploclub, on the Carretera de Vento in the Boyeros district. A round of golf costs $2; a lesson is $5.

You can simply **fish** on the surface with light spinning gear, or get in deep with heavy tackle. The price varies according to the size of the boat, the length of time, and the extras—bar, onboard lunch, etc.—provided. A 31- to 33-foot yacht accommodating six people costs $130 for 3 hours.

Horse lovers should check out the riding club at Havana's Lenin Park. The lush park covers some 30 square km (19 square mi) and has streams, lakes, and thick tropical vegetation.

For **jogging,** Havana's Malecón is ideal, but if you prefer more structured facilities, try the **Estadio José Martí** (Vedado, Calle G y 3), the **Ciudad Deportiva** (Av. Rancho Boyeros y Vía Blanca), or the **Complejo Deportivo Panamericano** (Pan-American Complex, Habana del Este).

The cost of **sailing,** like fishing, depends on the size of the boat; 3 hours on a 44-foot yacht will cost roughly $30 per person.

For a few dollars an hour, you can play **tennis** on a hotel court—nearly every hotel has one. Classes with a private instructor, the price is usually $5 per hour. The best courts are at the hotels **Tritón, Marina Hemingway, Copacabana,** and **Nacional** (clay) and in the **Pan-American Complex.**

Marina Hemingway (☞ Boat Tours *in* Havana Essentials, *above*) is the prime spot for **water sports,** whether it's diving, sailing, or fishing for swordfish. Scuba diving is especially popular, and fast launches can take you where you want to go. The prices range from $25 for a daytime dive to $30 for a night dive to $40 for a double session with two dives. Introductory courses, either in a pool or at a beach, cost $10 per hour.

You can also sign up for such courses at the **Copacabana, Comodoro,** and **Marazul** hotels. Snorkeling, including all equipment, costs $20; a session with lunch can run you $47.

Spectator Sports

Cuba's main spectator sports, **baseball** and **boxing,** are free. Check the local newspapers for game and match times and locations.

DINING

Havana has none of the frenzy of Europe or North America. The pace in Cuban bars and restaurants is calm (reservations rarely required), warm, and relaxed—possibly too relaxed. A lunch or dinner in the Cuban capital always seems to last longer than you anticipate. The cardinal rule: revise your notion of the "dinner hour."

Most of Havana's restaurants have similar offerings, featuring Caribbean seafood, red meat, and Creole cuisine. Lobster, grilled or *enchilada* (sautéed or stewed with hot red peppers), is flavorful. The large, tasty Cuban *camarón* (shrimp) are frequently prepared *a la plancha* (grilled). *Pargo* (porgy) and *cherna* (sea bass) are two ubiquitous whitefish, and both are recommended.

It may seem strange, but Creole cooking has become a specialty and is not offered in all restaurants. If you crave *frijoles dormidos* (black beans cooked in water or broth and seasoned with salt, pepper, and onion), fried pork skin, or *tasajo* (dried beef), don't count on finding it in just any establishment. La Bodeguita del Medio, Tocororo, Los Doce Apóstoles, La Cecilia, and El Aljibe are among the best places to sample Creole cuisine.

Meals in Havana are not cheap: It's difficult to find one for less than $20 per person. Add a cocktail and some shrimp, and the cost rises to $30 or more. As a precaution, always ask to see the wine list. A bottle of Faustino V white, which costs $5 in a store, can be priced as high as $25 in a restaurant. Most hotels offer a buffet—an option only if you want to dine quickly on mediocre fare.

For details on price categories, *see* the chart *in* On the Road with Fodor's at the front of this guide.

$$$$ **Abanico de Cristal.** Whether you order a Creole dish or a traditionally prepared platè of venison, this restaurant will not disappoint. Some of its carefully chosen recipes are generations old. The ambience, complete with violins, is perhaps the most luxurious in Havana. *Hotel Meliá Cohiba, Vedado, Av. Paseo e/1 y 3,* ☎ *33 36 36.* ⊙ *Noon–midnight.*

$$$$ **Comedor de Aguiar.** This restaurant has a great chef and elegant quarters in one of Havana's landmark hotels. The house specialty is whole shrimp served with rum flambé. *Vedado, Hotel Nacional, Calle O and 21,* ☎ *33 35 64.* ⊙ *Daily noon–1* AM.

$$$$ **El Cedrano.** The buffet table at this establishment in the Hotel Meliá
★   Cohiba has terrific offerings, including salmon, shellfish, serrano ham, and cheeses of exceptional quality. Excellent breakfasts are also served for $25 plus beverages. *Hotel Meliá Cohiba, Vedado, Av. Paseo e/1 y 3,* ☎ *33 36 36.* ⊙ *Noon–midnight.*

$$$$ **El Floridita.** This has been Cuba's most famous restaurant since the 1930s. Ernest Hemingway, John Ringling, and various Cuban presidents have been regulars here because of the excellent food, which is always well presented and well served. Don't leave the island without trying one of the daiquiris. *La Habana Vieja, Monserrate 557, at Obispo,* ☎ *63 10 60/63.* ⊙ *Daily 11:30* AM*–midnight.*

Havana Dining and Lodging

Hotels
Ambos Mundos, **18**
Bruzón, **9**
Capri, **5**
Caribbean, **14**
Colina, **8**
Habana Libre, **7**
Habana Riviera, **1**
Hostal Conde
Villanueva, **21**

Hostal Valencia, **20**
Inglaterra, **12**
Lido, **16**
Lincoln, **13**
Morro, **2**
Nacional, **4**
Plaza, **13**
Presidente, **3**
St. John's, **10**
Santa Isabel, **19**

Sevilla, **15**
Vedado, **11**
Victoria, **6**

Restaurants
Al Medina, **14**
Comedor de Aguiar
(Hotel Nacional), **3**
Don Giovani, **12**
El Barracón (lobby of
the hotel Habana
Libre), **4**
El Cochinito, **6**
El Floridita, **9**
El Patio, **11**

KEY

Hotels ●1

Restaurants ①1

El Polinesio, **5**

Emperador (ground floor of Focsá building), **2**

L'Aiglon (lobby of the hotel Habana Riviera), **1**

La Bodeguita del Medio, **10**

La Divina Pastora, **16**

La Torre (top of the Focsá building), **2**

La Torre de Marfil, **13**

Los Doce Apóstoles, **15**

Sierra Maestra (25th floor of the hotel Habana Libre), **4**

Terraza del Hotel Inglaterra, **8**

$$$$ **Labrasa.** Meat lovers take note: The Meliá Cohiba, which houses
★ Labrasa, is one of the few establishments in Cuba that has a license to
buy high-quality meat from abroad. The sirloin and the barbecued cut-
let are sure successes. *Hotel Meliá Cohiba, Vedado, Av. Paseo e/1 y 3,*
☎ *33 36 36.*

$$$$ **Tocororo.** Fresh, high-quality produce and simple preparation are the
★ hallmarks here. The house hors d'oeuvre, *pechitos de camarones*
(shrimp cakes), is a must-have, and the Creole and seafood (especially
grilled lobster) are famous. *Miramar, Calle 18, No. 302, e/3 y 5,* ☎
33 22 09. ☉ *Noon–midnight; until 2 or 3 AM if there are customers
waiting. Closed Sun.*

$$$ **1830.** Stop by this restaurant, which is housed in a 19th-century town
house, for a late dinner. At night, the gardens become a discotheque.
If the occasionally uneven cuisine doesn't work for you, maybe the danc-
ing will. *Vedado, Malecón y 20,* ☎ *33 967.* ☉ *Daily noon–midnight.*

$$$ **El Pavo Real.** For Chinese food, this is one of only a few places in Ha-
vana. Come only if you're absolutely dying for the stuff, though, as
the cuisine isn't especially distinguished and the prices are somewhat
inflated. *Miramar, El Puente de Hierro, Av. 7, No. 205, e/2 y 4,* ☎ *33
23 15.* ☉ *Daily noon–midnight.*

$$$ **El Polinesio.** Asian cuisine is the specialty at this recently opened restau-
rant in the Hotel Tryp Habana Libre. Polynesian chicken cooked over
hot coals before your eyes is just one of the standout dishes. *Hotel Tryp
Habana Libre,* ☎ *33 40 11.* ☉ *Noon–midnight.*

$$$ **Fiesta.** The service and quality have improved so much at this Span-
★ ish restaurant, that it now merits a star. The variety of offerings is sure
to thrill even the most hard-to-please palates. *Santa Fe, Marina Hemingway, Av. 5 y 248,* ☎ *33 11 50/57.* ☉ *Noon–midnight.*

$$$ **L'Aiglon.** If your tastes run to the international, L'Aiglon is for you.
The service is good; the food ranges from good to great. *Vedado,
Hotel Riviera, Paseo y Malecón,* ☎ *33 40 51.* ☉ *Daily noon–midnight.*

$$$ **La Casa de Quinta y 16.** Housed in a small, rustic ranch house beside
★ the Casa del Habano, La Casa will astound you with its beautifully
presented, well-prepared seafood and meat dishes. The prices are mod-
erate for this category. *Miramar, Av. 5 y 16,* ☎ *33 11 85.* ☉ *Noon–
midnight.*

$$$ **La Cecilia.** This restaurant has aspirations of greatness, and it's well
on its way. Creole cooking is the specialty, and there are also mixed
seafood grills. Dinner is only served till midnight, but there's dancing
that continues well into the wee hours. *Miramar, Av. 5 y 110,* ☎ *33
15 62.* ☉ *Daily noon–midnight.*

$$$ **La Divina Pastora.** Atop one of the artillery batteries that once defended
★ the harbor, this is, without a doubt, Havana's most beautifully situ-
ated restaurant. Come for the historic ambience, the seafood, and the
fantastic music group. Relax in the pleasant bar just above the water.
Habana del Este, Gran Parque militar Morro–Cabaña, ☎ *33 83 41.*
☉ *Daily noon–midnight.*

$$$ **La Pampa.** The specialty here is Argentine cuisine, fine meats, *chinchu-
lines* (grilled tripe stuffed with a mixture of garlic, parsley, lemon juice,
salt, and pepper), and *morcillas* (blood sausage). The prices don't al-
ways match the level of the service, but it's still a place to keep in mind.
Miramar, Hotel Comodoro, Calle 3 at 84, ☎ *33 55 51/59,* FAX *33 11
68.* ☉ *2–midnight.*

$$$ **La Piazza.** Pizza, pasta, and an excellent carpaccio are the draws. The
★ service isn't bad either. *Hotel Meliá Cohiba, Vedado, Av. Paseo e/1 y
3,* ☎ *33 36 36.* ☉ *Noon–midnight.*

$$$ **La Torre.** Situated on the 33rd floor of the Focsá Building, this was once
one of Havana's most select establishments, with deluxe private din-
ing rooms. Though the cuisine is not what it once was, the view of the

city is still fantastic. Stop by if only for a drink at the bar and a vista to remember. *Vedado, Altos del edificio Focsá, Calle 17 at M,* ☎ *32 46 30.* ☉ *Daily noon–midnight.*

$$$ Papa's. Seafood is the specialty here. *Santa Fe, Marina Hemingway, Av. 5 at 248,* ☎ *33 11 50/56.* ☉ *Daily noon–midnight.*

$$$ Sierra Maestra. From this, another food-with-a-view establishment (☞ La Torre, *above*), you can see the lights of El Morro fortress and La Habana Vieja. *Vedado, Hotel Habana Libre, 5th floor, Calle L at 23,* ☎ *33 40 11.* ☉ *7 PM–midnight.*

$$ Al Medina. The Middle Eastern food here is not half bad. *La Habana Vieja, Casa de los Árabes, Oficios 12,* ☎ *63 08 62.* ☉ *Thurs.–Tues. noon–11.*

$$ Don Giovani. This Italian restaurant is in an attractive colonial house near the Plaza de la Catedral. Though the cuisine is often undistinguished and the service can be slow, the historic ambience and the prices are terrific. *La Habana Vieja, Tacón 4,* ☎ *61 44 45 and 62 35 60.* ☉ *Noon–midnight.*

$$ El Barracón. You'll be hard pressed to find better Creole food anywhere
★ in Havana. The roast pork, the *masas fritas* (fried pork skin), the *yuca con mojo* (yucca with garlic butter sauce), and the frijoles dormidos are well prepared. The Creole desserts are winners, too. *Vedado, Hotel Habana Libre, Calle L at 23,* ☎ *33 40 11.* ☉ *Noon–midnight.*

$$ El Cochinito. The name means "little pig," and that's what you'll get— pork served innumerable ways—at this eatery in the heart of La Rampa. *Calle 23 e/H y I.* ☉ *Wed.–Sun. noon–10.*

$$ El Patio. This restaurant is in the courtyard of a palace on the Plaza de
★ la Catedral, and location is its main draw. Stop in if only for a beer or a coffee. *La Habana Vieja, Pl. de la Catedral,* ☎ *61 85 04 and 65 85 11.* ☉ *Noon–midnight.*

$$ El Ranchón (Diplorestaurante). Step into this ranch house surrounded by jungle, and just try to resist the Creole dishes on the menu. If your tastes are more worldly, there's international cuisine as well. Whatever your pleasure, the portions are large, the quality is high, and the prices reasonable. *Cubanacán, Playa, across from Palacio de las Convenciones, Calle 19 at 140,* ☎ *33 19 84 and 23 58 38.* ☉ *Daily noon–11:30.*

$$ La Bodeguita del Medio. One of Havana's great sanctuaries, the Bode-
★ guita, is a superb Creole tavern. Its mojitos are famous around the world, as is its absolutely authentic Cuban fare. Try the *picadillo* (finely chopped meat sautéed with onions, garlic, olives, and tomatoes), the tasajo, or the *arroz congri* (rice with spicy meat sauce). The chicharrones are also standouts, especially accompanied by a light bottled beer. Although lately the prices here have waxed and the quality waned, you can't beat the outstanding local flavor. *La Habana Vieja, Empedrado 256, e/Cuba y San Ignacio,* ☎ *62 44 98.* ☉ *Daily 11:30 AM–1 AM.*

$$ La Cascada. For a quick meal, try this well-stocked buffet complete with a cheese board and pastries. *Miramar, Hotel Comodoro, Calle 3 at 84,* ☎ *33 55 51/59.* ☉ *Daily 10–3 and 7–11.*

$$ La Giraldilla. Mexican food and Creole cuisine are served in this magnificent country villa on the outskirts of Havana. If the food doesn't impress you, the setting will. *La Coronela, Avenida 22 e/Autopista y 51,* ☎ *33 63 90 or 33 60 62.* ☉ *Noon–midnight.*

$$ La Terraza. This small spot in the picturesque village of Cojímare was
★ one of Hemingway's watering holes between fishing trips. As you might expect from a waterfront restaurant, seafood is the specialty. *Cojímar, Real 161, e/Río y Montaña,* ☎ *65 34 71.* ☉ *10 AM–11 PM.*

$$ La Torre del Mangia. Chefs who were trained in Milan have made this
★ *the* place for Italian cuisine. Any of the pasta dishes are sure to please as is the *parguitos entomatados del golfo* (gulf porgy with tomato). The

understated decor is in sync with the relaxed pace. *Miramar, Playa, Av. 5 e/40 y 42,* ☎ *33 24 50.* ☾ *Daily noon–11.*

$$ Morambón. Here you'll find both international and Asian cuisine, including a room where only Korean dishes are served. *Av. 5 at 32,* ☎ *23 4 89.* ☾ *Daily noon–midnight.*

$$ Parrillada del Hotel Copacabana. Expect good, reasonably priced bar-
★ becued meat. At the end of the meal, enjoy some ice cream beside the hotel's natural pool. *Miramar, Calle 1 at 44,* ☎ *33 12 63.* ☾ *10 AM–11 PM.*

$–$$ El Aljibe. Come here for real Cuban food, real cheap. The roast chicken
★ *con mojo* (with garlic sauce) and the *el aljibe* (combination plate of chicken, rice, beans, salad, meat, bread, and dessert) never fail to please. A meal rarely costs more than $15, and two orders will feed three. *Miramar, Calle 24 at 7,* ☎ *33 15 83/84.* ☾ *Noon–midnight.*

$ Dos Gardenias. Whatever you hanker, this eclectic place can probably meet your needs with a menu that includes Creole cuisine, Chinese food, and pizza. *Miramar, Calle 26 at 7,* ☎ *33 23 53.* ☾ *Noon–midnight.*

$ La Rueda. Though you'll have to travel a ways to get here and reser-
★ vations are a must, it's worth the extra effort. Enjoy a day in the country, listen to some Guajira music, and feast on *picante* (spicy) fricasee of goose. *El Chico, Carretera de Guajay, Calle 294, e/185 y 187,* ☎ *45 32 96.* ☾ *Daily noon–8.*

$ La Torre de Marfil. Excellent Chinese food and very low prices are the
★ norm at this establishment near the Plaza de Armas. *Calle Mercaderes e/Obispo y Obra Pía.* ☾ *Noon–10.*

$ Los Doce Apóstoles. Located in the Castillo de los Tres Reyes del
★ Morro and very near the restaurant La Divina Pastora (☞ *above*), Los Doce Apóstoles was another of the artillery batteries built to defend Havana. Today it houses this tiny restaurant, a very pleasant spot with attractive prices. The food is traditional Cuban: rice, beans, pork, and, for dessert, yams. Don't order anything else. *Habana del Este, Parque militar Morro-Cabaña,* ☎ *63 82 95.* ☾ *Daily noon–11.*

$ Terraza del Hotel Inglaterra. The fare—barbecued beef, pork, and chicken—and decor here are simple, and the view over La Habana Vieja is lovely. What's more, the Inglaterra, built in 1875, is one of the city's architectural gems. *La Habana Vieja, Prado 416,* ☎ *33 85 93.* ☾ *3–midnight.*

Privately Owned Restaurants (Paladares)

Privately owned restaurants, or *paladares,* were authorized by the Cuban government in 1994. They have become an important alternative for tourists because the prices are much lower ($10–$15 including a beverage and dessert) than those in state-run restaurants, and the food and service are often superior. Today, there are approximately 1,500 paladares in Cuba, half of them in Havana, principally in Vedado and Miramar.

Despite government restrictions such as limited seating (causing waits of up to an hour) and bans on the sale of beef, shellfish, or cigarettes, eating in a paladar can be gratifying. Many owners are professionals who opened such a business to survive economic crisis. They often serve up warm, illuminating conversation with their delicious dishes. Some places even have antique dishes, luxurious mahogany furniture, and fine silver.

Choose carefully, though, as there are many "improvised" paladares, where the sanitation is lacking, the food is poor, and the service is slow. Stick with the establishments listed below or ask around for recommendations. Also, call ahead to confirm that the paladar is still in business (at press time, there were reports of further government restrictions and rigorous new taxation policies) and to make reservations.

$ **Claro de Luna.** On the pier in the fishing village of Cojímar, 15 min-
★ utes by car from the center of Havana, this paladar specializes in fresh fish. Indeed, there's no better place for it—grilled, pickled, or rotisserie-cooked. The chef, Coqui, is a fisherman, who was in *The Old Man and the Sea* with Spencer Tracy. *Cojímar, Calle Real 20,* ☎ *65 18 37. Closed Mon.*

$ **Don Max.** Come here for meat, poultry, and fish dishes with a Creole touch. *Miramar, 119 Calle 2 e/1 y 3,* ☎ *23 72 81.*

$ **Doña Eutimia.** On the luxurious Plaza de la Catedral, this restaurant
★ offers excellent Creole cuisine. *Callejón de Chorro 62,* ☎ *61 51 63.*

$ **Eddie's Paladar.** The menu features outstanding traditional Cuban
★ dishes, such as Camagüey soup. The atmosphere is welcoming, and the place is often frequented by intellectuals, artists, and diplomats. *Vedado, Calle B 514, e/21 y 23,* ☎ *3 55 50.*

$ **El Bistrot.** This bar-restaurant serves up French cuisine and salads in a pleasant setting that faces the piers. *Vedado, Calle K and the piers, number 12,* ☎ *32 27 08.* ⊙ *6:30 PM–2 AM.*

$ **El Dragón de Oro.** Come here for good Chinese food and a comfortable atmosphere. *Playa, 1708 Calle 52, e/17 y 19,* ☎ *22 51 32.*

$ **El Fausto.** The pleasant surroundings add to your enjoyment of El Fausto's Creole and international dishes. *Playa, 901 Calle 84,* ☎ *22 47 69.*

$ **La Cocina de Lillian.** The carefully prepared and presented food will
★ enchant you as much as the ambience and setting. There's even a statue-filled patio. This is a must-visit. *Miramar, 1311 Calle 48, e/13 y 15, no phone. Closed Sat.*

$ **La Fiesta.** Pick your pleasure: pizza or Creole food. *Kholy, 2826 Calle 47, e/28 y 34,* ☎ *23 84 67.*

$ **La Guarida.** Here you can expect select international dishes and good
★ music in a setting that won't disappoint. *Centro Habana, 418 Calle Concordia, e/Gervasio y Escobar,* ☎ *62 49 40.*

$ **La Kakatúa.** The owner, Juan Carlos, was one of the pioneers of the
★ paladar. He offers high-quality Creole food, music, wine, and rum. *Calle 18 e/18 y 20,* ☎ *3 10 82. Closed Tues.*

$ **La Terraza de Playa.** Order the grilled fish—a specialty here—and enjoy your meal in the charming garden. *Playa, 907 Calle 80, e/9 y 11,* ☎ *23 37 31.*

LODGING

The absence of tourism for so long made Havana's hotel selection less than superb. For years, Cuba had no interest in developing the tourist industry because of the social problems that threatened to come with it. In the end, the country's economic woes left it no choice.

Plans for large-scale development of tourism were laid a little more than a decade ago, and many of today's shortcomings can be explained by a lack of experience. Service is poor, facilities run-down, and there are obvious discrepancies between price and quality. Several hotels have gone for 30 years without renovations and are in need of major repairs; if it's not the plumbing that breaks down, the air-conditioning doesn't work, or the hot water runs out, or the elevator takes forever. Hotels of more recent vintage can also have defects: slow communications, a lack of quality bars or restaurants, and poor service.

Five or six years ago the Ministry of Tourism undertook a program to restore and renovate some of the city's most beautiful hotels. Thanks to this initiative, travelers may now enjoy the Hotel Nacional, one of Havana's classic and most luxurious hostelries, as well as the Inglaterra and the Plaza, two hotels that strongly retain their colonial flavor and are in the historic section of the city. The Comodoro, the Copacabana, and the Château Miramar, with their beaches and natural pools on the Miramar coast, are also options. All of these are attractive hotels with acceptable service, and all have undergone recent renovation—a guarantee, of sorts, in today's Cuba.

In addition, in 1995 several hotels, among them the Habana Libre and the Neptuno, were taken over by European and Canadian hotel groups that have begun renovations with an eye to high-quality accommodations and services. The lovely Hotel Sevilla in La Habana Vieja was reopened in 1993 and is now an excellent choice. The Meliá Cohiba, a superdeluxe establishment next to the Riviera, opened its doors in mid-1995 under Sol-Meliá management, and is another fine alternative for well-heeled tourists and conventions. Likewise, the hotels Santa Isabel and Ambos Mundos and the Conde de Villa Nueva boardinghouse have recently been opened in the heart of La Habana Vieja.

Miramar is the farthest away from the historic center of Havana, as well as from the Playas del Este, but most of its hotels are on the beach, and there are plenty of nearby restaurants, bars, and nightclubs. The hotels of La Habana Vieja are ideal for night people and those who love history. (In all the hotels in this neighborhood, be very careful with cameras, bags, and rental cars; theft is common in this area.) Vedado hotels are newer and are also near the historic center and many major sights.

The economic opening of the Cuban government has permitted a new variety of boarding. Thousands of people rent out houses, rooms, or apartments in the city at reasonable prices, approximately between $20 and $30 per person per day. Some of these are excellent places, others only functional. You'll need recommendations, so ask around. Although it's not possible to compile a guide to these private residences, with a little effort you may be able to find splendid lodgings at good prices.

For details on price categories, *see* the chart *in* On the Road with Fodor's at the front of this guide.

$$$$ **Château Miramar.** This small hotel (50 rooms) has a magnificent swimming pool, ocean bathing, and thorough, personalized service. You also can't beat the location near the center of the city yet still on the beach. *Miramar, Calle 7 at 60,* ☎ *33 19 15 or 33 19 52/57.*

$$$$ **Hotel Meliá Cohiba.** Designed for comfort, each of the 462 rooms, of
★ which 120 are suites, has a minibar, satellite TV, and a telephone. Among the hotel's facilities are squash courts, a gymnasium, a solarium, a beauty salon, meeting rooms, and banquet halls. It also has shops, a discotheque, and 24-hour room service. *Vedado, Av. Paseo e/1 y 3,* ☎ *33 36 36,* FAX *33 13 33.*

$$$$ **Marina Hemingway.** This pier to the east of the capital accommodates private yachts and is the site of the annual Hemingway fishing tournament and the point of departure for cruises along the island. You can stay in one of the on-site hotel's 60 rooms or one of the 20 two-floor cabanas to the east of the marina. There are two restaurants, a mall, and a food store as well. *Santa Fe, Calle 248 y 5 Av.,* ☎ *33 11 50.*

$$$$ **Nacional.** Unquestionably Havana's most majestic hotel, when the
★ Nacional opened in 1930 it was the lodging of choice for such celebrities as Winston Churchill, the Prince of Wales, Buster Keaton, Ava Gard-

ner, and Marlon Brando. Set on a promontory that was once an artillery battery defending Santa Clara, the hotel has unmatched views of the sea, El Morro, and the Vedado district. The sixth floor has more amenities (it was set up for business travelers): fax service, international newspapers, separate check-in, and meeting rooms. The restaurants are excellent, and the rooftop terrace has stunning views of Havana. The service is good and the hotel was recently renovated. *Vedado, Calle 21 at O,* ☎ *33 35 64/67,* FAX *33 50 54.*

$$$$ **Santa Isabel.** Opened in early 1997, this hotel is in an 18th-century
★ palace once owned by the Count of Santovenia. Its beauty and location on the Plaza de Armas have made it a focal point of La Habana Vieja. It has 27 rooms, 11 of which are suites, a restaurant, a lobby bar, and a balcony. *La Habana Vieja, Calle Baratillo, e/O'Reilly y Obispo.*

$$$$ **Victoria.** This small (30 rooms), comfortable, family-run hotel is in the center of the Vedado district. Its convenient location and excellent service make it especially popular with business travelers. There is a good on-site restaurant. *Vedado, Calle 19 at M,* ☎ *33 35 65 or 78 20 65,* FAX *33 31 09.*

$$$ **Ambos Mundos.** Ernest Hemingway lived here during the 1940s, per-
★ haps drawn by the charm of the nearby colonial houses or, more likely, by the close proximity of the legendary El Floridita restaurant (☞ Dining, *above*). The hotel underwent extensive renovations and reopened in 1997. It now has 53 rooms (4 of which are suites), a bar, a cafeteria, a restaurant, and a balcony. *La Habana Vieja, Calle Obispo e/San Ignacio y Mercaderes,* ☎ *61 48 87.*

$$$ **Capri.** Before the revolution, the Capri was frequented by American gangsters and is still famous for Mario Puzo's reference to it in *The Godfather*. Although it's in urgent need of renovation, it has a few benefits: a small, pleasant pool on the top floor (the view is fabulous); an outstanding location next to the Habana Libre and the Nacional and a block from La Rampa; and two cabarets, the Capri and the Salon Rojo, that fill up every night. *Vedado, Calle 21 at N,* ☎ *33 35 71 or 33 37 23,* FAX *33 37 50.*

$$$ **Comodoro.** Though it's a ways from the historic sights, nearly at the end of the Miramar district, the Comodoro has swimming pools and a pleasant beach. It also has several nice bungalows. The hotel runs a tourism and hostelry school. *Miramar, Calle 3 at 84,* ☎ *33 20 28 or 33 20 14,* FAX *33 11 68.*

$$$ **Copacabana.** Here everything is new, in perfect condition, and close to the sea. The Caribbean washes at the hotel's foundations and forms a natural swimming pool. The service is average, but the views make up for it. Amenities include a discotheque, tennis and squash courts, and a marina from which you can fish or dive. *Miramar, Calle 1 e/44 y 46,* ☎ *33 10 37 or 33 12 63,* FAX *33 28 46.*

$$$ **Habana Libre.** This, the former Havana Hilton, has 534 rooms and is the city's largest hotel. Although currently being renovated, it is still open for business. Convenience is its calling card: it has a terrific location in the center of Vedado, at the start of La Rampa, and most of Havana's major tourist offices have spaces in the hotel. It also has a pool, a sauna, and a splendid view of the city from the 25th floor. The service has noticeably improved under the management of the Spanish Tryp chain. *Vedado, Calle L e/23 y 25,* ☎ *33 40 11,* FAX *33 31 41.*

$$$ **Habana Riviera.** The Riviera is being renovated and may yet again take it's place as a leading hotel. It's still open, so you can take advantage of its excellent location on the Malecón, Havana's waterfront promenade; its spacious rooms with sea views; and its splendid saltwater swimming pool. The service here is acceptable. *Vedado, Paseo y Malecón,* ☎ *33 37 33,* FAX *33 37 48.*

$$$ **Inglaterra.** Established in 1875, the Inglaterra is one Havana's oldest
★   hotels. Its perfectly preserved colonial architecture and its Spanish
        aura—with a marvelous interior patio decorated with coats of arms
        and Valencian tiles—make it a must-see, whether or not you stay here.
        The hotel is across from the Parque Central, very near the García
        Lorca Theater—formerly a Gallego palace—the Capitolio, and the
        commercial streets around San Rafael. Although this is an excellent
        place to immerse yourself in La Habana Vieja, be forewarned that ser-
        vice is slow and the communication systems are poor. *La Habana
        Vieja, Prado 416,* ☎ *33 85 93,* FAX *33 82 54.*

$$$ **Neptuno.** This hotel and the Tritón, its near neighbor, are among Mi-
        ramar's most important hotel complexes. The Neptuno is the newer
        of the two and, accordingly, the more recommendable. Constructed
        on the coral coast to the west of the city, it has a seaside swimming
        pool and operates an aqua-bar, a barbecue, two tennis courts, and a
        car rental service. *Miramar, Av. 3 at 70,* ☎ *33 16 06,* FAX *33 00 42.*

$$$ **Plaza.** On the corner of the Parque Central and the Gómez block, just
★   steps from the famous El Floridita (☞ Dining, *above*), the Plaza has
        neoclassical architecture and completely modernized rooms. There is
        no pool, but the rooftop terrace has terrific views of the old city and
        the Bay of Havana. *La Habana Vieja, Calle Zulueta 267 at Neptuno,*
        ☎ *33 85 83/90,* FAX *33 85 92.*

$$$ **Sevilla.** Folks have always raved about this hotel's beautiful patios and
★   Spanish-style fountains. Since its refurbishment, they can also rave about
        its pool, sauna, gymnasium, and other amenities. *La Habana Vieja, Tro-
        cadero 55 at Prado,* ☎ *33 85 66/69.* FAX *33 85 82.*

$$ **Hostal Conde Villanueva.** Constructed as a private residence in 1714,
★   this hostal retains a very welcoming colonial atmosphere. Its privileged
        location in the historic district is also a boon. *202 Calle Mercaderes,
        at Lamparilla y Habana Vieja.*

$$ **Hostal Valencia.** Just steps from the Plaza de Armas, this was the man-
★   sion of the Count de Sotolongo during the 18th century. It has 12 rooms,
        a marvelous interior patio, and a mezzanine bar with a warm atmo-
        sphere. *53 Calle Officios, e/Obra Pía y Lamparilla,* ☎ *62 38 01,* FAX
        33 31 09.

$$ **Horizontes Itabo.** Like the Tropicoco (☞ *below*), this hotel is on the
        Santa María beach, some 30 minutes from Havana by cars—perfect
        if you want to relax in the sun, but a little out of the way if you want
        to take in the sights. Among the facilities are a large pool and a *ranchón*
        (restaurant). Because it is outside the Havana city limits, communica-
        tion is poor; you must dial several area codes to call anywhere. *Santa
        María del Mar, Laguna de Itabo, Fuente de Madera,* ☎ *0–687–2581/
        89 or 0–687–2558/59.*

$$ **Kholy.** A prefabricated building, the Kholy has been nicely renovated
        and decorated with wicker furniture and floral-print cushions. It's
        surrounded by trees, not very far from the Tropicana cabaret, and 10
        minutes by car from La Habana Vieja. It has a pool. *Playa, Av. 49 at
        36, Kholy suburb,* ☎ *33 02 50 or 33 02 40/42.*

$$ **Panamericano.** This tourist complex is on the outskirts of the capital,
        very near Cojímar, and is part of the sports facilities built in 1991 for
        the Pan-American Games. It consists of a hotel and two apartment-
        hotels, both just steps from the beach. It is halfway between the Playas
        del Este and the city's historical quarter, and only 10 minutes from each.
        Its facilities and service are average. *Cojímar, Calle A y Av. Central,*
        ☎ *33 88 10,* FAX *33 80 01.*

$$ **Presidente.** The vestibule, corridors, restaurants, and some of the
★   rooms have paintings, ceramics, and other valuable art objects from
        the 1930s. Stay here to be near the Malecón, the cultural institute
        Casa de las Americas, and some of Havana's important theaters. You'll

find the Presidente comfortable, and its small pool with gardens are very pleasant in summer. *Vedado, Calzada y G,* ☎ *33 43 94,* FAX *33 37 53.*

$$ St. John's. This small hotel makes up for its service shortcomings and lack of a pool with moderate prices and a location on La Rampa, close to movie theaters, tourist offices, and international airlines offices. On its top floor is El Rincón del Feeling, where you can listen to performers sing romantic songs from the 1940s. *Vedado, Calle O e/23 y 25,* ☎ *33 37 40 or 33 41 87,* FAX *33 35 61.*

$$ Tropicoco. This hotel 25 km (16 mi) east of Havana is near the fine white sands and coconut trees of Playa de Santa María. The hotel offers an "all-inclusive" program ($60 per person) that includes lodging; breakfast, lunch, and dinner; Windsurf or catamaran rental; and drinks at the bar. *Santa María del Mar, Av. Sur e/Av. de Banderas y Calle 7,* ☎ *0–687–2531/39.*

$$ Vedado. On the same street as the St. John's (☞ *above*), this is a hotel for young people or travelers on tight budgets—those who plan to spend their time out and about, rather than lounging at their hotel. The Vedado has 194 rooms (very small but air-conditioned) and a pool. *Vedado, Calle O e/Humboldt y 25,* ☎ *33 40 72,* FAX *33 41 86.*

$ Bruzón. Along with the hotels of the Playas del Este, this is one of the least expensive lodgings in the Cuban capital. The 46 rooms, all doubles, are small, but each has a private bath and a telephone—although only 10 have televisions. The hotel is the home of the Rincón del Tango, which features *porteña* (Argentine) music. The location near the Plaza de la Revolución, however, is not ideal. *Plaza, Bruzón e/Pozos Dulces y Boyeros,* ☎ *70 35 31/33.*

$ Caribbean. The least expensive of all Havana hotels, the Caribbean sometimes experiences water shortages. It has no air-conditioning or television, but it does have fans and radios. It's strategically located on the Paseo del Prado, the border between Centro Habana and La Habana Vieja, very close the beginning of the Malecón. *Centro Habana, Prado 164, e/Colón y Refugio,* ☎ *62 20 71/73 or 33 62 33.*

$ Colina. This is a simple but well-situated establishment across from the
★ University of Havana at the start of Calle San Lazaro, which leads to the Paseo del Prado in La Habana Vieja. Look no farther for inexpensive lodgings with fairly good service and a convenient location. *Vedado, Calle L e/27 y Jovellar,* ☎ *32 35 35.*

$ Lido. The Lido is near the water *and* La Habana Vieja and has a colorful clientele (many Cubans stay here). The service, sadly, is mediocre to poor. It's only recommended for intrepid travelers. *Centro Habana, Consulado 210, e/Animas and Trocadero,* ☎ *33 88 14.*

$ Lincoln. Not only does the Lincoln have a good location but it also has color televisions and air-conditioning—true luxuries for a hotel in this price range. *Centro Habana, Galiano e/Virtudes y Animas,* ☎ *33 82 09.*

$ Morro. This small, 20-room establishment is just a block from the Malecón, between the Riviera and Presidente hotels. *Vedado, Calle 3 e/D y C,* ☎ *33 39 07/09 or 30 99 43.*

$ Playas del Este hotels. In Playas del Este there are many hotels that are inexpensive but of poor quality. All in all, they are not recommended, for what you save in lodging you'll spend on taxis. Their sole advantage is being right on the beach. **Atlántico Gran Caribe** (Avenida de Las Terrazas, Santa Maria del Mar, Habana del Este, ☎ *33 55 02, 33 55 23,* FAX *33 55 19*). **Bacuranao Islazul** (Vía Blanca km 15½, Bacuranao, Habana del Este, ☎ *65 76 45, 65 63 32*). **Las Brisas Horizontes** (Calle 11 e/1 y 3, Santa María del Mar [Ioma], Habana del Este, ☎ *24 69, 33 84*). **Mégano Horizontes** (Vía Blanca km 17, Santa María del Mar, Habana del Este, ☎ 44 41, 37 47). **Playa Hermosa Islazul** (Av. 5, corner of 470, Guanabo, Habana del Este, ☎ 27 74, 36 11).

THE ARTS AND NIGHTLIFE

Cinemas and Theaters

Note that movie houses and theaters in Cuba reduce their programming during the off season owing to the economic crisis affecting the entire island.

Cinemas

Centro Cultural Cinematográfico Yara. *Vedado, Pl. de la Revolución, Calle 23 y L,* ☎ 32 94 30. 🎟 $2. ☉ 12:30 PM–2 AM.

Centro Promotor del Humor Cina Acapulco. *Vedado, Pl. de la Revolución, Av. 26 e/35 y 37,* ☎ 395 73. ☉ 5 PM–midnight.

Charles Chaplin. *Vedado, Pl. de la Revolución, Calle 34 e/10 y 12,* ☎ 31 11 01. 🎟 $2. *Thurs.–Sun. at 6 and 9.*

Complejo Cultural Payret. *La Habana Vieja, Prado y San José,* ☎ 63 31 63. 🎟 $3. ☉ 12:30 PM–2 AM.

La Rampa. Cuba's cinematheque. Interesting cycles and series on actors and directors from different countries. *Vedado, Calle 23 e/O y P,* ☎ 76146.

Riviera. *Vedado, Calle 23 e/G y H,* ☎ 30 95 64.

Trianon. *Vedado, Línea y Paseo,* ☎ 30 96 48.

Theaters

Gran Teatro de la Habana. Formerly the García Lorca Theater. The Cuban National Ballet performs here. *Centro Habana, Prado y San Rafael,* ☎ 61 30 78. ☉ *Mon.–Sat. at 8:30, Sun. at 5.*

Sala El Sótano. *Vedado, Calle K e/25 y 27,* ☎ 32 06 30.

Sede del Conjunto Folclorico Nacional. *Vedado, Pl. de la Revolución, Calle 4 e/3 y 5,* ☎ 31 34 67. 🎟 $1.

Teatro Bertold Brecht. *Vedado, Calle 13 y 1,* ☎ 32 93 59.

Teatro de Guiñol Para Niños. *Vedado, Calle M e/19 y 21,* ☎ 32 62 62.

Teatro Hubert de Blank. *Vedado, Calzada, e/A y B,* ☎ 30 10 11.

Teatro Karl Marx. *Miramar, Playa, Calle 1 y 10,* ☎ 30 07 20.

Teatro Mella. *Vedado, Pl. de la Revolución, Línea y A,* ☎ 3–8696. ☉ *Thurs.–Sun. at 6 and 8:30.*

Teatro Nacional de Cuba. *Vedado, Pl. de la Revolución, Paseo y 39,* ☎ 79 60 11. ☉ *Thurs.–Sun. at 8:30.*

Cafés and Terrace Bars

Unlike other Caribbean cities, Havana is not famous for its bars and cafés or for the custom of sitting on an outdoor terrace with a glass of brandy or a frozen daiquiri. It is not so much that its residents have no wish to as that they have little opportunity. The few places that do exist are concentrated in La Habana Vieja and are, indeed, extraordinarily lovely. One is **El Mirador,** a terrace-bar attached to the restaurant La Divina Pastora (☞ Dining, *above*), on the channel leading into Havana's bay. An old battery of cannons is preserved here, a souvenir from the days of the Spanish and from which the wise and the fortunate now enjoy fine sunsets.

Only a few meters away from El Mirador are **Los Doce Apóstoles** (☞ Dining, *above*) and **El Polvorín,** two rustic taverns in the fortress of the Tres Reyes del Morro (Gran Parque Militar Morro-Cabaña). These three spots are exceptional; it would be criminal to leave Havana without visiting them.

On the Plaza de Armas, across the bay, are **La Mina,** a bar-restaurant with a very nice terrace, **Casa de las Infusiones,** and **Casa de la Natilla,** all ideal stops for the abstemious. Those who crave something alcoholic might try a mojito at the **Taberna del Galeón.**

If you walk up from the Plaza de Armas along O'Reilly and take a right at San Ignacio, you come to the Plaza de la Catedral. Here you will find the palace of the Marqueses de Aguas Claras, now a lovely bar and restaurant called **El Patio** (☞ Dining, *above*). Don't eat here, but do stop for an aperitif. Every day the square fills up with a delightful and crowded crafts market. Some of the strollers you see are doubtless recovering from a visit to **La Bodeguita del Medio** (☞ Dining, *above*), the most famous Creole tavern in Cuba, legendary for its mojitos, its chicharrones, and its traditional fare.

At the end of Calle Obispo, still in the district of La Habana Vieja but near the edge of Centro Habana, is the bar-restaurant **El Floridita** (☞ Dining, *above*), birthplace of the daiquiri. Founded more than 150 years ago, El Floridita is the most exclusive watering place in Havana, haunt of Hemingway and of politicos, actors, and writers of the '40s and '50s. As of this writing, the bartender Antonio Meilán, with more than 50 years in the profession, is still making drinks here. Its prices may be somewhat inflated, but El Floridita is not to be missed.

Sharing the same corner with El Floridita is the **Casa del Ron** (Obispo, e/Bernaza y Monserrate.) A little farther along, across the Parque Central, is the **Colonial Bar** in the Hotel Inglaterra (☞ Lodging, *above*).

There are plenty of bars in Habana Vieja where you can get a drink or a sandwich. In the Calle Montserrat are **La Zaragozana** and **El Castillo de Farnés,** and at Prado and Malecón is the open-air bar of the fortress **La Punta.** There are also reasonably good spots in the hotels **Plaza** and **Sevilla.**

Various Havana hotels have pleasant terraces on their top floors, with wonderful views of the city and acceptable, even reasonable, prices. Try the ones at the **Nacional** (21 y O); the **Plaza** (La Habana Vieja, Zulueta y Neptuno), where the bar is called El Solarium; and the **Inglaterra** (La Habana Vieja, Prado 416).

Among the interesting bars in the Vedado district are **El Turquino,** on the 25th floor of the Habana Libre (23 y L) and **La Torre,** on the top of the Focsa Building (17 y M).

In Miramar there are **La Maison** (Calle 16 at 3), which has a garden terrace well worth a visit and the bar-restaurant **La Cecilia** (Av. 5, No. 11010, e/110 y 112).

Cabarets and Discothèques

Over the past few years, along with the traditional Cuban cabarets with their dance shows and orchestras, there are now many discotheques and concert halls such as Los Van Van, Adalberto Álvarez y su Son, and the Charanga Habanera—all of which are very popular and busy till dawn. There are also late-night bars with jazz groups or interpretations of *feeling* (romantic music from the '40s and '50s). Consult the tourist office in your hotel to find out who is performing where and to check on the venue's status; some cabarets may be closed. It's also good to make reservations in these establishments.

Cabarets

Capri. Located in the hotel of the same name, the first-class Capri has two hour-long shows nightly, one at 10 and one at 12:30. *Vedado, Hotel Capri, Calle 21 and O,* ☎ *33 35 71 or 33 37 23.* 🔳 *$15. Closed Thurs.*

Parisien. This cabaret features disco music in deluxe surroundings. *Vedado, Hotel Nacional, Calle 21 y O,* ☎ *33 35 64/67.* 🔳 *$25.* 🕐 *Nightly.*

Salon Rojo. The Hotel Capri's second and less expensive cabaret also presents two shows a night, one from 10 to 11 and another from 12:30 to 1:30. *Vedado, Hotel Capri, Calle 21 y O,* ☎ *33 35 71 or 33 37 23. Closed Mon.*

Tropicana. This is the most famous, largest, and most luxurious of Havana's nightspots. Until 1959 the covered section in which smaller shows and live music are presented was a casino. The Tropicana sprawls beneath a canopy of palms and coconut trees. There are two elaborate outdoor shows, the first from 10:30 to midnight, the second from 1 AM to 2 AM. *Marianao, Calle 72 at 41,* ☎ *33 01 10.* 🔳 *from $30 to $70 per person depending on the table. Reservations essential.* 🕐 *Tues.–Sun. 9 PM–2 AM.*

Discotheques and Piano Bars

Ache. The Ache is open from 10 PM to 5 AM. *Vedado, Hotel Meliá Cohiba, Paseo e/1 y 3.*

Arcos de Cristal. This cabaret next to the Tropicana features musical combos. It is open from 10 PM to 3 AM. *Calle 72 y Av. 41. Reservations essential.*

Discoteca del Hotel Copacabana. Here the $10 cover charge does not include a drink. *Miramar, Calle 1 e/44 y 60.* 🕐 *9 PM–5 AM.*

Discoteca Habana Club. The disco in the Hotel Comodore also has a $10 cover charge with drinks extra. *Miramar, Hotel Comodore, Calle 84 at 3.* 🕐 *9 PM–5 AM.*

Discoteca Río Club. One of the most popular discotheques in the city, maybe becase the cover charge is only $5. *Calle O at 1 y Miramar.* 🕐 *Daily.*

Discoteca de la Marina Hemingway. This is open-air space at the marina. *Marina Hemingway, Jaimanitas.*

El Elegante. For a change of pace, check out this video-bar and jazz performance space. *Vedado, Hotel Riviera, Paseo y Malecón.*

El Pampero. Also known as the Rincón del Tango (Tango Corner), this is the only spot in Havana that features the tango and Argentine music. *Plaza, Hotel Bruzón, Bruzón e/Pozos Dulces y Boyeros.* 🔳 *Free.* 🕐 *11 AM–midnight. Closed Mon.*

El Rincón del Bolero. Come for boleros and *feeling* until 3 AM. *Miramar, Calle 7, corner of 26.*

La Maison. This terrace-garden presents a fashion show from 9 to 10, then performances by contemporary Cuban groups and soloists. The music ranges from *feeling* to traditional Cuban fare. *Miramar, Calle 16 at 7.* 🔳 *Free. Reservations essential. Closed Mon.*

Piano Bar del Hotel Meliá Cohiba. Every night except Monday there are performances by the excellent Cuban pianist, Frank Emilio, from 10 to 11. *Hotel Meliá Cohiba, Vedado, Av. Paseo e/1 y 3,* ☎ *33 36 36.*

Piano Bar del Presidente. Sometimes there's live performance by groups or soloists, other times there's recorded music. Check ahead. *Vedado, Hotel Presidente, Calzada y G.* 🕐 *10 PM–2 AM. Closed Fri.*

Piano Bar del Teatro National. Come for the jazz performances from 11 PM–2 AM and the warm setting. *Plaza de la Revolución.*

Pico Blanco. Also called Rincón del Feeling, here you'll find live romantic music and boleros from the '40s. There are also performances by

Cesar Portillo de la Luz Tuesday through Sunday as well as the combo Nueva Trova Cubana. *Hotel St. John's, Calle O y 23.* ✆ *$5 (drink included).*

Snack Bar del Hotel Plaza. Trios and small musical combos perform in the hotel lobby from 7 to 10:30 PM. There are also performances in the Solarium, on the hotel's top floor, after midnight. *La Habana Vieja, Hotel Plaza, Agramonte 267.*

Salsa Rooms

Café Cantante del Teatro National. For $10 you can salsa here till 3 AM; it's open cover charge. *Plaza de la Revolución.*

La Casa de la Música. Same deal as at the Café Cantante. *Miramar, Calle 18 e/33 y 35.*

La Cecilia. This open-air place is also open until 3 AM—but not every day. *Miramar, Avenida 5 y 110,* ✆ *33 15 62.*

La Tropical. Be somewhat cautious at this typical Cuban place as there are occasional scuffles. *Playa, Calle 41, corner of 42.*

Palacio de la Salsa. There are salsa performances every day except Monday. The usual $10 cover charge may vary depending on the orchestra. It's open 11 PM–3 AM. *Hotel Riviera.* ✆ *33 40 51.*

EXCURSIONS FROM HAVANA

There are numerous excursions and outings from Havana, from tracing the steps of Ernest Hemingway to visiting the magnificent Botanical Gardens. Various agencies and corporations offer packages. The principal agencies are: Havanatur, Cubatur, Cubanacán, and Gaviotatours (☞ Visitor Information *in* Havana Essentials, *above*).

If possible, however, try to arrange these excursions on your own rather than joining organized tours, which inevitably have rigid schedules and group meals and preset menus.

Botanical Gardens. In the Botanical Gardens, 25 km (15½ mi) south of Havana, palm trees are the featured attraction, but you can also admire a Japanese garden and countless varieties of bougainvillea and orchids. Tours take up to three hours and their prices vary depending on the package.

Encounter with Hemingway (Reencuentro con Hemingway). This tour in air-conditioned buses includes a visit to La Vigía, Ernest Hemingway's Havana residence in the village of San Francisco de Paula, now a museum. It also stops in Cojímar, the fishing village from which the writer once set out in his yacht *Pilar* and the setting for his novel *The Old Man and The Sea.* ✆ *$10, not including lunch; $27 with lunch.* ☉ *Departures daily at 8:30 AM except Tues. and rainy days. Duration: 4 hrs.*

In Hemingway's Tracks (Por la Ruta de Hemingway). This tour follows a route similar to the one described above but includes a cocktail at the Bodeguita del Medio and lunch in the restaurant 1830. ✆ *$25.* ☉ *Departures daily at 9 AM and 2 PM except Tues. and rainy days. Duration: 4 hrs.*

Playas del Este. This bus tour takes you to the long, white-sand beaches 20 km (12 mi) east of Havana—Guanabo, Santa María, or Mégano—all with coconut palms and fine sand. ✆ *$10.* ☉ *Departures daily at 9 AM and 2 PM. Duration: 4 hrs.*

Visit to the Partagás tobacco factory. This bus tour takes you through one of the most prestigious cigar factories in the world, on Calle Industria between Barcelona and Dragones, very near La Habana Vieja.

It includes a drink and a handful of Havana cigars as well as free time for shopping. ✉ *$10.* ⊙ *Departures weekdays and alternate Sats. at 9 AM and 2 PM. Duration: 3 hrs.*

Special-Interest Tours

All-Day Excursions

Cayo Largo. This plane trip to a paradisiacal Cuban key with virgin beaches (☞ Chapter 2) includes a seafood lunch and a yacht tour. ✉ *$94.* ⊙ *Departures daily at 6 AM, returning at 6:30 PM.*

Guamá. This air-conditioned bus tour to the crocodile breeding area and a Taino native Caribbean village on the Tesoro Lagoon in the Ciénaga de Zapata. ✉ *$35.* ⊙ *Departs at 7:30 AM, returns at 6:30 PM.*

Isla de la Juventud. Owing to its numerous inlets and its irregular coastline, this island was a well-known pirate refuge in the 16th and 17th centuries. This, along with its coral banks, make it a Caribbean paradise. The plane tour includes a boat excursion to the international diving area, swimming at a virgin beach, a seafood lunch, and a visit to the Colony Hotel. ✉ *$89.* ⊙ *Departs at 6:15 AM, returns at 6:30 PM.*

Santiago de Cuba. The tour includes the flight to Cuba's second city and the colonial capital until 1589; a visit to the house of the conquistador and first governor of Cuba, Diego Velázquez; and tours of El Morro, the fortress guarding the magnificent bay of Santiago, and of the city's historic center (☞ Chapter 4). ✉ *$139.* ⊙ *Departs at 6 AM, returns at 7 PM.*

Soroa. Travel by bus to this famous orchid grove in the Rosario mountains (☞ Chapter 2). There are also a swimming pool and a natural waterfall, and the bus tour includes lunch. ✉ *$30.* ⊙ *Departs at 8 AM, returns at 4 PM.*

Trinidad. One of the first seven towns founded by the Spanish, Trinidad is famous for its colonial architecture and the miraculous preservation of its buildings and its cobblestone streets (☞ Chapter 3). This plane excursion includes a tour of the city, visits to a ceramics studio and a tobacco factory, a drink in the traditional Canchánchara tavern, and lunch and beach time at the Hotel Ancón. ✉ *$79.* ⊙ *Departs at 6:30 AM, returns at 4:30 PM.*

Viñales. Visit the Viñales Valley (☞ Chapter 2). The tour, on an air-conditioned bus, includes a brief walk through the town of Pinar del Río, a visit to a tobacco factory, a stop at the Guayabita del Pinar rum factory, a Creole lunch, a tour of the Cueva del Indio (Indian Cave), and a look at the prehistoric mural. ✉ *$39.* ⊙ *Departs daily at 7:30 AM, returns at 6:30 PM.*

Varadero. This tour gives you a day on the beach at Varadero (☞ Chapter 2) and includes a guided trip on an air-conditioned bus. ✉ *$27 without lunch, $39 with lunch.* ⊙ *Departs daily at 7:30 AM, returns at 6 PM.*

Overnight Excursions

Cienfuegos. The trip, in an air-conditioned bus, begins with a visit to the village of Santa Isabel de las Lajas, birthplace of the king of Cuban folk music, Benny Moré. Creole lunch and lodging in the Hotel Jagua, a night outing to a cabaret, and a cruise across the bay are included. ✉ *$89.* ⊙ *Departs at 7 AM, returns at 7 PM.*

Trinidad. Situated in the mountains and near the sea, Trinidad is considered a living museum. It was founded in 1514 by Diego Velázquez, and its buildings and squares are perfectly preserved. The bus tour combines visits to museums, churches, bars, and ceramics shops with an overnight stay at the Motel Trinidad. ✉ *$120.* ⊙ *Departs at 7 AM, returns at 7:30 PM.*

Varadero. The trip to Varadero and back in an air-conditioned bus includes an overnight stay with half pension. ✉ *$135.* ☉ *Departs 7:30 AM, returns at 4:30 PM.*

Viñales. This tour of Pinar del Río in an air-conditioned bus includes lodging in a hotel in the Viñales Valley (half pension) and a visit to Cayo Levisa. ✉ *$99. Departs at 7 AM, returns at 7 PM.*

Varadero, Cienfuegos, and Trinidad. Why not take a whirlwind tour of three nights, three cities? This trip includes lodging in the Hotel Paradiso in Varadero, the Jagua in Cienfuegos, and the Ancón, on the beach of the same name, in Trinidad, in a double room (half board the first two nights and full board the third). ✉ *$225.*

2 Western Cuba

PINAR DEL RÍO

The landscape in the western province of Pinar del Río is a succession of contrasts—from the rocky heights of its Sierra de los Órganos and Sierra del Rosario and its unusual *mogotes* (flat-top hillocks) to its hidden beaches and pristine forests. The fertile tobacco fields are also an important part of the land; the quality of the tobacco produced here has, for centuries, been famous. If it is routinely accepted that Cuban cigars are the best in the world, connoisseurs know that the very highest quality leaves are those from the county of Vuelta Abajo, which extends west of the provincial capital to the towns of San Luis, San Juan, and Martínez. The Pinar del Río's proximity to Havana, its many attractions, and its plentiful tourist facilities make it a great place to explore.

Numbers in the margin correspond to points of interest on the Western Cuba map.

Exploring

From Havana to Pinar del Río and Beyond

Leave Havana on the six-lane freeway that heads west; the landscape will soon make you feel very far from the great metropolis. Royal palms, the national symbol, and other tropical vegetation begin to appear, as do *bohíos,* the traditional peasant houses made of wood and palm leaves. Some 70 km (43 mi) from the capital, just as you enter the province of Pinar del Río, you will see the turnoff to Soroa to the right. The steep road to this tourist complex in the upper reaches of the Sierra del Rosario passes small towns and tunnels under leaves of red *flamboyans* (flame) and carob trees. Rocky peaks occasionally appear above the thick tropical forest. Much of the area is part of natural reserves—thousands of acres of wooded highlands, where, among other creatures, there are hummingbirds only an inch long, said to be the world's smallest birds.

On the right side of the road, a sign points you to some **waterfalls** on the Manantiales River. After leaving your car and paying the entry fee of $1, walk through the woods for 10 minutes or so until you reach the top of the cascade. Don't forget to bring a good insect repellent: The abundant bugs can definitely ruin your walk—if not your day. Walk another 10 minutes to the bottom, where there's a natural swimming pool and a terrific view of the falls.

Back on the road to Soroa, continue until you reach the **orquideario,** a superb 35,000-sq-km (22,000-sq-mi) grove devoted exclusively to orchids. Canary Islands botanist Tomás Felipe Camacho labored over this botanical garden for nine years and dedicated it to his daughter. It contains some 700 orchid varieties from all parts of the world. Entry

❶ costs $2. Beyond this, you come to the tourist town of **Soroa,** and 2 km (1 mi) outside it, you begin to climb more and more steeply until you reach the crest of a mountain.

NEED A
BREAK?

El Castillo de las Nubes (the castle of the clouds) restaurant is atop the highest peak in the area and is housed in a remarkable stone structure. The stunning view from here extends over the entire palm-canopied valley; on a clear day, you can see as far as the Isla de la Juventud. The menu consists of simple dishes of meat and fish accompanied by locally grown fruit.

Continue west on the highway. To the south of the road there is a large, sparsely populated area containing Maspotón and Las Víboras, two

❷ of Cuba's largest game preserves. **Pinar del Río,** the provincial capital

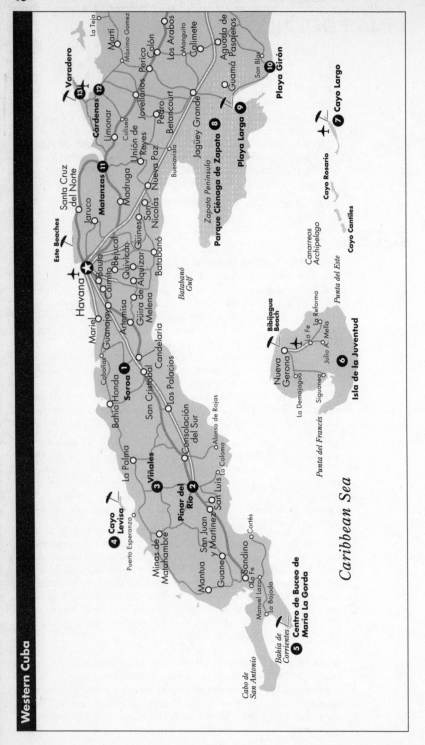

La Teja

Martí

Máximo Gómez

Varadero

13 ✈

12

Colón

Los Arabos

Calimete

Manguito

Perico

Colón

Aguada de
Guamá Pasajeros

San Blas

10

Playa Girón

Cárdenas

Limonar

Coliseo

Jovellanos

Pedro
Betancourt

Jagüey Grande

8

Playa Larga

9

Cayo Largo

7

Unión de
Reyes

Madruga

Nueva Paz

Parque Ciénaga de Zapata

Cayo Rosario

Matanzas

11

Santa Cruz
del Norte

Jaruco

San
Nicolás

Guines

Buenavista

Zapata Peninsula

Cayo Camiles

Este Beaches

Havana

✈ ⭐

Bauta

Caimito

Bejucal

Quivicán

Melena

Batabanó

Batabanó
Gulf

Canarreos
Archipelago

Punta del Este

Mariel

Guanajay

Artemisa

Güira de
Alquízar

Candelaria

Cabañas

Bahía
Honda

Soroa

1

San Cristóbal

Los Palacios

Consolación
del Sur

Alonso de Rojas

La Coloma

Bibijagua
Beach

La Reforma

La Fe

R. Mella

Nueva
Gerona

Julio A. Mella

6

Isla de la Juventud

La Palma

Viñales

3

**Pinar del
Río**

2

San Luis

San Juan
y Martínez

La Demajagua

Siguanea

Punta del Francés

4 Cayo
Levisa

Puerto Esperanza

Minas de
Matahambre

Mantua

Guane

Cortés

Sandino

La Fe

Manuel Lazo

La Bajada

5 Centro de Buceo de
María La Gorda

Bahía de
Corrientes

Cabo de
San Antonio

Caribbean Sea

of some 125,000 inhabitants, is 176 km (109 mi) from Havana. Although it is one of Cuba's fastest growing cities, there are few tourist attractions. You should, however, visit the **Donatien Tobacco Factory** (Maceo 157) to see the work that goes into the production of cigars, or stop by the **Casa de la Trova** (musical society; Gerardo Medina e/Isidro de Armas y Martí) for some traditional Cuban tunes. The city center also has remarkably preserved, early 20th-century wooden houses with columned porticoes. Be sure to stop at a bar to try the local drink, *guayabita del pinar,* made with rum and locally grown guava.

3 The standard route continues to **Viñales,** 27 km (17 mi) farther west. This small city seems frozen in time—a perfect 19th-century urban ensemble. Even more interesting is the valley surrounding it, a lovely plain dotted with mogotes. These hillocks were formed during the Upper Jurassic period, making them the oldest rock formations in Cuba. Beneath many of them are caverns and rivers that form one of the most notable subterranean networks in the Americas. The hotels **La Ermita** and **Los Jazmines** are two excellent observation posts overlooking the valley.

From Viñales, take the road to Minas de Matahambre. After 3 km (2 mi) you come to the turnoff to the **Mural de la Prehistoria** (Prehistoric Mural) in the Dos Hermanas Valley. This immense painting completely covers the vertical wall of a mogote, and it depicts the entire evolutionary process of the Sierra de los Órganos—from prehistoric apes to Homo sapiens. The mural, restored in 1980, is 120 meters (394 feet) high and 180 meters (590 feet) wide. It was painted between 1959 and 1962 by Leovigildo González, a disciple of the great Mexican muralist Diego Rivera.

Backtrack to Viñales and take the road toward Puerto Esperanza to complete your tour of the valley. The road wanders through little towns nestled under the mogotes and then gradually descends to the sea. After crossing Ancón Pass you come to the **Cueva de José Miguel** (José Miguel Cave) on the left with its interior cabaret, and, farther along, the famous **Cueva del Indio** (Indian Cave). Discovered by local farmers in 1920, this cave once contained a settlement of the Guanahatabeyes, hunter-gatherers who inhabited the region. A flight of steps, nearly overgrown with vegetation, leads to the entrance. The cave is some 1,700 meters (5,575 feet) long, but you are restricted to the 550 meters (1,804 feet) that are lit, the first 250 meters (820 feet) of which you explore along a well-worn path. The cave's curious rock formations resemble, with a little imagination, human and animal figures. At the end of the path you board a small motorboat that takes you along the river and out through another opening. There is a restaurant at the cave's main entrance, and just across the road from it are a small restaurant and a guest house.

Two km (1 mi) farther along are the **sulphur and mineral springs of San Vicente,** with a hotel for people taking the cure. The average water temperature is 31°C (88°F), except for the mineral springs, which are cold and potable.

Just beyond the springs, turn left at the crossroads toward San Cayetano, and you soon reach **Puerto Esperanza,** a small fishing village where **4** boats make the 45-minute crossing to **Cayo Levisa.** (You need your passport to take the boat, and it's a good idea to arrange a stay at this tiny key with its virgin beaches through your travel agency at home or in Havana or Pinar del Río). Also near Puerto Esperanza is the village of **El Rosario.** The guest house here is a good place to stay while you explore more of the northern coast.

From Pinar del Río to the Guanahacabibes Peninsula

From Pinar del Río you can also journey toward the western tip of the island. Leave the city on the Nacional I, which travels through tobacco fields dotted with drying sheds made of palm fronds. Twenty-three kilometers (14 mi) to the west, the road passes through **San Juan y Martínez,** whose main street is lined with columned houses painted in different colors. Just before entering the village you will see the turnoff to **San Luis.** These towns are in the heart of **Vuelta Abajo,** which produces the world's finest tobacco. The road continues on toward Sandino across a region of lagoons, some of which—Pesquero Lagoon in particular— are crowded with local fishermen. Farther along, past the town of Manuel Lazo, you cross a dense forest. In places, the teeming vegetation is covered with crabs, some of which will raise their huge claws as you approach.

When you come to Bahía de Corrientes, you will have to pass through a military checkpoint in the town of La Bajada. You then continue to the left along the ocean for 15 km (9 mi) to reach the **Centro de Buceo de María la Gorda** (Maria la Gorda Diving Center), one of Cuba's top underwater exploration centers. Unlike other diving meccas, such as those on the Isla de la Juventud, these areas are close to the shore, so you don't lose so much time on the boat getting to and from a dive site. The water here is an intense indigo, as beautiful as any in the Caribbean.

On the other side of the La Bajada is the **Guanahacabibes Peninsula,** listed by UNESCO as a Biosphere Preserve. It is Cuba's largest forest preserve and home to countless animal and plant species in danger of extinction. Because it was so remote, it became a refuge for the island's indigenous peoples during the Spanish invasion. To visit the area you will need camping gear and a permit from the tourist office.

Dining and Lodging

For details on price categories, *see* the charts *in* On the Road with Fodor's at the front of this guide.

Cayo Levisa
DINING AND LODGING

$$$$ **Cayo Levisa.** This small, well-run vacation center is near a 2-km (1-mi) stretch of pristine beach. The restaurant keeps no strict hours. *Cayo Levisa. 20 cabins with bath and air-conditioning. Restaurant, bar, beginning diving courses. Meals included.*

María la Gorda
DINING AND LODGING

$ ★ **Centro de Buceo María la Gorda.** Although designed with divers in mind, this tourist center is a good choice for anyone who simply wants quiet and seclusion. The food is excellent, and the upbeat staff make the atmosphere very pleasant. *Centro Internacional de Buceo de María la Gorda, Municipio Sandino,* ☎ *04 31 21. 8 2-room apartments, 3 houses with 3, 4, and 5 rooms. Restaurant, bar, tourist shop, game room.*

Pinar del Río
DINING

$ **Rumayor.** The specialty of this house, decorated with motifs inspired by African cults, is smoked chicken. Of the fish dishes, the *cherna frita* (sea bream sautéed in butter with garlic and onions) is a standout. *Carretera de Viñales, Km 1,* ☎ *8–63051.*

$$ **Pinar del Río.** The city's largest (and best) hotel is a good base for those traveling without a car. Organized tours to the nearby sights depart from here. *Calle Martí at the highway,* ☎ *50 70/77. 149 rooms with bath and air-conditioning. Restaurant, bar, swimming pool, store, nightclub, game room, car rental, tourist office.*

Other hotels in the area include the **Vueltabajo Islazul** (Calle Martí, corner of Rafael Morales, ☎ 53 63) and the **Hacienda Las Lagunas** (Carretera Central, Km 182, Candelaria, Pinar del Río), both of which are in the mountains, and **La Víbora** (Carretera Central, Km 82, Candelaria, ☎ 29 58 48 and 29 45 28). For a beach setting, try the **Villa Laguna Grande** (Guanaba Peninsula, Cabibes, Pinar del Río, ☎ 24 30). The recently renovated **Hotel Mirador de San Diego** (San Diego, Pinar del Río) offers country surroundings, and the **Horizontes Pinar del Río** (Calle Martí at the highway, Ciudad de Pinar del Río, ☎ 50 71/78) is a downtown hotel.

Puerto Esperanza

$ **Villa Rosario.** Occupying an old mansion that once belonged to a local landholder and later became the Communist Party headquarters, this hotel and restaurant has been in operation since 1900. It is a hub from which to explore an area somewhat off the beaten track. The restaurant's specialties include boiled lobster and fried meats. *Granja Rosario, Puerto Esperenza,* ☎ *938 28. 4 rooms, 2 with bath. Restaurant, bar. Reservations essential.*

Soroa

$$ **Soroa.** This tourist resort consists of various facilities strewn across a hillside in the Sierra del Rosario. Forty-nine cabins and two restaurants are grouped around the pool. To get to the Castillo de las Nubes restaurant (☞ Exploring, *above*) and nine rental houses, you must climb a few more miles to the mountaintop. *Carretera de Soroa, Km 8, Candelaria,* ☎ *85–21 22. 49 cabins and 9 houses, all with bath and air-conditioning. 3 restaurants, bar, swimming pool, shop, nightclub.*

$$ **Hotel Moka.** Situated 10 km (6 mi) outside Soroa, the streams, lakes, and ravines of the Sierra Rosario make the Moka's setting special indeed. *Autopista Habana-Pinar del Río, Km 51, Cayajabos, Pinar del Río.* ☎ *33 55 16, 2921, 2996.*

Valle de Viñales

$ **Casa de Don Tomás.** This eatery occupies the oldest house (circa 1822)
★ in Viñales and has a small garden at the back of it. Try the *delicias de Don Tomás* (a rice dish with ham, pork, lobster, and sausage) or the *tasajo a lo campesino* (peasant-style dried beef). *El Trapiche* cocktail is a house creation. The Trío Romance musical group performs during lunch. The service here is impeccable. *Calle Salvador Cisneros 141.*

$ **Mural de la Prehistoria.** The ranch next to the Mural de la Prehistoria serves an excellent peasant lunch of roast pig, *arroz moro* (Moorish rice), and fried or boiled meats. *Mural de la Prehistoria. No dinner.*

$$ **La Ermita.** Perched on a promontory overlooking the valley of Viñales,
★ La Ermita has one of the best panoramic views in Cuba. The restaurant has a large terrace open to the valley and is highly recommended. *Carretera La Ermita, Km 2,* ☎ *932 04. 64 rooms with bath and air-*

conditioning. Restaurant, bar, swimming pool, sports facilities, tourist shop, parking.

$$ **Rancho San Vicente.** This hotel is in a spa, so you can indulge yourself with a program of medicinal baths. *Carretero de Puerto Esperanza, Km 38, ☎ 932 00. 32 rooms with bath and air-conditioning, 14 cabins with bath. Restaurant, bar, swimming pool with sulfuric water, store, nightclub, game room.*

$ **La Casa del Marisco.** This tiny, new establishment is across from the
★ entrance to the Cueva del Indio. The restaurant does a fine job preparing dishes with prawn caught in the river that flows through the cave. *Carretera de Puerto Esperanza, Km 38. 3 rooms with bath. Restaurant, bar, 24-hr room service, crafts shop.*

Nightlife

At the **Restaurant Rumayor,** on the outskirts of Pinar del Río, a small folklore ensemble ($5 cover charge) entertains on Monday and Tuesday; Thursday through Sunday a larger group ($15 cover charge) takes over. Performances generally start at about 10 PM, and afterward there is dancing to recorded music. *Carretera a Viñales, Km 1.5, ☎ 35 07.*

The **Dancing Light Cuevas de Viñales** is inside the Cueva de José Miguel, in the Viñales Valley. The unusual location is what makes the place especially attractive. *Carretera Puerto Esperanza, Km 36, ☎ 32 03. Opens at 10 PM.*

ISLA DE LA JUVENTUD

Exploring

Cuba comprises more than 4,000 islands and keys. The next in size
❻ after the main island is the **Isla de la Juventud** at 3,060 sq km (1,900 sq mi). Part of the Canarreos Archipelago, it is often overlooked in tours of the country, but it is a highly regarded destination for divers, its main visitors.

The island was formerly known as the Isla de Pinos, owing to its abundant pine forests. Columbus discovered it in 1494 on his second voyage to America. At that time the island was virtually uninhabited and its dense vegetation made it a favorite refuge for pirates during the 17th and 18th centuries. It is the subject of countless tales and legends, including the claim that this was the spot Robert Louis Stevenson had in mind when writing *Treasure Island.*

The island remained remote until Castro's revolution, when it became an experimental work-study center. Thousands of young people helped to transform the island into a major citrus-producing area. Its new name, Island of Youth, is a tribute to that effort.

Along the length of **Punta del Francés** there are some 56 diving areas, with alluring names such as the Túnel del Amor (Tunnel of Love), Pasaje Escondido (Hidden Passage), and Barco Hundido (Sunken Ship). Calm and transparent waters, an impressive coral reef, underwater caves, and a great variety of fauna make for some underwater excursions. Although it's quite a distance from the base at the Hotel Colony to the diving zone, the splendid scenery en route makes the trip worthwhile.

Diving may be the main attraction, but it is not the only one. Near both Punta del Este and Nueva Gerona, the island's main town, there are numerous **caverns** containing splendid pre-Columbian paintings. The best known are the seven paintings at Punta del Este, discovered in 1910 by the survivors of a shipwreck. The images in the main cave are made up of red and black circles connected by a red arrow pointing east-ward. Some argue that these were celestial signs. The tourist office at the Hotel Colony organizes excursions to the caves.

The majority of the island's beaches are of white sand, but the black-sand beach at **Bibijagua,** 10 km (6 mi) from Nueva Gerona on the island's north coast, is very popular.

Dining and Lodging

For details on price categories, *see* the charts *in* On the Road with Fodor's at the front of this guide.

Nueva Gerona

DINING

$$ **El Río.** If meat doesn't tempt you, try one of the many Cuban seafood dishes at the El Río. *Calle 32, e/35 y Carretera La Fe,* ☎ *2–3217.* ☉ *Daily noon–9:45.*

$ **El Cochinito.** As the name suggests, this restaurant specializes in roast suckling pig. *Calle 39 at 24,* ☎ *2–2809 and 2–4451.* ☉ *Daily noon–10.*

$ **El Corderito.** Next door to the Cochinito, this is the place to go for lamb. *Calle 39 at 22,* ☎ *2–2400.* ☉ *Daily noon–9:45.*

LODGING

There are several very affordable places to stay in the area. Try **Motel Las Codornices** (Antigua Carretera La Fe, Km 4.5, ☎ 2–3349), **Rancho El Tesoro** (Carretera La Fe, ☎ 2–4089), or **Villa Gaviota Isla de la Juventud** (Nueva Gerona–La Fe Highway, Km 1, ☎ 2–3290 and 2–4486).

Playa Roja

DINING

$$ **Arco Iris.** This is the place for fish and shellfish. *Carretera de Siguanea, Km 41, International Center of Buceo el Colony,* ☎ *246 57.* ☉ *Daily 11–5.*

DINING AND LODGING

$$$ **Hotel Colony.** The Colony is the base for the International Diving Center. Here you can rent scuba equipment as well as arrange tours to other sights in the area. *Carretera de Siguanca, Km 42,* ☎ *9–8282 and 9–8181. 77 rooms with bath and air-conditioning. Restaurant, bar, pool, shops, nightclub, currency exchange, tourist office.*

CAYO LARGO

Exploring

❼ Situated at the eastern end of the Canarreos Archipelago, **Cayo Largo** (Long Key) is a small, 38-sq-km (24-sq-mi) island whose ecological balance has been almost perfectly maintained. Yet it is also one of the most fashionable Cuban resorts owing to its endless sun-baked beaches of snow-white sand that border an incredible turquoise sea. A handful of hotels with all the imaginable amenities completes the package. Come and be pampered by hotel staff used to catering to the whims of an oh-so international clientele. Forget all your cares amid the sun, sand, and service. Lose yourself in one of many isolated spots, places where it seems you are the first person ever to set foot. Tortoises are even confident enough to lay their eggs on some of the beaches.

Visits here are usually part of a package combining transportation, accommodations, meals and beverages, and activities—one of the very few all-inclusive packages offered in Cuba. Cayo Largo is a fixed item in the lists of most tour operators, so you can book a trip here from home or at any Cuban tourist office.

Arriving and Departing

There are daily flights from Havana and Varadero, respectively 285 km and 274 km (177 mi and 170 mi) away. Weekly flights are available from Camagüey and Santiago. On flights from any of these cities, request a window seat—the planes never climb very high and the views of the coral reefs as you approach the island are unbelievable. Recently, charters have also been initiated from Canada, Mexico, and Grand Cayman Island. Note that if you arrive on such an international flight (or by private yacht) and you don't plan to travel elsewhere in Cuba, you won't need a visa. If you arrive and decide you *do* want to see more of the country, it's not too late; you can obtain a visa in Cayo Largo.

Upon arrival, you will probably be taken directly to a reception in a cane-roofed structure to be greeted by a choral group singing Cuban songs. Although most flights arrive early in the morning, the welcome always includes a complimentary seafood cocktail and a rum drink—a lively way to start the day. After some dance performances, you will be whisked away to your accommodations. (Together, the four hotel complexes make up Club Aventuras.) From that point on, the key is yours.

Getting Around

You can rent a motorbike or a car or take the bus that runs from Club Aventuras to Playa Sirena, the most popular beach and the departure point for all boating excursions. Among the other favored beaches are Lindamar, Blanca, Los Cocos, Tortugas, and Luna.

Excursions and Organized Activities

There are several organized excursions. One of the shortest is a ride across to **Cayo Iguana,** a nearby island and nature preserve inhabited exclusively by iguanas. The cost is $12 a person, and departures take place as soon as enough people have signed up.

On **Cayo Cantiles** nature preserve there are monkeys and other wildlife. On this full-day excursion you can practice your snorkeling and fish for lobsters that you will later be served for dinner. The trip costs $62 per person.

Among the other possibilities are diving on a coral reef ($14 for 45 minutes); deep-sea fishing ($132 for 4 hours, $222 for 8 hours, divided up among the participants); sky diving ($20 dollars for 20 minutes; 6-person minimum); an all-day catamaran excursion ($57 per person; 4-person minimum); or a one-day visit to Cayo Rico ($37 per person).

Dining and Lodging

For details on price categories, *see* the charts *in* On the Road with Fodor's at the front of this guide.

Dining

$ **Taberna del Pirata.** Don't let the thatched roof and beachside snack shanty appearance fool you; this bar-restaurant serves excellent lobster. Wash it down with ice-cold beer and enjoy the band that plays popular Cuban songs. Just be sure to slather yourself with mosquito repellent before you go lest you be both dinner and a diner. *Playa Sirena.*

Dining and Lodging

$$$ Isla del Sur. The rooms of this somewhat nondescript hotel form a single block. Ask for one with a view of the Caribbean. The restaurant, Los Canarreos, has a reasonable buffet; meals are included in the price of your room. *Playa Lindamar,* ☎ *33 31 56 and 79 42 15,* FAX *33 31 56. 59 rooms with bath and air-conditioning. Restaurant, bar, satellite TV, pool, hairdresser, international communications center, shop, car and motorbike rentals.*

$$$ Villa Capricho. The rustic style of the buildings in this compound is very much in keeping with the Cayo Largo ambience. The Merlin Azul restaurant offers paella and salads for lunch and fish dishes for dinner; meals are included in the price of your room. *Playa Lindamar,* ☎ *33 31 56 and 79 42 15,* FAX *33 31 56. 60 cabins with bath and air-conditioning. Restaurant, bar, satellite TV, shared marina, shop.*

$$$ Villa Coral. Here the look is that of a colonial village. The newest parts of the hotel are a little too far from the pool, so let the staff know if you want to be close this amenity. Il Ciao del Cayo restaurant specializes in Italian cuisine; at lunch only pizza and salad are available. Meals are included in the cost of the room. *Playa Lindamar,* ☎ *33 31 56 and 79 49 15,* FAX *33 31 56. 72 rooms with bath and air-conditioning. Restaurant, bar, satellite TV, pool, shop, tourist information office.*

$$$ Villa Iguana. This series of bungalows is arranged in blocks along the beach. For sea views, request one in the front row. The restaurant, El Gavilán, serves only buffets at lunch and dinner. Meals are included in the cost of your room. *Playa Lindamar,* ☎ *33 31 56 and 79 49 15,* FAX *33 31 56. 114 bungalows with bath and air-conditioning. Restaurant, bar, satellite TV, pool, shop, tourist office.*

Another lodging option is the **Hotel Pelícano** (☎ 33 31 56 and 79 42 15, FAX 33 31 56), also on the beach.

THE ZAPATA PENINSULA

Exploring

The Zapata Peninsula is covered by a marsh and was, for centuries, inhabited only by a few fishermen and peat cutters. This nature preserve is easy to reach from Havana: Follow the A-1 to the turnoff for Playa Larga, 142 km (88 mi) from the capital.

Before you reach the turnoff, however, stop at **La Fiesta Campesina,** a former estate that is now a rest area with interesting exhibits. Don't miss the collection of trees and fruit-bearing plants: Mamey, coffee, mangoes, cherries, guavas, cherimoya, oranges, lemons, bananas, avocados, and pineapples all grow here. There is also a small zoo with iguanas, deer, tortoise, doves, and parrots, as well as other exotic birds, including the South American coot. Surrounded by all this exotic flora and fauna, sample the region's rum drink, the *fiesta campesina,* or have a Creole coffee, which is served in small clay cup with a piece of sugarcane.

Back on the road, you'll pass through the **Central Azucarero Australia** (Australia Sugar Mill). Here you will see a reminder of the early years of the revolution that brought Fidel Castro to power, one of the first such sights on this tour. In 1961, during the invasion by anti-Castro forces at the Bay of Pigs, Castro set up his headquarters in this sugar mill. Today a small museum recalls the event with memorabilia.

❽ The road continues into the **Parque Ciénaga de Zapata,** or Zapata Marshlands Park. A little farther along you come to **La Boca,** a series of tourist facilities next to a **crocodile farm.** The farm has more than

3,000 crocodiles, which are raised here as much to protect the species as to exploit them for their commercial value. A tour of the farm (☞ $3) allows you to watch the beasts snooze in the mud. In the ranch house you can sample roast crocodile tail ($7 per serving), said to be an aphrodisiac.

Launches take you from La Boca to **La Laguna del Tesoro** (Treasure Lagoon) and **Guamá.** The route passes along a channel cut through the vegetation. Some 16 sq km (10 sq mi) in area, this is Cuba's largest natural lagoon. Legend attributes its name to an incident in early colonial times. When the Spanish conquered this territory, they rounded up the native tribesmen next to the lagoon. The captives flung their treasure into the water rather than surrendering it to the enemy.

After crossing the lagoon, the launch takes you to the Guamá Tourist Center. Built to replicate a Taino village, the center is a complex of cabins on tiny islands that are linked by bridges. In one there's a sequence of 25 life-size sculptures that depict the daily activities of the indigenous people, the work of artist Rita Longo. Guamá is also a great place to fish for trout, shad, and *manjuarí,* a combination of fish and reptile. These strange creatures are considered "living fossils" and can be as much as a meter long.

9 From La Boca, continue through the marshlands until you reach the sea at **Playa Larga,** at the head of the Bahía de Cochinos (Bay of Pigs). Many people believe this to be the best beach on Cuba's south coast. An international bird-watching center has been established here, and you can spend hours spying on exotic tropical birds. If you are lucky you may even get to see the *zunzuncito,* which is considered to be the world's smallest bird and, like other hummingbirds, can remain suspended in flight while drinking nectar from flowers, its only sustenance.

The road follows the east coast of the Bay of Pigs to Playa Girón. Among the attractions on this route are the **cenotes,** deep-rock pools or submerged caves, only a short trek through the forest. You can dive down into the transparent waters to admire the odd geological formations and look for the blind fish that inhabit them.

10 Where the bay meets the sea, you come to the **Playa Girón.** This was another key location in the 1961 landing of anti-Castro forces, though it took its name from an earlier visitor, the French pirate Gilbert Girón. A little farther down the coast is **Caleta Buena,** famous for its natural pool. Route 3–1–16, which you have been following since the turnoff to La Fiesta Campesina, turns inward at Playa Girón, toward Yaguaramas, where it connects with 3–1–2. From this point you can proceed to Cienfuegos and Trinidad. This stretch of road is in poor shape, and is usually impassable after a storm. Check on its condition ahead of time; if it's closed, you will have to backtrack to the junction with A-1.

Dining and Lodging

For details on price categories, *see* the charts *in* On the Road with Fodor's at the front of this guide.

Laguna del Tesoro

DINING

$ **La Boca.** La Boca restaurant offers a variety of dishes and is the perfect stop if you plan to visit the crocodile farm. *Carretera Central Australia a Ciénaga de Zapata, Boca, Laguna del Tesoro,* ☎ *2458.*

$$ **Villa Horizontes Guamá.** This cluster of cabins that resemble *caneyes,*
★ the traditional dwellings of the indigenous Taina, rises above the small
islands at the end of the lagoon. *Laguna del Tesoro,* ☎ *2458. 44 cabins with bath and air-conditioning, 3 accommodating 4 persons. Restaurant, bar, pool, boat charters, fishing excursions, crafts shop, nightclub.*

Playa Girón

DINING AND LODGING

$ **Villa Horizontes Playa Girón.** Make this large vacation complex your
base for diving excursions in the cenotes and in Caleta Buena. *Playa
Girón.* ☎ *7810, 7812, 4118, and 4110. 196 bungalows, most with
bath and air-conditioning. Restaurant, bar, pool, sports facilities, fishing and diving excursions, shop, car rental.*

Playa Larga

DINING AND LODGING

$ **Villa Hoteles Playa Larga.** From here you can hit the beach, go fishing, head out for bird-watching—whatever your pleasure. *Playa Larga,*
☎ *7219, 7225, and 7219. 48 cabins with bath and air-conditioning.
Restaurant, bar, bicycle and car rental, fishing excursions.*

HAVANA TO VARADERO

The traditional village of Varadero has 12 km (7 mi) of exquisite fine-sand beaches. It is on the Hicacos Peninsula, a long slender arrow northeast of Matanzas that faces the Straits of Florida and nearly touches
the Tropic of Cancer. From the drawbridge at Paso Malo lagoon to
Punta de Molas, the peninsula is nearly 19 km (12 mi) long, and its
tip is the northernmost point in Cuba. Its average width is only 700
meters (2,296 feet); at its widest point, between Punta Hicacos and the
Clarck estuary, it measures a mere 1,200 meters (3,936 feet).

There are small, isolated high points along the length of the peninsula.
These plateaulike formations with their horizontal stratification are separated by either sandy areas or mangrove swamps and have numerous grotto openings. They are part of the ancient dunes of the Santa
Fe Formation, which dates back some 80,000 years. They show unmistakable signs of marine erosion several meters above the present
sea level, indicating that the sea level has dropped.

Although it has become quite a resort in recent years, Varadero has
retained its charm. New structures have been built to blend in with
earlier wooden ones; there are no high rises here. The main longitudinal roads are the Avenida Kawama, Avenida 1, Avenida de las Américas, and the Autopista del Sur (Southern Highway). Streets running
perpendicular to these avenues are numbered consecutively from 1 to
69. The streets in the Villa Cuba section follow alphabetical order from
A to L.

Exploring

The road from Havana to Matanzas and on to Varadero is an easy, diverting drive. Coming out of the Havana Bay tunnel you are on Via
Blanca, the two-lane highway to Matanzas that passes through Playas
del Este. Some 80 km (50 mi) out of Havana is the Bacunayagua
Bridge, the highest in Cuba. It is 313 meters (1,027 feet) long and 16
meters (52 feet) wide, and was completed in July 1959. On the left,
before the bridge, is a small bar on a low hill; from here the view of
the Yumuri Valley is terrific. The valley lies at the eastern end of the
Habana-Matanzas ridge and is one of the most interesting geograph-

Varadero

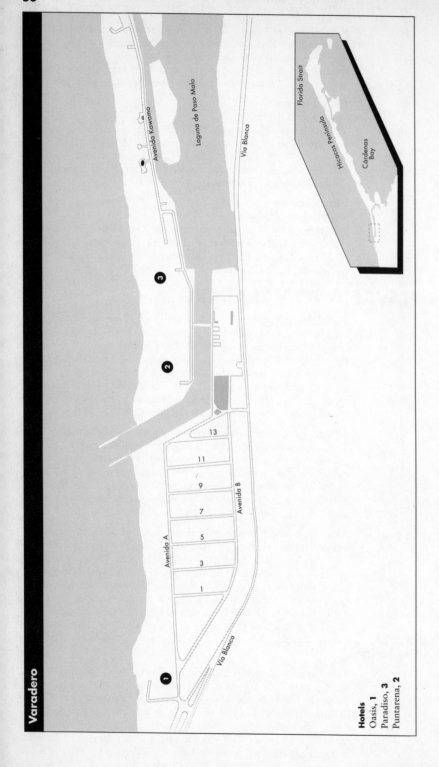

Florida Strait

Hicacos Peninsula

Córdenas Bay

Avenida Kawama

Laguna de Paso Malo

Vía Blanca

Avenida A

Avenida B

Vía Blanca

1

3

5

7

9

11

13

Hotels
Oasis, **1**
Paradiso, **3**
Puntarena, **2**

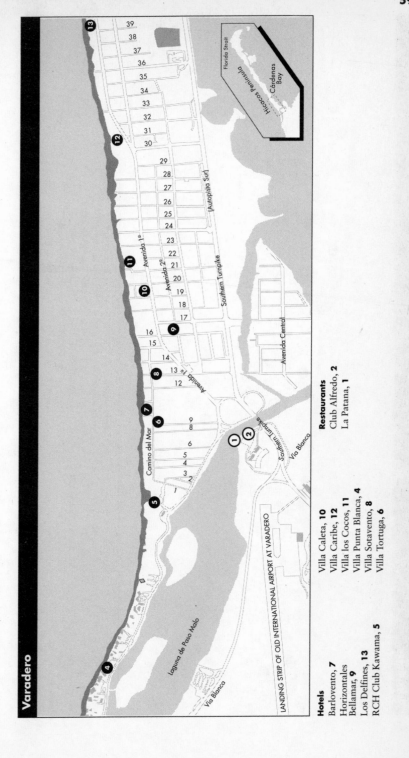

Varadero

39
38
37
36
35
34
33
32
31
30
29
28
27
26
25
24
23
22
21
20
19
18
17
16
15
14
13
12

Florida Strait

Hicacos Peninsula

Cárdenas Bay

Avenida 1ª

Avenida 2ª

(Autopista Sur)

Southern Turnpike

Avenida Central

9
8
6
5
4
3
2
1

Avenida 1ª

Camino del Mar

Southern Turnpike

Via Blanca

Via Blanca

Laguna de Paso Malo

LANDING STRIP OF OLD INTERNATIONAL AIRPORT AT VARADERO

Hotels
Barlovento, **7**
Horizontales
Bellamar, **9**
Los Delfines, **13**
RCH Club Kawama, **5**

Villa Caleta, **10**
Villa Caribe, **12**
Villa los Cocos, **11**
Villa Punta Blanca, **4**
Villa Sotavento, **8**
Villa Tortuga, **6**

Restaurants
Club Alfredo, **2**
La Patana, **1**

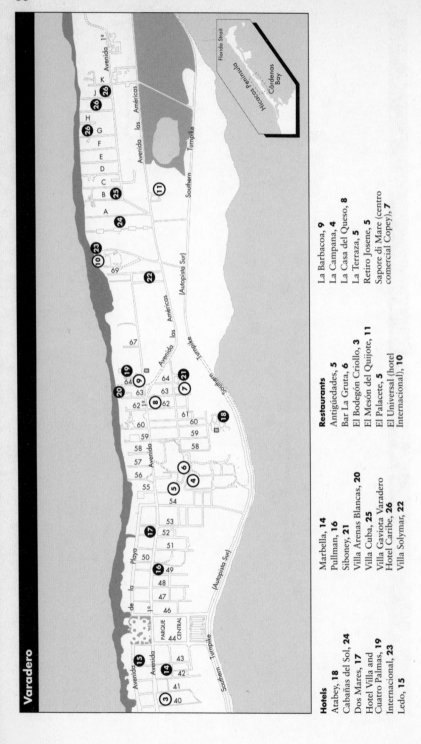

Varadero

Florida Strait

Hicacos Peninsula

Cárdenas Bay

Hotels

Atabey, **18**
Cabañas del Sol, **24**
Dos Mares, **17**
Hotel Villa and
Cuatro Palmas, **19**
Internacional, **23**
Ledo, **15**

Marbella, **14**
Pullman, **16**
Siboney, **21**
Villa Arenas Blancas, **20**
Villa Cuba, **25**
Villa Gaviota Varadero
Hotel Caribe, **26**
Villa Solymar, **22**

Restaurants

Antigüedades, **5**
Bar La Gruta, **6**
El Bodegón Criollo, **3**
El Mesón del Quijote, **11**
El Palacete, **5**
El Universal (hotel
Internacional), **10**

La Barbacoa, **9**
La Campana, **4**
La Casa del Queso, **8**
La Terraza, **5**
Retiro Josene, **5**
Sapore di Mare (centro
comercial Copey), **7**

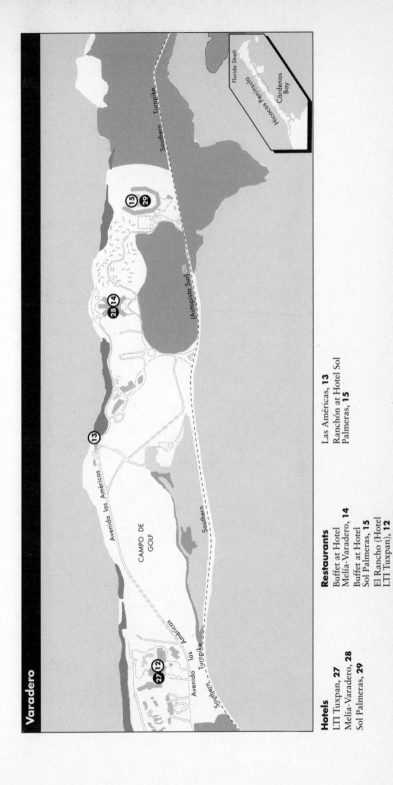

Varadero

Hotels
LTI Tuxpan, **27**
Melía-Varadero, **28**
Sol Palmeras, **29**

Restaurants
Buffet at Hotel
Melía-Varadero, **14**
Buffet at Hotel
Sol Palmeras, **15**
El Rancho (Hotel
LTI Tuxpan), **12**
Fuerreventura (Hotel
Melía-Varadero), **14**

Las Américas, **13**
Ranchón at Hotel Sol
Palmeras, **15**

Varadero

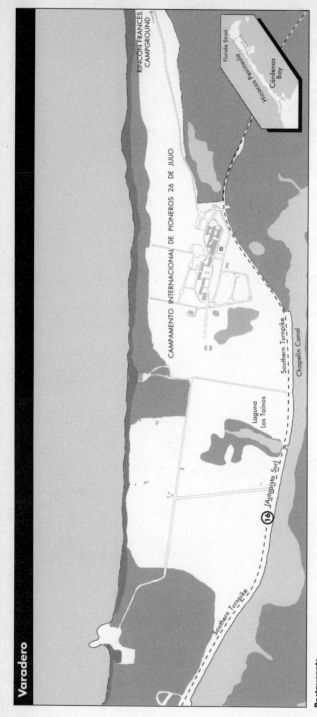

Restaurants
Marina Chapelín, **16**

ical landscapes in Cuba. To see it you have to drive some 10 km (6 mi) to the south off the road to Varadero. The valley is 8 km (5 mi) wide and surrounded, except to the west, by hills. It was formed into a natural amphitheater by the Yumurí River and its tributaries.

About 20 km (12 mi) from the Bacunayagua Bridge is the city of **Matanzas,** the capital of a province of the same name. It lies on the Bay of Matanzas, the deepest (600 meters/1,968 feet) in Cuba. Matanzas extends across undulating hills and valleys crossed by rivers flowing into the bay. It has several bridges and beautiful mansions on the riverbanks, for which reason it is also sometimes called "the Cuban Venice."

There are several especially interesting buildings in the city center. The **Sauto Theater,** opened in 1863, is a fine example of the neoclassical style. The lovely interior frescoes were painted by the architect himself, Daniel Dal Aglio. Also worth seeing are the **Museo Farmacéutico** (Pharmaceutical Museum) and the **Palacio del Junco** (1842), both of which are on Calle Milanés next to the Plaza de Armas. Other structures of interest are the **Aduana** (Customs Building), built in 1826 and now the Palacio de Justicia (Supreme Court); the **Casa de la Trova y el Escritor** (House of the Troubador and the Writer), built in the late 18th century and one of the city's oldest residences; and the **Cuartel de Bomberos** (Fireman's Barracks) in the demolished artillery battery of San José de La Vigía.

Finally, near the Matanzas exit there is the **Cueva de Bellamar,** a cave with extraordinarily beautiful crystals and stalactites. Other caves along the way to Varadero are the **Cueva Grande de Santa Catalina** and the **Cueva del Muerto** (Cave of the Dead).

From Matanzas to Varadero there is a toll highway, which costs $2. Five kilometers (3 mi) east of Matanzas you come to **Cárdenas,** a village typical of the province and one famous for its many bicycles and carriages, its Arrechabala rum factory, and its surrounding henequen plantations. It is very pleasant to stroll through the streets of Cárdenas, but you may want to make it a side trip from **Varadero** rather than a stop along the way.

In Varadero

Car Rentals
At almost any hotel you can rent cars, four-wheel-drive vehicles, and motorbikes. In any case, there are offices of **Cubacar** in the hotels Meliá Varadero (☎ 66 70 13), Tuxpan (☎ 66 76 39), and Sol Palmeras (☎ 66 73 59.) **Havanautos** is in the Paradiso-Puntarena Complex (☎ 66 71 20) and **Transautos** can be reached at ☎ 66 73 32.

Habanos
Cigar smokers must stop by **Casa del Habano** (Avenida 1, between 63 and 64) for the best brands stored under the best conditions.

Dining

Unless otherwise indicated a meal will cost from $20 to $40 per person. We do not include addresses or opening times for all the restaurants—most of them are very well known.

Antigüedades. Dine on simple dishes amid antique furniture recovered from the great mansions of the local bourgeoisie. Lobster, shrimp, and filet mignon—all grilled—are standouts. *Calle 56 at 1, Parque Josone,* ☎ *2933.*

Bar La Gruta. This is a good place to stop during a walk around the lake in the Parque Josone.

Barbacoa. Here you'll find an international menu. *Hotel Meliá Las Américas.* ☎ *66 76 00.* 🕐 *Noon–midnight.*

Buffets at the hotels Sol Palmeras and Meliá-Varadero. For a fast, tasty meal try these buffets. If you can't find what you need, the wait staff will attend to it quickly. *Hotel Sol Palmeras, Autopista del Sure,* ☎ *33–70–09 and 33–72–09. Hotel Meliá-Varadero, Carretera del as Morlas-Veradero,* ☎ *33–70–13.*

Capri. At this restaurant on the beach you'll find Italian fare. *Calle 43 at the beach,* ☎ *62117.*

Cayo Libertad. If the Barbacoa (☞ *above*) is crowded, try the international dishes here. *Marina Dársena de Varadero.* 🕐 *10 AM–midnight.*

Club Alfredo. Here you'll find good pizza at reasonable prices ($15 per person). *Villa Tortuga, at the entrance to Varadero, near La Patana,* ☎ *62243 and 64115.*

Dante. This is another stop if you're in the mood for Italian. *Calle 1 y 56,* ☎ *63319.* 🕐 *Daily 12:30–4 and 7–midnight.*

El Bodegón Criollo. Feast on typical Cuban food while listening to the trio that performs here regularly. *Av. de la Playa at 40,* ☎ *62180.* 🕐 *Noon–10.*

El Criollo. As it's name suggests, Creole food is the specialty here. *Avenida 1 at 18,* ☎ *63297.*

El Galeón. This is a great place for seafood. *Marina Gaviota Varadero,* ☎ *66292.*

El Mesón del Quijote. The menu of Spanish dishes is limited, but the food is good. *Carretera de las Américas, opposite the Villa Cuba,* ☎ *62975.* 🕐 *10 PM–midnight.*

El Palacete (formerly El Principal). Food-lovers take note: This luxurious establishment is working hard to become *the* place for fine dining. The international menu includes homemade pâtés, lobster, and leg of lamb. *Calle 56 at 1,* ☎ *2933.* 🕐 *12:30–midnight.*

El Rancho. Come here for outstanding grilled meats. The *butifarra* sausage is not to be missed. *Hotel LTI Tuxpan, Carretera de las Américas, Km 3.5,* ☎ *33524 and 66524.* 🕐 *10 PM–2 AM.*

★ **Fuerteventura.** The exquisite decor in this small restaurant in a five-star hotel will whet your appetite. The Spanish food, from the straightforward chicken with lobster to the most sophisticated Basque specialties, is creatively prepared. Don't skip the gazpacho. *Hotel Meliá-Varadero, Autopista del Sur,* ☎ *6–6221 and 33 70 13.* 🕐 *5–12:30 AM.*

Grill Picante. If you're craving Mexican, this is the place. *Villa Cabañas del Sol,* ☎ *63011.*

Halong. Look no farther for Chinese food. *Camino del Mar at 12,* ☎ *63787.* 🕐 *Daily 3–11.*

La Arcada. This is yet another option if your palate prefers international cuisine. *Hotel Meliá Las Américas,* ☎ *66 76 00.* 🕐 *7 AM–midnight.*

La Barbacoa. Stop in for grilled surf or turf delights. *Hotel Villa and Cuatro Palmas, Calle 64 at de la Playa,* ☎ *63435.* 🕐 *noon–midnight.*

La Campana. This *mesón* (tavern) serves Creole food and specializes in grilled meats. There's a Cuban country fest nightly at 9. ☎ *3306.*

La Casa del Queso. The specialties here are cheese, meat, and chocolate fondues—a change of pace from traditional Varadero restaurant fare. *Av. de las Américas at 64, across from the Hotel Villa y Cuatro Palmas.* 🕐 *1–1.*

La Patana. The setting is a rustic barge moored at the entrance to Varadero. There are only eight tables, so service is a dream. If you like, you can select your lobster, *pargo* (grouper), or *chernas* (sea bass) and scoop it out of the tank yourself.

La Terraza. This establishment enjoys a prime location next to the docks. It is an ideal place for an aperitif or a *mojito* (rum, lemon, and ice and garnished with mint leaves).

Las Américas. This restaurant is in a house that once belonged to American millionairess Irene Dupont and has been kept as it was when she lived here. If the family photographs and books in the dining room don't intrigue you, perhaps the sea views will. The prices are excessive—bordering on abusive—but the setting makes a visit highly recommended. *Autopista del Sur,* ☎ *33 70 13.* ☉ *10 AM–10:30 PM.*

Mallorca. This is yet another of Varadero's Spanish restaurants. *Avenida 1, corner of 61,* ☎ *63101.* ☉ *Daily noon–11.*

Marina Chapelín. Some 20 boats a day set out from this marina on tours of area keys and reefs. It has two dining room–salons where you can select your lobster from a tank. One of the salons is glassed in and air-conditioned, a cool haven from the mosquitos. *Autopista del Sur, Km 21, Punta Hicacos,* ☎ *66 75 50.* ☉ *9 AM–midnight.*

Mediterráneo. The cuisine is distinctly international here. *Avenida 1, corner of 54,* ☎ *62460.* ☉ *Daily noon–3 AM.*

Mi Casita. Here, fish and shellfish reign supreme. *Camino del Mar e/11 y 12,* ☎ *63787.*

Retiro Josone. Formerly the vacation home of the head of the Arrechabala rum factory in Cárdenas, the Retiro is now a notable dining complex. It includes a small lake, four restaurants, several gardens, and an unusual spot called El Rincón de los Enamorados (Lovers' Corner). *Calle 1 e/56 y 59,* ☎ *6–2044, 6–2740, or 6–2933.*

Sapore di Mare. Most of the Italian food here is undistinguished, though the pizzas are good. *Hotel Atabey-Siboney, Av. 2 at 64,* ☎ *33 71 58.* ☉ *Noon–10.*

Taberna Dortmunder Kneioe. Add this to your list of places that serve international dishes. *Camino del Mar e/13 y 14,* ☉ *Daily noon–10.*

Lodging

Varadero hotels are generally less expensive than those in Havana. Location is key: The best beaches are those between Calle 55 and Punta Hicacos; the worst, those in the Via Blanca and Kawama areas. Choose your hotel accordingly. All but the most budget of places have terraces and restaurants. Some even have musical combos that play in the evening till midnight. In addition, many of these hotels offer bicycle and motorbike rentals and almost all of them rent equipment: Windsurfers, catamarans, and the like.

The hotels in the $$ category have similar amenities, whether they are cabins, bungalows, or simple hotel rooms. These generally include air-conditioning and radios—seldom TVs; pools; restaurants and bars; or cars, motorbikes, and bicycles for rent. Villas come with a refrigerator.

Some of the hotels in the $ category may have been recently renamed, but you will have no trouble finding them if you ask for them by the names given here. They usually have radios, air-conditioning (only a fan in a few cases), and a safe; some, such as the Pullman, even have a pool.

For details on price categories, *see* the chart *in* On the Road with Fodor's at the front of this guide.

$$$$ **Hoteles Tryp Paradiso Puntarena, Tryp Gran Caribe Sierra Club.** The architecture of these two hotels, very massive and sturdy, disrupts the serenity of Varadero. The beach leaves much to be desired, but the hotel has many amenities. *Av. Kawama,* ☎ *66 71 21/24,* ℻ *66 70 74. 518* *air-conditioned rooms with televisions, telephones, and safes. Restaurants, cafeterias, snack bar, pool, sports and recreational activities, stores, telex and fax services, car rental, private parking.*

$$$$ **Internacional Varadero.** Although the Internacional is a little run down and the service is only average, the best beach in Varadero is at its doorstep. *Av. de las Américas,* ☎ *66 70 38/39,* FAX *66 72 46. 163 rooms with air-conditioning, televisions, and telephones. Terrace grill next to the beach, sauna, gymnasium, game room, nightclub, car rental, tourist office.*

$$$$ **LTI Bella Costa Cubanacán.** *Carretera de las Américas.* ☎ FAX *66 72 10.*

$$$$ **LTI Tuxpan.** *Av. de las Américas, Km 3.5,* ☎ *66 75 60,* FAX *66 75 61.*
★   *235 rooms with air-conditioning, radios, and telephones. 2 restaurants, bars, cafeteria, tea salons, pool, barbershop, beauty parlor, stores, convention rooms, safe.*

$$$$ **Meliá Las Américas.** The most luxurious of the Meliá hotels, this mod-
★   ern Grupo Sol establishment opened in 1994. *Carretera de Las Morlas–Varadero,* ☎ *66 76 00 and 66 75 25. 18 suites and 250 rooms. Breakfast buffet, 24-hr room service, satellite TV, 3 pools, hairdresser, beach.*

$$$$ **Meliá-Varadero.** You could spend your entire vacation without ever
★   leaving this deluxe hotel or lifting a finger, owing to its emphasis on service. The only drawback is the beach on which it sits, by no means the best on the peninsula. The suites have color televisions, VCRs, and minibars. *Carretera de Las Morlas–Varadero,* ☎ *66 70 13,* FAX *66 70 12 or 33 71 62. 490 rooms and 7 suites with air-conditioning, telephones, and terraces with ocean views. Restaurant, bar, cafeteria, grill, pool, squash, volleyball, private park, diving and other water sports, boutique, child care, children's area, medical services, conference room, telex and fax services.*

$$$$ **Sol Palmeras.** The service here is excellent as is the beach. All rooms
★   have air-conditioning, telephones, and radios; some have TVs. *Autopista del Sur,* ☎ *66 70 09,* FAX *66 70 08. Restaurants, bars, grill, pool, tennis, child care, conference rooms, car rental, excursions to nearby beaches.*

$$$ **Arenas Doradas.** New facilities are the draw at this establishment with 316 rooms (24 of which are suites). The pool, the discotheque, and the laundry service also make it attractive. *Carretera de Las Morlas,* ☎ *66 81 50/56,* FAX *66 81 59.*

$$$ **Bella Costa.** This relatively new hotel has 382 rooms—including 76 bungalows—a pool, a Jacuzzi, a discotheque, and laundry services. *Avenida de las Américas,* ☎ *66 72 10,* FAX *66 72 05.*

$$$ **Brisas del Caribe.** The new rooms are pluses here as is the cost—the price for a double room includes all fees and services, except phone, fax, massage, laundry, and champagne. There is a gym, a discotheque and bike and water-sports-equipment rental. *Carretera de Las Morlas,* ☎ *66 80 30,* FAX *66 80 05.*

$$$ **Cabañas del Sol.** This hotel is beautifully situated very close to the sea.
★   The cabins were renovated a few years ago; some have private baths. *Av. de las Américas,* ☎ *63011 and 33 72 36,* FAX *33 72 46. Same facilities as the Internacional.*

$$$ **Club Varadero Super Club Resort.** Here the price of a room includes
★   breakfast, lunch, and dinner; drinks at the bar; all hotel services; and Windsurfer or catamaran rental. *Av. de las Américas, Km 3,* ☎ *66 70 30 and 66 70 31,* FAX *66 70 05.*

$$$ **Coral Gaviota.** At this beachside complex you can stay in a hotel or a cabin. The air-conditioned rooms have TVs, telephones, safes, and minibars. *Calle K, La Torre,* ☎ *66 72 40,* FAX *63018. Restaurant-buffet, pool, hairdresser, sports facilities.*

$$$ El Caney. At the far end of the peninsula, the small Caney has only six double rooms, all with air-conditioning and TVs. *Autopista del Sur, Punta Hicacos,* ☎ *56 39 14.*

$$$ Gran Hotel. This large hotel has 331 rooms, including 21 honeymoon suites, six regular suites, and two rooms completely equipped for travelers with disabilities. There is a freshwater swimming pool, a play area for children, a Jacuzzi, and a discotheque. *Carretera de Las Morlas, Km 115,* ☎ *66 82 43,* FAX *66 82 02 and 66 82 30.*

$$$ Hotel Villa and Cuatro Palmas. This complex, across from the com-★ mercial center of Varadero and on a magnificent beach, is brand new. All rooms have 10-channel TVs, telephones, safes, and minibars. *Av. de la Playa at 64,* ☎ *66 70 40,* FAX *66 72 46. Pool, volleyball, windsurfing, catamaran and boat rental, daily sports and activities program, boutique.*

$$$ Iberostar Hotel Villa Barlovento Complex. This hotel offers bar service on the beach. *Calle 11 and Camino del Mar,* ☎ *71 40/44,* FAX *66 72 18. Beauty parlor; boutique; car, motorbike, and bicycle rental.*

$$$ Riu Las Morlas. This recently opened 148-room establishment lists a pool, a discotheque, massage services, and laundry services among its amenities. *Carretera Las Américas,* ☎ *66 72 30,* FAX *66 72 15.*

$$$ Sol Club La Sirena. Of this hotel's 244 rooms, two are suites. The price includes all fees except telephone, fax, laundry, massages, and champagne. *Avenida de las Américas y Calle K, La Torre,* ☎ *66 80 70,* FAX *66 80 75.*

$$$ Villa Cuba Gran Caribe. This complex near the Dupont residence has pleasant one-, two- or three-room, air-conditioned houses—some with private bath—on a magnificent beach. *Calle C y 1, La Torre,* ☎ *62975,* FAX *33 72 02. Pool, stores, game rooms, motorbike rental.*

$$$ Villa Punta Blanca. *Residential Development Kawama,* ☎ *66 70 90. 337 rooms with air-conditioning and private baths. Pool, tennis; car, motorbike, and bicycle rentals.*

$$$ Villas and Bungalows Cuatro Palmas. Here, the villas have from two ★ to six rooms with air-conditioning, kitchens, and TVs. The 122 bungalows have air-conditioning, satellite TVs, and telephones. *Av. de la Playa at 64,* ☎ *66 70 40. Same facilities as the Hotel Villa and Cuatro Palmas (☞ above).*

$$ Atabey. The building is a nondescript prefabricated affair far from the beach, but the pool and the 134 comfortable rooms with bath and telephone are definite pluses. *Calle 61 y 3,* ☎ *63013.*

$$ Dos Mares. This is a modern villa of 36 rooms, including two suites for families with children, a restaurant and a solarium. It is in the center of Varadero, but it's still near the beach. *Av. 1 y 53,* ☎ *62702.*

$$ Hotel Horizontes Bellamar. The apartments here have refrigerators, radios, and air-conditioning; some have private baths. The beach is average. *Calle 17 at Av. 2,* ☎ *63014 and 33 72 47,* FAX *66 72 46. Beauty parlor, game room, motorbike and bicycle rental.*

$$ Oasis. Constructed during the 1950s, this hotel is somewhat noisy. The beach is rocky, not white sand. *Vía Blanca, Km 130, at the entrance to Varadero,* ☎ *66 73 80/86.*

$$ Villa Caribe. The Villa has 124 rooms, a restaurant, pool, a bar on the beach, a game room, and bike and motorbike rentals. *Av. de la Playa y 30,* ☎ *63310.*

$$ Villa Kawama. This old group of bungalows recently doubled its number of rooms to 207 and has added recreational facilities. Despite all the upgrades, the service remains slow. *Residential Development Kawama,* ☎ *33 71 55 and 33 71 56.*

$$ Villa Sotavento. This 255-room villa is a no-frills establishment, but ★ it is fully air-conditioned and next to the sea. *Calle 13 y Camino del Mar,* ☎ *62953.*

$$ **Villa Tortuga.** This pleasant villa has 139 rooms, a restaurant, tennis courts, and a bar on the beach. There are bike, motorbike, and car rentals. *Calle 9 e/Camino del Mar y Boulevard,* ☎ 62243.

$$ **Los Delfines.** The Los Delfines is modest, but it's next to the sea. *Av.*
★ *de la Playa y 39,* ☎ 63815.

$$ **Pullman.** This is an older establishment with considerable atmosphere,
★ a beautiful lobby, a restaurant, a bar, and economical rooms. *Av. 1 e/49 y 50,* ☎ 62575.

$$ **Villa Solymar.** At this modest villa, some of the 555 rooms have shared
★ baths. *Av. de las Américas,* ☎ 62217.

$ **Apartamentos Herradura.** In this horseshoe-shape building surrounding the coast you'll find 33 apartments with living room, dining room, and completely equipped kitchen. *Av. de la Playa e/35 y 36,* ☎ 63703.

$ **Mar del Sur Horizontes.** This is another aparment-hotel option. *Av. 3, corner of 30,* ☎ 66 74 82.

$ **Villa Caleta.** The Caleta has 30 rooms around a pool and a group of bungalows that face the sea. *Calle 19 y 1,* ☎ 63515 and 63514.

Nightlife

Cabarets

Anfiteatro de Varadero. The open-air show here tries to rival that of the Tropicana in Havana.

Cabaret Continental. At midnight, after the show, the cabaret becomes a discotheque. ☎ 63011. ☉ *Tues.–Sun. 10 PM–2 AM. Reservations essential.*

Cabaret La Cueva del Pirata. This is another nightspot in a natural cave. After the show there is dancing. *Carretera de las Américas, Km 11,* ☎ 63324. ☉ *Mon.–Sat. 9 PM–3 AM. Reservations essential.*

Santiago. *Hotel Meliá Varadero,* ☎ 66 70 13. ☉ *Daily 7 PM–3 AM.*
Sol Palmeras. *Hotel Sol Palmeras,* ☎ 66 70 09.

Discothèques

Discoteca Caribbean. *Centro Comercial, Av. 1 y 60.* 🖃 *$10 (includes drink).* ☉ *Until 5 AM.*

Discoteca La Bamba. *Hotel Tuxpan, Av. de las Américas, Km 3.5,* ☎ 66 75 66. 🖃 *$10 (includes drink).* ☉ *Until 5 AM.*

Discoteca La Salsa. *Kawama Peninsula, Hoteles Gran Caribe Sierra Club and Paradiso Puntarena,* ☎ 66 71 25 to 29. 🖃 *$10 (includes drink).* ☉ *Until 5 AM.*

El Kastillito. *Av. de la Playa y 49,* ☎ 63888. ☉ *9 PM–2:45 AM.*

La Rada. *Vía Blanca, Km 132 (La Bahia dock).* ☉ *9 PM–3 AM.*

La Cascada. *Hotel Meliá Las Américas,* ☎ 66 76 00. ☉ *Daily 9 PM–2 AM.*

Rincón Latino. *Hotel LTI Bella Costa Cubanacán,* ☎ 66 72 10. ☉ *Daily 10 PM–3 AM.*

Riu Mambo. *Hotel Riu Las Morlas,* ☎ 63913. ☉ *Daily 10 PM–3 AM.*

3 Central Cuba

CIENFUEGOS

The people of Cienfuegos are proud of their city and constantly tout it as la linda ciudad del mar (the lovely city of the sea) or, more emphatically, la perla del sur (the pearl of the south). Tucked into the southern coast of the island—just 250 km (155 mi) from Havana—Cienfuegos makes a good excursion from the capital.

The luminous bay, Bahí de Jagua, is visible from almost any point in Cienfuegos owing to the Malecón, or waterfront boulevard—the longest in Cuba. Columbus passed through in 1498 on his second voyage, and 10 years later Sebastián de Ocampo carefully explored the bay during his wanderings. The Bahí de Jagua is one of the safest harbors imaginable, and, because of it, the original indigenous enclaves and the early Spanish settlements flourished. Pirates working these seas also found it attractive. Chronicles record the visits of Henry Morgan and Sir Francis Drake, among others, as early as 1540. The fortress Nuestra Señora de los Ángeles de Jagua was constructed in the mid-18th century, both to defend the town and to prevent the traffic in contraband between its inhabitants and foreign vessels. It continues to dominate the harbor's narrow entrance.

Technically, the city of Cienfuegos is not very old. According to the records, it was officially founded on April 22, 1819, by Louis D'Clouet and 45 French colonists from Bordeaux. D'Clouet himself, though originally French, was a Spanish subject, having been born in New Orleans, then a possession of the Spanish Crown. The city was first christened Fernandina de Jagua, recognizing both King Fernando VII and the indigenous name for the spot (according to local mythology, the jaguar is the mother of all women). The city's strategic location attracted settlers from all over. By 1821 colonists had already arrived from Baltimore, New Orleans, and throughout the Caribbean. Ten years after its founding, the city's name was changed to honor Cuba's governor, José Cienfuegos.

Numbers in the margin correspond to points of interest on the Central Cuba and Exploring Trinidad maps.

Exploring

❶ **Cienfuegos** is laid out on a rectilinear grid. Of its hotels, only the **Jagua** is within the city proper, thus it is the logical spot to begin this tour. The hotel stands almost at the end of Punta Gorda, and, from the terraces on the hotel's upper floors, you can enjoy a bird's-eye view of the point. In this part of the city, the houses are from a very early era and have whitewashed walls and roof tiles darkened by time. Almost completely surrounded by water, this little neighborhood—with its tree-lined streets and ubiquitous fishermen—is the perfect place for a stroll.

Just across from the hotel (and practically a part of it) is the extraordinary **Palacio del Valle** (Valley Palace). Built between 1912 and 1917, this imposing mansion reflects the eclectic taste of its original owner. Although the structure has a predominantly Moorish appearance, if you look closely, you will also see Romanesque, Gothic, Byzantine, and Baroque features. Presently it houses a restaurant.

The Palacio del Valle is some 2 km (1 mi) from the city center, so to continue this tour you must hire a taxi or rent a car. On your left, as you drive along Calle 37, are several interesting buildings, among them the old **Cienfuegos Yacht Club** and other sports centers or social clubs. Farther along, the street opens onto the waterfront and be-

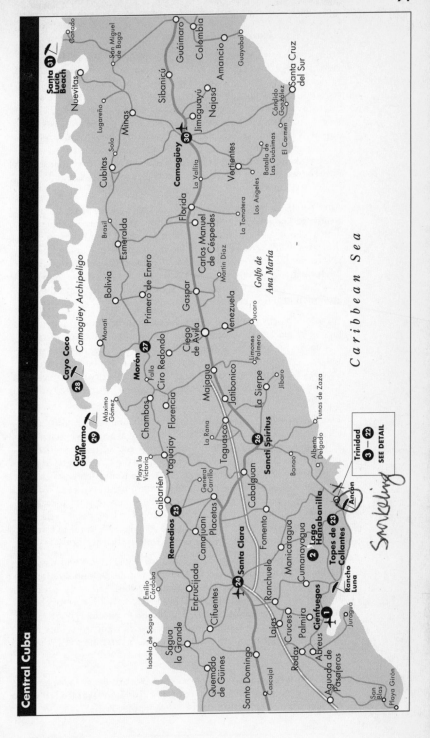

Central Cuba

Santa Lucía Beach **31**

Cayo Coco **28**

Cayo Guillermo **29**

Morón **27**

Remedios **25**

Santa Clara **24**

Cienfuegos **1**

Lago Hanabanilla **23**

Topes de Collantes **2**

Rancho Luna

Ancón

Camagüey **30**

Sancti Spíritus **26**

Trinidad **3** — **22**

SEE DETAIL

Snorkeling

Caribbean Sea

Golfo de Ana María

Camagüey Archipelago

comes the Malecón, more than 1 km (½ mi) long. The open space on the right is the **Plaza de la Revolución.**

When it leaves the water, the Malecón becomes the **Paseo del Prado,** the city's main thoroughfare. From here, resume the tour on foot. This boulevard is where the locals congregate; a walk along it will show you something of daily life in Cienfuegos. All of Paseo del Prado is studded with monuments, busts of illustrious Cienfuegos natives and Greek steles or plaques. The facades of the houses along it have porticoes supported by columns and are painted in brilliant colors—orange, green, blue, or yellow. Horse-drawn carriages add to the exotic atmosphere. The paseo begins in front of the **Teatro Luisa,** in a little park that serves as a rendezvous point before and after theater performances and as the city's nerve center.

After you leave the Teatro Luisa you will pass an ice-cream shop, the **Heladería Coppelia;** several pizzerias; a movie theater; a puppet theater; a school; and a number of restaurants, shops, and bookstores. At the end of the Paseo del Prado, retrace your steps for two or three blocks and turn right onto either 56 or 54, also known as **San Carlos** and **El Boulevard,** respectively. On either street you can look in the shop windows, watch children playing, and see couples out for a stroll as the afternoon begins to cool down.

After four blocks you come to **Parque José Martí.** A majagua tree that grew here marked the center of the original town, which consisted of a square with five blocks on each side. At that time, this was dense jungle, of which only a single ceiba tree remains. The buildings around the park reflect important chapters in the city's history up through the first decades of this century, and the entire area is considered a national monument.

Like the Paseo del Prado, the park is filled with monuments: busts, sculptural groups, a statue of José Martí, a triumphal arch, and even a pair of lions. At the corner of San Carlos is the **cathedral.** Note its stunning stained-glass window with depictions of the 12 apostles. On your right, as you leave the cathedral, is the **Teatro Tomás Terry,** which was built by a sugar baron in 1890 and is still in use today. Even if there is nothing scheduled, peek inside at the three tiers of seats, the ceiling frescoes, and the typical fin de siècle decor. The high point in the theater's history was when Enrico Caruso sang here. A statue in Carrara marble of Tomás Terry, the founder, stands at the entrance.

Continuing counterclockwise around the square, you will pass the **Biblioteca Provincial** (Provincial Library) and the **Galería de Arte,** established in an early colonial building in 1986. Across the park, on the corner, is the **Casa de la Cultura,** in a lovely early 20th-century building known as the **Palacio Ferrer.** The **Museo Provincial** is on the same corner. In this 19th-century structure you can admire rooms filled with the type of furniture and decorations favored by the 19th-century bourgeoisie.

NEED A
BREAK?

Stop in at **El Palatino,** situated on the same block as the museum, for something to drink. The building dates from 1842 and was the first secular structure in Cienfuegos to be built with a portico.

Excursions from Cienfuegos

Jardín Botánico

A trip to the Botanical Garden—the oldest in Cuba and considered one of the finest tropical gardens in the world—is highly recommended.

Though it's not far from town, you'll need to hire a taxi, rent a car, or sign up for a group tour at the tourist office in your hotel. The garden was established as a study center in 1901. Botanists were determined to develop new and more profitable strains of sugarcane. They soon included other plants in their research, and in time amassed a general collection. Today, there are some 2,000 varieties of tropical and sub-tropical plants from five continents, including 89 different kinds of rubber plants, 23 types of bamboo, 241 medicinal plants, 248 timber-producing trees, 69 different orchids, and 400 types of cactus. The highlight is the collection of 307 varieties of palm trees.

The garden is 18 km (11 mi) from Cienfuegos along an unmarked road. Leaving the Hotel Jagua, follow Calle 37 to Avenida 18. Turn right and go four blocks to Calle 45, then take a left. You will pass the municipal stadium. When you come to the Clinica Estomatológica, turn right again onto Avenida Cinco de Septiembre. This street leads out to the Rancho Luna beach, from which you must take the turnoff to the Circuito Sur. (Once you're outside the city, it's best to ask for directions at every junction along the way). The garden's entrance is just before the Pepito Tey sugar mill. The $2 admission fee includes an informative, often amusing, guided tour. A small bar next to the parking area serves refreshments.

Boat Tour of the Bay

Boat tours, which depart from the major hotels and normally take about five hours, include a visit to the **Castillo de Jagua.** Below this fortress is the fishing village of **Perché,** in which many of the houses are built on wooden pilings over the water. You may have time for a meal at the **Casa del Pescador** ($20 to $30) and a swim before the tour starts back.

Eastern Ceinfuegos Province

Although Cienfuegos Province is fairly flat, the eastern part of it includes the **Sierra del Escambray,** one of Cuba's three major mountain ranges. Rent a car or arrange a tour at your hotel. If you drive yourself, you could make this the start of an excursion to Trinidad. Leave Cienfuegos via Avenida 64 (the Trinidad road). After a few kilometers take the fork to the left, toward Cumanayagua. This road leads through lovely farmland, and the landscape becomes increasingly hilly and green as you climb. Stop at **Lago Hanabanilla,** an artificial reservoir that attracts both fishermen and vacationers. You can tour the lake on a yacht or take one of the walking itineraries along the shore. One walk leads to the **Casa del Campesino,** a traditional working farm. You can visit the family's home, admire the small cultivated gardens, and sample a coffee brewed in a manner hundreds of years old. The walk continues to the Río Negro restaurant, where you can have lunch.

Dining and Lodging

For details on price categories, *see* the charts *in* On the Road with Fodor's at the front of this guide.

Cienfuegos

DINING

$$ Finca La Isabela. Situated in an old estate on the outskirts of Cienfuegos, this restaurant draws an international clientele. Some of the rooms are preserved as a museum. The house specialties are roast pig and the Isabel cocktail. A musical combo usually performs at dinner. *Carretera de Rancho Luna, Km 1,* ☎ *7606.*

$$ Palacio del Valle. This impressive palace next to the Hotel Jagua has ★ been converted into a restaurant whose menu is the most varied in the city. The ground-floor dining room was once a drawing room, and it is graced with a spectacular staircase. Carmen Iznaga, a niece of the poet Nicolás Guillén, sings and plays the piano during dinner. *Jardines de Hotel Jagua, Punta Gorda,* ☎ *3021 and 3025.* ⊙ *10–9.*

$ ★ **Casa del Pescador.** Nestled at the entrance to the bay across from Castillo de Jagua and the village of Perché, this small restaurant is strong on seafood—fish, shrimp, lobster, and *caguama* (tortoise). Cool breezes make the terrace a refreshing place for lunch. *Punta La Milpa, Carretera de Pasacaballo a La Milpa,* ☎ *8160.* ⊙ *8 AM–midnight.*

DINING AND LODGING

$$ **Hotel Pasacaballo.** Before this was a hotel, it was the spot from which Spanish troops ferried their horses across the harbor. Cienfuegos is 22 km (14 mi) away. *Carretera de Rancho Luna, Km 22,* ☎ *96280/90. 180 rooms with bath and air-conditioning. Restaurant, bar, pool, shop, tourist office.*

$$ **Hotel Horizontes Rancho Luna.** If you want to stay on the beach, this is the place. If touring Cienguegos is your calling, however, it may not be ideal as it's 16 km (10 mi) from the city. *Carretera de Rancho Luna, Km 16,* ☎ *48120/23. 225 rooms with bath and air-conditioning. Restaurant, bar, pool, shop, car rental, tourist office.*

$$ **Jagua.** This Jagua has a great location at the tip of Punta Gorda in Cienfuegos. From its upper terraces there are splendid views of the bay. The nightly cabaret show is also a treat. *Punta Gorda, Calle 37, No. 1, e/0 y 2,* ☎ *3021/25,* 🆁🅰🆇 *66 74 54. 145 rooms with bath and air-conditioning. Restaurant, bar, pool, nightclub, shop, tourist office.*

Another beachfront hotel in the Cienfuegos area is the **Cubanacan Faro Luna.** *Playa Rancho Luna, Carretera de Pasacaballos, Km 18,* ☎ *5582.*

Lago Hanabanilla
DINING

$$ **Río Negro.** Take the launch from the Hotel Hanabanilla ($2) to this lakeshore ranch-restaurant for the house specialty, *pollo saltón a la piña* (chicken with pineapple), an invention of the chef. An excellent musical group plays during meals.

DINING AND LODGING

$$ **Hotel Hanabanilla.** Situated on the edge of the lake, this is a good base camp for trout-fishing excursions. *Salto del Hanabanilla, Municipio Manicaragua,* ☎ *86932, 49125 and 49125. 127 rooms with bath and air-conditioning. Restaurant, bar, pool, store, tourist office.*

TRINIDAD

Trinidad is a colonial gem, a place where the past lives on. Unlike other colonial cities in the Americas, Trinidad has few historical monuments, splendid palaces, or imposing cathedrals. What is so astonishing about the place is that the buildings, the streets, and the way of life are just as they were a century or two ago. There are no billboards or souvenir shops to break the spell. Trinidad belongs entirely to the Trinitarios, the people who live here. Its cobbled streets, the roofs of ancient tiles, the barred windows, and the horse-drawn carts are not mere decorations for the benefit of tourists.

Trinidad is one of the seven towns founded by Diego Velázquez. After an initial reconnaissance of the island in 1508, Sebastián de Ocampo recommended founding a city at Jagua—now Cienfuegos, just to the west—to take advantage of the excellent harbor. Velázquez toured the entire region and selected this site instead. As a conquistador and soldier he preferred a more densely populated spot. Moreover, the gold that had been discovered was much closer to Trinidad than it was to Jagua.

Initially the city developed rapidly thanks to the area's gold mines. But from the beginning Trinidad's history was marked by alternating prosperity and decline. In bad times, many of its inhabitants moved on. When Hernán Cortés set out from here on his conquest of Mexico, he took many Trinitarios with him. The city's golden age occurred during the 17th and 18th centuries, owing to the flow of contraband and sugar and the exploitation of slave labor. The 19th century brought widespread cultivation of the sugar beet in Europe, reducing the demand for cane sugar; the century also saw the abolition of slavery. Slowly but inexorably, Trinidad's splendor faded. During the first half of the 20th century, the city was simply forgotten, left to become a desolate, almost ramshackle, little town.

Renovation and restoration began in 1965, when the city was declared a national monument. In 1988, UNESCO recognized Trinidad as a World Heritage Site, along with the nearby Valle de los Ingenios (Valley of the Sugar Mills). Today it is once again a city of extraordinary charm.

Exploring

The best way to explore Trinidad is on foot. Its historic center is a tangle of irregularly cobbled streets that are difficult for cars to negotiate, so don't even think of driving. Slip into a pair of comfortable walking shoes and set out with the certainty that you will find something delightful around almost every corner. This itinerary covers the major sights, but don't hesitate to abandon the route if you find yourself drawn in a different direction. In Trinidad you will do well to let chance be your guide. In the text that follows, the contemporary street names are occasionally followed in parentheses by the traditional ones—still used by the locals.

❸ Begin at the **Plaza Mayor,** or Main Square, in the very center of town. This was where the original settlement was founded by the Spanish. Around the square are some of the finest buildings from the colonial era, a charming ensemble that will take you back into the 18th and 19th centuries. The center of the square is a park surrounded by trellises and planted with palm trees. The large painted vases decorating one end were made in a local ceramics shop. Of the buildings around
❹ the square, the only two-story one is the **Palacio Brunet,** which houses the **Museo Romántico,** a collection of objects from the late-18th and early 19th centuries. Although Trinidad is small, it has many museums, and this is one of the most interesting. This building dates from 1741, when it had only one floor; the upper story was added much later. Two centuries have passed, and still it is one of the few two-story structures in Trinidad. Its 13 rooms are filled with period furniture, utensils, and paintings—affording a singular look into a typical 19th-century Trinidad household. You'll be inspired by the mahogany staircase, the marble floors, the interior patio, and—especially—the view of the square from the long balcony on the second floor. *Plaza Mayor, Calle Fernando Hernández Echerri (Cristo).* 🖼 *$2. Closed Mon.*

To the left of the museum, on the other side of Calle Simón Bolívar
❺ (Desengaño), is the **Iglesia de la Santísima Trinidad.** The present church was built in the late 19th century on the spot formerly occupied by the Parroquial Mayor (main parish church). Although it is not one of Cuba's most beautiful religious structures, it is worth a visit. Its collection of religious images, some of which date from the 17th century,

Exploring Trinidad

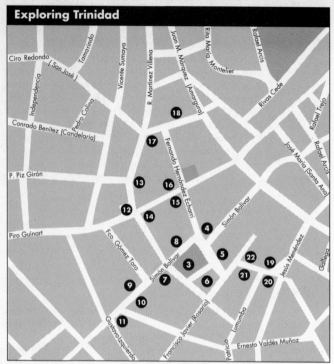

Alexander von
Humboldt House, **21**

Archivo Histórico
Municipal, **15**

Ayuntamiento y
Carcel, **14**

Casa de Alderman
Ortiz, **7**

Casa de la Trova, **20**

Casa del Corsario, **18**

Fondo de Bienes
Culturales, **10**

Iglesia de la Santísima
Trinidad, **5**

La Canchánchara, **13**

La Luna, **17**

Mansión de los
Conspiradores, **22**

Museo de Arqueología
Guamuhaya, **8**

Museo de Arquitectura
Trinitaria, **6**

Museo Histórico
Municipal, **9**

Palacio Brunet, **4**

Palacio Iznaga, **11**

Plaza Mayor, **3**

Plazuela de Segarte, **19**

Plazuela Real del
Jigüe, **12**

Torre del Antiguo
Convento de San
Francisco de Asís, **16**

include the interesting *Cristo de la Vera Cruz,* carved in Spain in the
18th century. One of the church's two altars is made of various precious Cuban woods.

6 Continuing clockwise around the square, you come to the **Museo de Arquitectura Trinitaria.** The building it occupies, the Casa de los Sánchez Iznaga, was originally two structures built in the 18th century. This is the only Cuban museum devoted to colonial construction techniques, with displays of different types of masonry, grillwork, windows, and doors. But the building itself is appealing, particularly its impressive timber roof. *Plaza Mayor.* ✉ *$1. Closed Fri.*

Across the plaza and to the left of the Museo de Arquitectura Trini-
7 taria is the **Casa de Alderman Ortiz,** now an art gallery showing contemporary Cuban artists; some of the work is for sale. This structure was built in the early 19th century for Ortiz de Zúñiga, who was both the city's mayor and a pirate-ship outfitter. The long balcony is one of the finest in Trinidad. Inside, some of the original decor has been preserved. It is thought that, before leaving for Mexico in 1518, Hernán

Cortés lived in the building that originally stood here. The present building once housed an archaeology museum, which has been moved to Sancti Spíritus, the provincial capital.

❽ The Casa Padron, on the fourth side of the square, now houses the **Museo de Arqueología Guamuhaya.** Guamuhaya was the name given to the region by the indigenous peoples, and the museum is devoted to their culture. *Calle Simón Bolívar 437.* ✉ *$1. Closed Thurs.*

Leave the Plaza Mayor and head down Calle Simón Bolívar (Desengaño). On either side of the street are mansions built by the wealthy families who owned the sugar mills. On the right, in the Palacio Can-
❾ tero, is the **Museo Histórico Municipal,** which traces the history of Trinidad from its beginnings in 1514. *Calle Simón Bolívar e/Gómez Toro y Gustavo Izquierdo.* ✉ *$1.50. Closed Wed.*

❿ In the pretty building across the street is the **Fondo de Bienes Culturales** shop, where you can buy embroidered items, wooden objects, and
⓫ antiques. On the next corner is the **Palacio Iznaga,** an example of the eclectic architecture of the 19th century and another of the city's rare two-story buildings.

Turn right on Calle Gustavo Izquierdo (or de Gloria). At the first corner you come to, you will see one of the Ministry of Tourism stores (the other is on Calle Francisco Javier), offering handicrafts of all kinds. This street has a number of 18th-century structures that were once hostels. You'll also pass the bus station.

When you come to Calle Piro Guinart (La Boca), turn right. A short
⓬ way down the street is the **Plazuela Real del Jigüe.** This is where the Spanish expeditionaries celebrated their first Christmas Mass in 1513, even before the city was founded. A plaque commemorates the event—however its mention of Fray Bartolomé de las Casas is erroneous, as he did not take part. The mass was, in fact, celebrated by Juan de Tesín, the priest who tried to convert the native chieftain Hatuey, leader of the first anticolonial rebellion. El jigüe—the tree in the center of the square—was planted in 1929. It has been a tradition to keep such a tree growing here to commemorate the original one from 1513.

NEED A
BREAK?

Turn left on Calle Rubén Martínez and rest your feet at **La Canchánchara,** which has a courtyard and live performances of traditional music. The name of the establishment is also the name of the house specialty: a drink made with brandy, lemon, honey, mineral water, and ice. Tradition holds that the recipe was invented by the *mambises,* 19th-century revolutionary guerrillas. The only difference between the original version and the one served today is that the former was consumed hot. The *guarapo* (sugarcane extract) here is also excellent. The Renaissance-style building, with its cedar frame roof, once belonged to Pablo Vélez, a nobleman and dealer in contraband, who conducted his shady business here rather than having to receive pirates and privateers at his family estate.

Return to the Plaza Real del Jigüe, and on the left-hand corner, at Calle
⓮ Piro Guinart 302, are the remains of the old **ayuntamiento y carcel** (town hall and jail). Look closely at the wall, where a section has been left unworked to show the 18th-century masonry of stone and lime.

⑮ On the next corner, you come to the **Archivo Histórico Municipal.**
⑯ Across the way, in front of a small square, stands the **torre del antiguo Convento de San Francisco de Asís** (tower of the old Saint Francis of Assisi Convent). The tower is all that remains of a convent that closed in the last century owing to a dearth of novices. The church was used again while the new parish church was under construction. Once that project was completed, the convent church passed into government hands and was rented out as an art gallery. It was subsequently demolished and replaced by this one in the Baroque Havana style. The building now houses the **Museo de la Lucha contra los Bandidos** (Museum of the Battle against Outlaws). Here you can see documents relating to the campaign against anti-Castro militias in the Escambray from 1959 to 1965. *Calle Fernando Hernández y Boca.* ⌨ *$1. Closed Mon.*

Turn left between the tower and the square, and continue along Fernando Hernández (Cristo) to its intersection with Calle Ciro Redondo
⑰ (San José). On the latter, a little to the left, is **La Luna,** one of the city's most charming taverns; it has been in operation since the 19th century. The pink house across the street dates from 1735 and is one of Trinidad's oldest. The yellow one next door, No. 261, is the so-called
⑱ **Casa del Corsario.** It was built in 1754 for the French pirate captain Carlos Merlín. During the heyday of piracy, Trinidad had an entire neighborhood inhabited by pirates: El Fotuto. Along with Bayamo and Remedios, Trinidad was a favored base for the corsairs who attacked enemy ships to loot them of their treasures.

Continue to the corner and turn right on Calle Juan Márquez (Amargura). Two houses practically facing each other have crosses on their facades. They are two of the 14 stations on the **Recorrido del Vía Crucis** (The Way of the Cross) followed during Easter Week celebrations. The route is mainly confined to calles Amargura, Real, and San Antonio.

There are 18th- and 19th-century structures all along Calle Amargura. As you walk down it you will pass two unfinished buildings that allow you to see early construction techniques. If you turn right on Calle Jesús
⑲ Menéndez (Alameda), it will lead you to the **Plazuela de Segarte.** Just before this square, the **Callejon de Galdos** leads off to the left. Here you find the house that once belonged to José María Galdós, the uncle of Benito Pérez Galdós, the Spanish Dickens and Dostoevsky all in one. Look at the windows in the little square and the nearby buildings; they represent some of the most elaborate woodworking in all of Trinidad.

NEED A   In the Plazuela de Segarte is the **Casa de la Trova,** where, as at all of
BREAK?   Cuba's traditional music societies, performances are given almost daily. At the end of the patio there's a record store and a small bar where you can enjoy the music while you have a drink. The house was built in 1777, and its interior walls are decorated with fascinating popular motifs.

As you leave the Casa de la Trova, on the left, on Calle Fernando Hernán-
㉑ dez (Cristo), you will pass the **house where Alexander von Humboldt stayed** during his time in Trinidad in 1801. Across the street is the so-
㉒ called **Mansión de los Conspiradores,** where, in the mid-19th century, members of the revolutionary group known as La Rosa Cubana held their meetings. On the right is a wide stairway leading to the Casa de Fernández de Lara, which has one of the most beautiful roofs in Trinidad. On the other side of the stairway is the Iglesia de la Santísima Trinidad and the Plaza Mayor, where your tour began.

Excursions from Trinidad

No visit to Trinidad is complete without an excursion through the nearby **Valle de San Luis,** or **Valle de los Ingenios** (Valley of the Sugar Mills). With Trinidad, it forms the district designated by UNESCO as a World Heritage Site. At one time it was home to 43 mills, primitive factories operated by slave labor that produced some 80,000 tons of sugar a year.

Leave Trinidad by way of the Carretera de Sancti Spíritus and, after a steep climb of 2 km or 3 km (1 or 2 mi), you will come upon a spot with a panoramic view of the valley. The best-preserved structure is the **Torre de Manacas-Iznaga,** an unusual tower rising 45 meters (148 feet) above the broad sugar fields 14 km (9 mi) from Trinidad. You cannot miss it, for it stands out in the middle of the landscape and the turnoff is very clearly marked.

Built of stone, brick, and steel, the tower consists of seven identical segments. It was constructed between 1835 and 1845 by Alejo María del Carmen e Iznaga, and was the stuff of legend from the start. One story relates that it was built as the result of a wager between Alejo and his brother Pedro. Alejo was to erect a tower and Pedro to dig a well; the one who built highest or dug deepest would be the winner. It is important to point out, however, that no well has ever been found. According to another tale, the tower was built as a prison for the rancher's unfaithful wife. This is also improbable inasmuch as Alejo left everything he owned to his widow. Finally, it is said that he constructed the tower to oversee the slaves and watch for runaways. This sounds more logical, as anyone who climbs to the tower on top of the structure can see. The quality of its construction, however, suggests that the tower was conceived as much as a monument as a practical structure. Other mill buildings around the tower include the owner's house and slaves quarters. A restaurant is planned for the near future to help stimulate tourism in the valley, which is to become a gigantic museum of slavery.

If you hanker for a quick change of temperature and landscape, you can leave the coastal lowlands, climb into the Sierra del Escambray, and head for the tourist complex at **Topes de Collantes.** Leave the city by way of the Carretera de Cienfuegos and cross the Guaurabo River; just before the town of Piti Fajardo, take the turnoff to the right and begin the climb into the mountains. The whole tour is only 19 km (12 mi) along a good road. Don't forget to bring a sweater, even if it's steaming hot in Trinidad. The difference in temperature is remarkable, and a great relief in the torrid days of summer. The other road leading to Topes, from Manicaragua on the other side of the mountain, is in very poor shape.

Topes de Collantes was developed in the 1950s as a sanatorium for sufferers of respiratory problems and is now a tourist center. From here you can set out to explore either on foot or on horseback. This is also a good place for fishing. One of the most interesting sights in the area is the **Salto de Caburní,** an impressive waterfall 75 meters (246 feet) high in the mountains. The climb is strenuous, and only recommended for those in good physical condition.

Dining and Lodging

For details on price categories, *see* the charts *in* On the Road with Fodor's at the front of this guide.

Trinidad

DINING

$$ **Trinidad Colonial.** Situated in a restored colonial house and decorated
★ with period furniture, this restaurant is considered the city's finest. The specialties are fish and seafood prepared according to Creole recipes and accompanied by *fufú de plátano* (fried bananas). A trio plays popular Cuban songs. *Calle Macco 402, e/Rosario y Colón,* ☎ *3873.* ☉ *10–10.*

DINING AND LODGING

$$$ **Ancón.** This modern beachside hotel is on the Ancón Peninsula, which
★ separates the Caribbean from the Casilda Inlet, 12 km (7 mi) out of Trinidad. All the rooms have sea views. *Playa Ancón, Carretera María Aguilar,* ☎ *4011 and 3155,* ℻ *66 74 24. 208 rooms with bath and air-conditioning. Restaurant, bar, pool, discotheque, shop, game room, car rental, tourist office.*

$$ **Hotel Horizontes Costasur.** Only a short distance from Ancón, this is an economical option if a beach sojourn is what you crave. *Playa Ancón, Carretera María Aguilar,* ☎ *6100 and 6190. 131 rooms with bath and air-conditioning. Restaurant, bar, pool, sports complex, shop.*

$$ **Motel Horizontes Las Cuevas.** Although this motel doesn't have as
★ many facilities as the Ancón, it's better situated for those who are interested in spending time in Trinidad. It takes its name from the large number of caverns in the area, one of which houses a discotheque. *Finca Santa Ana,* ☎ *2340, 3640, or 4003. 114 rooms with bath. Restaurant, bar, pool, discotheque, stores, tourist office.*

Topes de Collantes

DINING AND LODGING

$$$ **Topes de Collantes.** This complex, built around the original sanatorium,
★ is unlike any other in the Caribbean. At an altitude of 800 meters, it is recommended for those more interested in mountains than the beach. *Topes de Collantes, Escambray,* ☎ *42–40117 and 42–40330. 300 rooms including the hotel, the rest center, cabins, and houses, all with bath and air-conditioning. Restaurant, bar, indoor pool, hairdresser, sauna, bowling, gymnasium, stores, discotheque, game room, library, photography studio, tourist office.*

THE ROAD TO REMEDIOS

On many Cuban itineraries, the province of Villa Clara is often noted only as an area to speed through while traveling east–west on the main highway, the Carretera Central. Yet if you skip this region, you will miss one of the country's great treasures: the town of Remedios. Its history, architecture, and popular festivals make this settlement of some 17,000 people a prime destination.

Exploring

Santa Clara

㉔ The gateway to the area is the provincial capital of **Santa Clara,** 300 km (186 mi) from Havana and easily reached by way of the Carretera Central. Although it has few sights, students of recent Cuban history will appreciate the fact that it was Che Guevara's capture of Santa Clara that proved the decisive blow that brought Castro to power on January 1, 1959. The heart of town is the **Parque Vidal,** which has a few interesting buildings around it, including the **Teatro La Caridad**—one of the most famous theaters in Cuba and another one in which Enrico Caruso once performed—and the **Palacio Municipal** (Town Hall). Also facing the park is the **Hotel Santa Clara Libre,** the facade of which still displays bullet holes from the battle that ended the revolution. The quiet streets around the square, with their traditional shops, are worth a brief stroll. The park is famous for the thousands of birds that roost in its trees and make a deafening din.

One of the most unusual monuments in Santa Clara is the **armored train.** This is part of the train that was derailed (it was filled with soldiers and military matériel) during the assault on the city in late 1958. It stands next to the road to Remedios.

The 43-km (27-mi) road from Santa Clara to Remedios takes you through a countryside of gentle hills, palm trees, farmland, and small villages. Twenty-five kilometers (16 mi) out of Santa Clara you come to the most important of these villages: **Camajuaní.** At the entrance to town you may be surprised to find images of a toad and a goat; these are the symbols of the two sections of the village that vie with each other to build the most spectacular float for the Carnival festival.

Remedios

25 **Remedios** has one of the most beautifully preserved downtown areas in Cuba—some architectural experts maintain that it is better preserved than even Trinidad. Entering Remedios is like leaping back in time. There are almost no cars, and if you do see one, it will be an American model from the '40s or '50s. Most people get around by **horse-drawn carriage.** Remedios is one of three Cuban towns—Bayamo and Cárdenas are the others—that continue to truly rely on carriages as a means of transportation. Although carts and carriages are used in other Cuban cities, it is often out of current necessity rather than because of tradition.

Remedios dates from 1542, when a group of colonists established themselves on one of the keys off the nearby northern coast. Pirate attacks twice forced them to move until they arrived at the present spot 8 km (5 mi) inland. Attacks continued nonetheless, and in 1689, 18 Remedios families fled farther inland and founded the town of Santa Clara. Legend has it that local demons may have contributed to their determination to flee. It is known that some of them returned to Remedios to convince their former neighbors to join them. In an attempt to "persuade" the residents, they razed the town, leaving only the church standing. In the 18th century Remedios prospered and became a major cultural center. At the beginning of the 19th century it was heavily damaged by fire; most of the surviving colonial buildings are from that era.

The focus of any visit to the city is the Plaza de Isabel II (now Parque Martí), which lies between the two principal churches, **San Juan Bautista** and the **Bien Viaje.** The former is of considerably greater interest historically and artistically, however, the latter has a much more important place in the hearts of the Remedios citizens. Begin your tour at the Church of San Juan Bautista, which has stood here since 1578. Don't be deceived by its plain facade; great treasures await you inside. The altar is a splendid structure of cedar inset with gold, and the ceiling is teak carved with Moorish motifs. The walls are covered with carvings and religious paintings, the most startling of which is a pregnant Immaculate Virgin.

On the sidewalk next to the church are two traditional bars that open onto the square. The first, **La Fe,** serves only natural drinks of anise and mango. The second, **El Louvre,** lists croquettes and other light fare on its menu. Both establishments are perfect examples of meeting places unaltered by the passage of time, in their decor as well as in their offerings.

On this same sidewalk is the nightclub **Las Leyendas,** the only place in Remedios where you can watch a show or drink a beer. Farther along, you pass by the Hotel Mascotte, a small 14-room establishment that is almost always full despite a traditional policy—at least on paper— that guests stay at least three nights. This archaic requirement prevented the hotel from becoming the sort of place where people booked a room for the sole purpose of "illicit carnal commerce," thus depriving "respectable travelers" of a chance to rest. It was in this hotel, in 1899, that General Máximo Gómez met with a representative of U.S. President McKinley to deal with the discharge of the mambises, the fighters for Cuban independence in the Spanish-American War.

Continuing along this street, leaving the square to your right, you come to the **Museo de las Parrandas Remedianas** (Museum of the Revels of Remedios). Las Parrandas (revels or carousings) in Remedios is one of three traditional Cuban fiestas (the others are Carnival in Santiago de Cuba and Charanga de Bejucal in the province of La Habana). The museum has displays of *trabajos de plaza* (floats), lamps, flags, fireworks, banners, and other items required for a successful celebration.

Although the exact origins of this fiesta are uncertain, there is one story that seems likely. In the first half of the 19th century, on cold early mornings between the 16th and 24th of December, the locals celebrated masses called *de aguinaldo,* which preceded Midnight Mass, or Misa del Gallo, on Christmas Eve. Apparently, attendance was not as high as the parish priest would have liked. Hoping to frighten his flock into coming to church, he took to the streets with some youngsters and stirred up as much pandemonium as he could. It's not known to what extent he succeeded in getting parishioners to mass; what is certain is that the hell-raising was so appealing that ever since, the people of the town have prowled the streets on the nights leading up to Christmas Eve. The festival is now held on the Saturday that falls before the 26th. The whole town takes part, divided into the two neighborhoods, El Carmen and San Salvador, which compete with each other with floats and fireworks. Each group prepares secretly for months. Part of the game throughout the year is the business of infiltrating the "enemy camp" to spy or perhaps even attempt sabotage. The mascot of the Carmelitas is the *gavilan,* or hawk; that of the Sansarices (from the San Salvador district), the rooster. Fiesta night includes displays of the finished floats, traditional music performances, firecrackers, and a parade of townspeople who carry colorful banners.

Return to the square and walk along the side across from San Juan Bautista till you reach the **Buen Viaje** on your left. This small church is not of much architectural or historic interest, but the people of Remedios are very fond of it—witness the array of ex-votos at its entrance, a veritable compendium of popular faith.

On the last side of the square is the **Museo de Música Alejandro García Caturla,** in what was the founder's birthplace. This elegant 19th-century mansion contains a wealth of memorabilia from the life and work of this musician-cum-lawyer who broke with all the conventions

of his time. He took a black woman for a mistress, and his composi-
tions were often inspired by African music. He was also an incorruptible
lawyer and judge—which is why he was assassinated.

Sancti Spíritus

㉖ Return to Santa Clara and continue along the Carretera Central to **Sancti
Spíritus.** If you are short on time, you can quickly get a sense of the
city's flavor with a visit to the **Parque Serafín Sánchez.** Commonly called
the Parque Central, this large square is surrounded by neoclassical buildings, shops, and the **Hotel Perla.** Don't miss the narrow colonial streets
around the **Parroquial Mayor,** a church constructed during the 17th,
18th, and 19th centuries. A third point of interest is the **bridge over
the Río Yayabo,** the only surviving stone-arch bridge in Cuba. **Calle El
Llano,** which has several houses from the last century and is an ideal
spot for a quiet stroll, leads away from the bridge. If you have a pas-
sion for colonial art, be sure to visit the nearby **Museo de Arte Colonial** (Calle Plácido 64; closed Mon.).

Just outside Sancti Spíritus, in the foothills of the Escambray, you
come to **El Zaza,** a man-made lake famous for its abundant trout. Nearby
are the caves of the **Hornos de Cal** (Lime Ovens) and **Sierra de Banao,**
once inhabited by indigenous peoples. You can arrange tours of these
caves at the Hotel Zaza, which is on the lakeshore.

Dining and Lodging

For details on price categories, *see* the charts *in* On the Road with Fodor's
at the front of this guide.

Sancti Spíritus

DINING AND LODGING

$$ **Villa Rancho Hatuey.** This villa-hotel is right next to the Carretera Cen-
tral—perfect for a rest in the middle of a long excursion. *Carretera Cen-
tral, Km 383,* ☎ *2–6015 and 2–6406. 10 bungalows and 12 rooms
with bath and air-conditioning. Restaurant, bar, pool, sports facilities,
store, parking, tourist office.*

Santa Clara

DINING AND LODGING

$$ **Cubanacán La Granjita.** In the country, but close to the airport and to
the center of Santa Clara, this recently opened villa is a modern alter-
native to the Hotel Los Caneyes. *Santa Clara, Carretera de Maleza,
Km 2.5,* ☎ *26051 and 26052. 24 rooms with bath and air-conditioning.
Restaurant, bar, pool, sauna, gymnasium, horseback riding, store,
game room, movie theater, parking, tourist office.*

$$ **Hotel Horizonte Los Caneyes.** The rooms are in cabins that look like
caneyes, the rounded structures of the indigenous peoples. Rest assured,
though, that they have creature comforts undreamed of by the Taino
tribes. Many Cubans honeymoon here. *Av. de los Eucaliptus y Car-
retera de Circunvalación,* ☎ *4512 to 4515,* ℻ *33 50 09. 90 rooms
with bath and air-conditioning. Restaurant, bar, pool, shop.*

$ **Santa Clara Libre.** This 10-story hotel towers over the Parque Vidal.
The facade is still pockmarked from the bullets fired during the battle
of Santa Clara, when Che Guevara took the city. There is a good view
of the town from the top-floor bar-restaurant—otherwise, the hotel has
little to recommend it. *Parque Vidal 6, e/Marta Abreu y Trista,* ☎ *27548
to 27550. 159 rooms with bath and fan. Restaurant, bar, store, night-
club.*

FROM MORÓN TO CAYO COCO

The province of Ciego de Ávila is at Cuba's geographic center. Halfway between Havana and Santiago de Cuba, is the province's eponymous capital city. Among its few sights are the remains of a fortress from the Spanish-American War (War of Independence). Many people are drawn to the region for fishing and other outdoor activities as the game preserves here are virtually unmatched on the island. Most people, however, come for the spectacular coast. Along Cuba's northern shore—from the Hicaco Peninsula (Varadero) to the Bahía de Nuevitas in the province of Camagüey—are 465 km (288 mi) of *cayos* (keys). This untamed region is virtually uninhabited. Separated by channels and inlets that create interior lagoons, the keys form the Sabana-Camagüey Archipelago. To the north of them are huge coral reefs.

Exploring

Morón

27 Until the 19th century, the region's most important town was **Morón**, today a small, quiet community with a leisurely rhythm of earlier times. It's the perfect base from which to explore the coast. One of the first things you notice on arriving in Moróm is the statue of a *gallo* (gamecock) next to the modern clock tower across from the Hotel Morón. The story of the gamecock began in the southern Spanish town of Morón de la Frontera, in the province of Cadiz. Tradition tells of a popular rebellion that "plucked" a much-hated officer who strutted about "like a gamecock" and abused his power. To celebrate their triumph the rebels erected a monument of a plucked gamecock. This story is the basis of the Spanish expression *"sin plumas y cacareando"* ("featherless and crowing"), which is aptly used to describe someone who has been stripped of power and dignity without fully realizing it. During the 18th century, Spanish immigrants brought the story with them when they settled the Cuban Morón, and the city became known as La Ciudad del Gallo, or Gamecock City. Even though the Cuban gamecock always retained his feathers, it was kept as a symbol of the rebellion of the oppressed against authoritarian power. During the last two centuries there have been several gamecock monuments; the current one dates from 1982. A loudspeaker on the clock tower plays the gamecock's crowing daily at 6 AM and 6 PM. Near this square you can hire a horse-drawn carriage for a tour of the city.

Heading north from Morón, on the way to the cayos, you pass very close to the **Laguna de la Leche** (Milk Lagoon), so named because its waters have a milky color owing to deposits of sodium carbonate. The lagoon attracts large numbers of birds and is a good observatory. As you continue north, you will see a singular-looking settlement that seems more Belgian than Cuban. This is the town of **Isla de Turiguanó**, an immense livestock-breeding ranch.

Cayo Coco

28 The most spectacular feature of the 42-km (26-mi) road between Morón and **Cayo Coco** is the way it runs across and all but through the water. There are 17 km (11 mi) of roadway built by pouring enough stone and landfill into the shallow flats to create a roadbed. Racing across this corridor is exhilarating. On a calm, clear day when the sun is high, sea and sky seem fused. With luck, you'll see fish jumping from the transparent waters around you and, as you approach the key, you'll encounter great colonies of pink flamingos in the lagoons.

Cayo Coco is a nature preserve where as many as 159 different kinds of birds have been sighted.

The beach on this key, one of the largest keys of the Camagüey Archipelago, is outstanding. Plans are afoot to transform the 22-km (14-mi) stretch of sand into a major tourist center. For now, the landscape remains virtually untouched. Three-fourths of its surface is covered with forests and jungles containing wild horses, wild boar, and free-range livestock. Ironically, there are few coconut palms; the key's name comes from a species of bird—the coco—that lives in its forests. Head for the 3-km (2-mi) beach at **Las Coloradas,** where you can rent horses and hammocks. There is also a restaurant that serves lunch. In 1992 a huge, five-star hotel, the Guitart Cayo Coco, was opened on the beach at **Palma Real** (Royal Palm).

Cayo Guillermo

The other key with lodging and tourist facilities is **Cayo Guillermo.** To reach it you can either make the short drive from Cayo Coco or take a boat from the fishing-cooperative port at Punta Alegre, which is 67 km (42 mi) from Morón. At 13 square km (8 square mi), Cayo Guillermo is much smaller than its neighbor. Its three beaches are 5 km (3 mi) long overall and pleasant places to rest in the sun or to embark on diving excursions to the coral reefs.

Dining and Lodging

For details on price categories, *see* the charts *in* On the Road with Fodor's at the front of this guide.

Cayo Coco

DINING AND LODGING

$$$ **Tryp Cayo Coco.** This new complex covers several acres of beachfront land. Indeed it is so large, it seems more a small city than a hotel. The place can accommodate your every whim, and it's completely isolated from the bustle of the world outside. One restaurant, La Fontanita, specializes in Italian food; El Dorado serves fish and seafood; and El Caribeño has Creole cuisine. *Playa Palma Real,* ☎ *30 13 11. 458 rooms with bath and air-conditioning. 5 restaurants, bar, banquet hall, 2 pools, hairdresser, sports facilities, shop, car rental.*

$$$ **Nuevo Club Cayo Coco.** Opened at the end of 1996, this hotel is also managed by the Spanish Tryp chain and combines tropical vegetation with colonial architecture. ☎ *301 300. 502 rooms. 3 restaurants, 4 bars. The all-inclusive cost per person is $70 a day off season, $95 a day peak season.*

Cayo Guillermo

DINING AND LODGING

$ **Cojinar Gran Caribe.** Everyone calls this tiny hotel La Casita. It has no pretensions and is a good place for sunbathing or arranging diving excursions. *Cayo Guillermo,* ☎ *33 52 21. 8 rooms with bath and air-conditioning. Restaurant, bar, boat outings.*

Morón

DINING AND LODGING

$$ **Cubanacán Morón.** Make this your hub while you explore the region. It is near both the beaches and the game preserves. *Av. Carafa,* ☎ *3901 to 3904, 4432 and 3076. 144 rooms with bath, most with air-conditioning. Restaurant, bar, pool, hairdresser, shop, car rental, tourist office.*

FROM CAMAGÜEY TO SANTA LUCÍA

Exploring

On the Carratera Central, halfway between the provincial capitals of Ciego de Ávila and Las Tunas, is **Camagüey.** It is the third most important city on the island and has grown rapidly in the last few decades. Approaching it by car, you cannot help but be astonished at the new structures that tower along the ring road, most of them government office buildings. The contrast between this wide avenue and the narrow alleyways of the historic heart of the city is striking.

Camagüey is another of the seven towns founded by Diego Velázquez, but as is the case with nearly all of them, its present location is not the original one. Its name has been changed as well; until 1903 it was known as Santa María del Puerto del Príncipe. The site Velázquez selected in 1515 was on the Punto del Guincho, near Nuevitas, a port city at the far end of the bay of the same name. The following year the settlement was moved to the bank of the Caonao River, in the northwest part of the province, where the land was better and fresh water was more abundant. Some years later indigenous tribes wiped out the new community, and the colonists moved to an inland site near the junction of the Hatibonico and Tínima rivers and the native village of Camagüei. The new city's chief livelihood was the breeding of livestock, and in spite of the monopoly imposed by the Spanish authorities, local breeders developed a thriving contraband trade with the Dutch, French, and English Caribbean islands. Pirates were by no means blind to the wealth in Puerto del Príncipe. Henry Morgan and his men sacked the city in 1668, almost completely destroying it. Another attack followed in 1679. To deter these plunderers, the citizens rebuilt the city with a labyrinth of streets designed to confuse invaders. Puzzling forks led to squares where attackers might be ambushed. Even today, it's easy to become disoriented.

A daylong tour on foot is the best way to see Camagüey. Begin at the **Plaza de los Trabajadores** (Workers' Square), an irregular space surrounded by buildings of different styles. At one end is the **Museo Casa de Ignacio Agramonte.** Agramonte, often referred to simply as El Mayor (the Major), was an important leader in the Cuban War of Independence, and he took part in 45 battles. Cuban music enthusiasts will recognize him as the hero of a well-known Silvio Rodríguez song. Although the rooms of this museum, his birthplace, have all the trappings to which wealthy 19th-century Camagüey families were accustomed, the piano is the only piece that actually belonged to the Agramontes. Documents and eyewitness accounts of the war are also displayed. *Calle Ignacio Agramonte 459.* ✆ *$1.* ☉ *Tues.–Sun.*

Opposite the museum is the 18th-century **Iglesia de la Merced.** If you cut diagonally across the square and walk up Calle Padre Valencia, you come to the **Teatro Principal,** built of marble and glass in 1850. Today the theater has frequent performances by the Camagüey Ballet.

Returning to the square, head down Calle Salvador Cisneros to the heart of Camagüey with its colonial era houses. Some of them are quite somber; neither as impressive nor as colorful as those in other cities, they reflect the taste of the rural bourgeoisie. Note that many houses have a shady central patio—a distinguishing feature—and their windows often have interesting grillwork. Many also have the immense *tinajones,* or ceramic jars, in their patios. These were such fixtures in the early years that they became a symbol of the city. Camagüey always had water problems, and it was customary to store rainwater in these huge vented containers. The technique used to make them was developed in Spain.

At Salvador Cisneros 258 is the **Centro de Promoción Cultural,** which has exhibits of work by Cuban artists and jazz concerts. Across the street, at No. 259, there is a puppet theater that offers performances on Friday, Saturday, and Sunday at 3 and 10. Next door is the **Palacio de Justicia** (Court House), in a mid-18th-century building that was once a seminary. Turn right on Hermanos Aguero. On the first corner, you come to the **birthplace of Cuban poet Nicolás Guillén.** This modest house, which opened as a museum in 1992, is filled with the poet's possessions, and contains a sizable library for the study of his works. A little farther along is the **Plaza de Bedoya,** at the end of which is the **Iglesia del Carmen,** in very poor condition. This stretch of street, with its colonial houses painted in different colors, seems more typical of a small village than of a city of 300,000 inhabitants.

Retrace your steps to Plaza de Bedoya and go down Calle Martí, which has some very old houses, notably the one at the intersection with Calle 28 de Enero. Two blocks down is the **Parque Ignacio Agramonte.** At one side of the park is the **cathedral** and in the park's center is a monument to El Mayor. Also bordering the park is the **Casa de la Trova** (Musical Society), where local musicians gather in the evenings for choral singing. *Calle Salvador Cisneros 171.* ✉ *$1.* ☺ *Tues.–Fri. 5–8:30, weekends 8–11.*

Continue down Salvador Cisneros and after passing the **Palacio Bernal,** now occupied by the Academy of Sciences, turn right on Calle Ángel for two blocks to the **Plaza de las Cinco Esquinas** (Plaza of the Five Corners). On one corner stands one of the oldest houses in Camagüey, an unusual squat structure with a very irregular floor. Turn left on Matías Verona and you come to the **Plaza de San Juan de Dios,** with a beautiful ensemble of buildings, mainly from the 18th century.

NEED A BREAK?	One of the restored colonial buildings on the Plaza de San Juan de Dios houses the **Parador de los Tres Reyes.** It serves nothing but beer and *chorizo* (sausage) and has a predominantly Cuban clientele. Stop by for a bit of local charm. Reservations are essential (☎ 980 80).

The **Convent of San Juan de Dios,** built in 1728, occupies one whole side of the square. You can visit the small ceramics shop inside. Surely one of the more memorable events to take place on this square occurred after Ignacio Agramonte had been killed in battle. His corpse was brought here and ceremonially blown to pieces before the remains were cremated. A plaque bearing the words of the Silvio Rodríguez song in celebration of Agramonte commemorates the moment.

Take a right on Calle Hurtado, then bear right again when you reach Padre Olallo (known as Pobres), a long, serpentine street that leads to the Hotel Plaza. Along the way, you will see a triangular plaza from which two narrow alleys lead off to the right. The first is **Funda del Catre,** famous for being the narrowest street in Cuba. Take the left-hand street, Bartolomé Masó until you reach a park. There, shift over to the next street running parallel to Masó, Avellaneda, and you come to the **Palacio Pichardo,** site of Camagüey's first high school. A little farther on you pass the birthplace of the writer **Gertrudis Gómez de Avellaneda.** Still farther along, on Ignacio Agramonte, turn to the left and you will see the tower of the **Iglesia de la Soledad,** a mid-18th-century Baroque structure with splendid frescoes inside. Most Cuban churches are closed when there are no services in progress; this one is an exception.

Continue down Ignacio Agramonte, one of the commercial arteries of the city. On the corner is a pizzeria, usually with a long line of customers outside. To the right are the Cabaret Colonial, two movie theaters, a video theater, and the tourist office (the folks here can help you plan an excursion, but they don't have printed information on the city itself). Across the street, at No. 447, there is a pharmacy that specializes in medicinal plants. A little farther down you will find yourself at the Ignacio Agramonte house, where the tour began.

Playa de Santa Lucía

If you would like to flop on a beach near Camagüey, your best bet is ③ **Santa Lucía,** a destination that is especially popular with Canadian and German tour groups. Tour operators tend to book whole blocks of rooms, and independent travelers are well advised to reserve in advance during high season.

The 96-km (60-mi) drive from Camagüey to Santa Lucía takes a couple hours on a road that winds through fields and small towns. It also passes near the ruins of an old sugar mill, the chimney of which can be seen from a considerable distance. The major towns on the route are Minas and San Miguel de Baga.

Santa Lucía is a marvelous, 19-km (12-mi) strip of white sand protected by a coral reef. In addition to the usual resort activities, it has an international diving center and horseback excursions. Its hotels arrange tours to Cayo Sabinal, a huge key with still more terrific beaches; the San Hilario fortress; and the Columbus Lighthouse on Ponta Maternillo.

Dining and Lodging

For details on price categories, *see* the charts *in* On the Road with Fodor's at the front of this guide.

Camagüey

DINING

$$ El Ovejito. The colonial house in which this restaurant is situated has
★   been beautifully restored (of note are the friezes on the walls of the salon). The specialty here is lamb; feast on it while listening to the trio Voces Latinas. *Calle Hermanos Aguero 280,* ☎ *92524. Dinner only. Closed Mon.*

$$ La Campana de Toledo. The seafood dishes here are served on a typi-
★   cal patio, complete with immense tinajones. *Plaza de San Juan de Dios.* ☺ *Daily 9–5.*

DINING AND LODGING

$$ Cubanacán Maraguán. This little villa consists of a series of cottages in a garden. It's quiet, restful, and just a bit isolated. *Camino de Guanabanilla, Circunvalación Este,* ☎ *72017 and 72170. 35 rooms with bath and air-conditioning. Restaurant, bar, pool, game room, sports facilities, store, car rental, tourist office.*

$$ Hotel Horizontes Camagüey. This hotel is one of the city's best despite its location so far from the city center. *Av. Ignacio Agramonte,* ☎ *72015. 142 rooms with bath and air-conditioning. Restaurant, bar, pool, store, cabaret, tourist office.*

$$ Plaza. Very near the train station, the Plaza was built in 1907 for the
★   convenience of rail travelers. It was renovated in 1990, and is very popular with Cubans. You may like it despite the lack of some creature comforts. The restaurant has a special way of preparing goat. *Calle Van Horne 1,* ☎ *824 13. 67 rooms, some with bath and air-conditioning. Restaurant, bar, shop.*

$ Gran Hotel. This somewhat traditional hotel is right in the heart of Camagüey. *Calle Masco 67, e/Agramonte y General Gomez,* ☎ *92093.*

Santa Lucía
DINING

$$ La Casa de Argélico. If you're spending a few days on the beach, try this affordable eatery. A lobster lunch will cost you about $20. *Playa Santa Lucía, Nuevitas.*

$ King Fish. Near the beach in a little village of painted wooden houses at the end of Playa Santa Lucía, the tiny, unpretentious King Fish serves simple seafood dishes. *Playa Santa Lucía, Nuevitas.*

DINING AND LODGING

$$ Club Amigo Mayanabo. Although it was one of the first hotels geared for international tourists (it opened in the 1970s), the Club Amigo has been relatively well maintained. *Playa Santa Lucía, Nuevitas,* ☎ *36184 or 36185. 225 rooms with bath and air-conditioning. Restaurant, bar, pool, sports facilities, horseback tours, diving classes, store, car rental, tourist bus.*

$$ Golden Tulip Club Caracol. Opened in November 1991, this establish-
★ ment consists of a cluster of small buildings next to some prime beach. *Playa Santa Lucía, Nuevitas,* ☎ *335043. 150 rooms with bath and air-conditioning. Restaurant, bar, pool, hairdresser, sports facilities, horseback tours, diving classes, stores, discotheque, car rental, tourist office.*

$$ Golden Tulip Club Coral. This hotel complex next to the Golden Tulip Club Caracol is very modern. Like its neighbor, it has many amenities. *Playa Santa Lucía, Nuevitas,* ☎ *6265, 36347, or 36109. 298 rooms with bath and air-conditioning. Restaurant, bar, pool, sports facilities, horseback outings, diving classes, shop, discotheque, car rental, tourist office.*

$ Cubanacán Tararaco. At this modest motel-like accommodation, be sure to ask for one of the 26 rooms that have sea views. *Playa Santa Lucía, Nuevitas,* ☎ *36222 or 36310. 56 rooms with bath and air-condition-ing. Restaurant, bar, diving lessons, store, open-air cabaret, car rental, tourist office.*

$ Hotel Cuatro Vientos. This place is modest, but you can't beat its location on the beach. *Playa Santa Lucía, Nuevitas,* ☎ *33 54 33.*

4 Eastern Cuba

FROM HOLGUÍN TO GUARDALAVACA

The tourist brochures on Holguín boast that this area has the oldest tradition of tourism in Cuba. The pamphlets go on to cheekily explain that the first "tourist" in Cuban history arrived here on October 27, 1492—the day that Christopher Columbus sailed into Bariay Cove and discovered Cuba on his first voyage to America. The bay where he anchored is now part of Bariay National Park, a huge reserve that stretches from the town of Gibara to Nipe Bay. It includes 35 beaches—among them the beautiful Guardalavaca—and all the little islands along the coast.

Numbers in the margin correspond to points of interest on the Eastern Cuba and Exploring Santiago de Cuba maps.

Exploring

❶ Not only is the provincial capital of **Holguín** a good place from which to explore the eastern beaches, but it gives you a chance to see a typical Cuban city—one that's relatively free of the trappings of tourism. When the heat of the day has passed, the people of Holguín head for the **Plaza Calixto García**, the hub of local life. It's ringed with colonial houses, and behind their colonnades are traditional shops, bookstores, a library, a museum, photographers' studios, and the Casa de la Trova (Music Society). The most noteworthy building is the **Museo Municipal de Historia** (Municipal History Museum). Built in 1862 as a dwelling and grocery store, it later became the headquarters of the municipal government. It is popularly known as La Periquera (the Parakeet House), a name it has borne ever since Cuba's first War of Independence, when it sheltered Spanish soldiers during a rebel attack. The Spaniards wore green uniforms, and behind the building's barred windows they looked like parakeets in a cage. The museum is devoted to the history of the town and the island from pre-Columbian times to the present. *Calle Frexes.* ⊘ *Tues.–Sun. noon–7.*

Two other nearby museums are the **Carlos de la Torre Natural History Museum** (Calle Maceo), with an outstanding collection of shells, and the **birthplace of Calixto García** (Intersection of Calle Frexes and Calle Miró), which has exhibits on the life of this general in the War of Independence. The **Plaza de la Revolución** also bears the name of Calixto García, and it is adorned with a mausoleum containing his remains and a large bronze statue. This square is where large meetings and celebrations are held.

For a panoramic view of Holguín, climb the **Loma de la Cruz** (Hill of the Cross). By car, take the road that runs around and through the outskirts of town; on foot, you can climb up the 450 steps. There's a lookout with a cross, which gives the hill its name—the first one was placed here in 1790. The hilltop is the site of a religious festival on May 3, and affords a splendid view of the entire city spread out below you.

Another excellent view is from the **Altura de Mayabe** (Mayabe Heights), a hill 8 km (5 mi) from the city. From here you can see the entire Mayabe Valley, with its immense palm groves, cultivated fields, and huts scattered hither and yon. On these slopes is a tourist area with a fine replica of a **peasant dwelling**. Inside are the furnishings and tools found in a traditional Cuban house. There is also a small farm, with 15 different kinds of animals and 23 varieties of fruit trees. (If you have the stomach for it, you can select the animal you wish to eat). During meals there's a floor show of traditional songs and dances.

Eastern Cuba

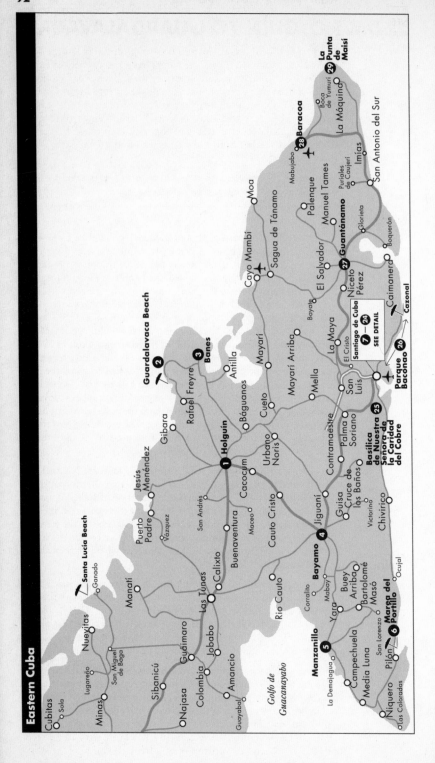

Cubitas
Sola

Lugareño
San Miguel de Baga
Minas
Nuevitas
Sibanicú
Guáimaro
Najasa
Colombia
Jobabo
Amancio
Guayabal

Santa Lucía Beach

Manatí
Puerto Padre
Jesús Menéndez
Vázquez
San Andrés
Las Tunas
Calixto
Buenaventura
Maceo
Cauto Cristo
Río Cauto

Golfo de Guacanayabo

La Demajagua
Manzanillo **5**
Campechuela
Media Luna
Niquero
Las Coloradas
Pilón **6**
San Lorenzo
Masó
Bartolomé
Buey Arriba
Mabay
Corralito
Yara

Bayamo **4**
Marea del Portillo **6**
Ocujal

Gibara
Rafael Freyre
Banes **3**
Guardalavaca Beach
2

Báguanos
Cueto
Antilla
Mayarí
Cacocum
Urbano Noris
Holguín **1**

Jiguaní
Guisa
Cruce de los Baños
Victorino
Chivirico

Cauto
Moa
Sagua de Tánamo
Cayo Mambí

Mayarí Arriba
Mella
San Luis
Palma Soriano
Contramaestre

Basílica de Nuestra Señora de la Caridad del Cobre
25

Palenque
Manuel Tames
El Salvador
La Maya
El Cristo
Bayate

Baracoa **28**
Mabujabo
Boca de Yumurí
La Máquina

La Punta de Maisí **29**

San Antonio del Sur
Imías
Puriales de Caujerí
San Antonio del Sur
Guantánamo **27**
Niceto Pérez
Glorieta
Boquerón
Caimanera

Cazonal
Parque Baconao **26**

Santiago de Cuba
7 — **24**
SEE DETAIL

NEED A
BREAK?
In the tourist complex Mirador de Mayabe look for the **Taberna de Pancho** (Pancho's Tavern). Its most startling feature is the presence of Pancho himself, a donkey with a marked weakness for beer. His record is 46 bottles in one day. The house specialties are sausages and cracklings, washed down with beer. There are two sittings for lunch, at noon and at 2 (to the accompaniment of a trio), and another two for dinner, at 6 and 8 (with mariachis). *Altura de Mayabe.*

From Holguín it is 50 km (31 mi) to Guardalavaca along a road that winds through farmland and small towns. The most interesting feature of the countryside is the **Silla de Gibara** (Saddle of Gibara), a curiously shaped mountain reminiscent of a saddle that Columbus described in his journal. Nearby is where the explorer first sighted the coast of Cuba. When you come to Rafael Freyre, turn left to visit the **monument** that marks the exact spot, on the shore of a narrow bay of coral rock. In fact, there are two monuments. Some years ago a smaller one with a commemorative plaque was erected where it was thought that Columbus landed. It is now believed that he actually first set foot on land across the cove, and a new monument, a series of truncated columns, is being constructed at the site. The road leading to it is in terrible condition in spots, so unless you have a consuming interest in history, skip this trip. Nearby is the **Playa Don Lino,** a small stretch of white sand with a grove of wild grapes behind it. It is a quiet place (there's one small hotel) protected by two coral reefs.

2 Back on the main road, you soon come to the beach of **Guardalavaca.** This large shelf of sand runs along the edge of a sea tinted every possible shade of blue. The beach also has many trees that provide welcome shade. Although Guardalavaca is not as well known as other Cuban beach areas (most of the visitors here are on package tours from Canada and Germany), it is undergoing major development. In a few years, it may well become a principal tourist destination.

3 Either return to Holguín or continue 20 km (12 mi) southeast of Guardalavaca to the small town of **Banes.** At least a third of Cuba's archaeological riches have been discovered in Holguín Province, notably in Banes, where you'll find the **Museo Indocuban,** a comprehensive museum devoted to the aboriginal culture. Among its treasures are a large collection of ceramics as well as jewelry and other objects often made of shells, bone, clay, and stone. The most interesting piece is a solid-gold human figurine 4 centimeters (1¾ inches) high.

Dining and Lodging

For details on price categories, *see* the charts *in* On the Road with Fodor's at the front of this guide.

Guardalavaca

DINING

$ **El Ancla (the Anchor), El Patio, and El Cayuelo (the Islet).** These three restaurants are part of the Guardalavaca tourist complex, though they are not in any of the hotels. All are relatively new and offer a good selection of local dishes in which, not surprisingly, seafood is often the main ingredient. *Playa Guardalavaca, Banes.*

DINING AND LODGING

$$$ **Cubanacán Atlántico.** The comfortable, modern Atlántico has outstanding amenities, including a restaurant that serves good Italian and shellfish dishes. *Playa Guardalavaca, Banes,* ☎ *30180. 233 rooms with bath and air-conditioning. Restaurant, bar, pool, beach sports, horseback tours, shop, game room, car rental, tourist office.*

\$\$\$ **Cubanacán Guardalavaca.** The rooms are in bungalows grouped around the pool. Opened in 1991, the entire complex is attractive and gleaming. The only drawback is that it is not right on the beach. *Playa Guardalavaca, Banes,* ☎ *30221 and 30121 to 30124. 136 rooms with bath and air-conditioning. Restaurant, bar, pool, beach sports, horseback tours, shop, car rental, tourist office.*

\$\$ **Cubanacán Turey.** This Cubanacán establishment is right on the beach. *Playa Guardalavaca, Banes,* ☎ *30195 to 30197.*

\$ **Hotel Gaviota Marina de Naranjo.** Although it's somewhat outside the main tourist area, this hotel is within easy reach of the beach. *Carretera a Guardalavaca, Bahía de Naranjos,* ☎ *25395.*

\$ **Río de Mares Sol Meliá.** Also somewhat removed from the action at Guardalavaca, the Río de Mares is on Playa Estero Ciego (Blind Inlet Beach). *Carretera a Guardalavaca, Playa Estero Ciego,* ☎ *30102 or 30115,* FAX *33557.*

Two other affordable lodging options in the area are **Club Río de Luna Sol Meliá** (Carretera a Guardalavaca, Playa Estero Ciego, ☎ 30102 and 30202, FAX 35571) and **Delta Las Brisas Cubanacán** (Playa Guardalavaca, ☎ 33 53 01 and 33 50 73).

Holguín
DINING

\$\$ **Polinesio.** This restaurant is on the 12th floor of one of the city's tallest buildings and has a very good view. The specialties are grilled chicken and pork and Asian dishes such as fried rice. *Av. de los Alamos, e/Garayalde y Pepe Torres.*

\$ **Pico Cristal.** The windows of this restaurant, on the third floor of an office building, overlook the goings-on in Parque Calixto García. The menu leans toward international cuisine. *Calle Libertad y Martí.*

DINING AND LODGING

\$\$ **Hotel Horizontes Pernik.** The name commemorates Georgi Dimitrov, a national hero born in Pernik, Bulgaria. Although the hotel's size and its impressive marble foyer truly seem to honor Georgi, its poorly maintained facilities and so-so restaurant would make him less than proud. *Av. Jorge Dimitrov y Av. XX Aniversario,* ☎ *48 10 11 or 48 10 81. 202 rooms with bath and air-conditioning. Restaurant, bar, pool, hairdresser, shop, nightclub, car rental, tourist office.*

\$ **El Bosque.** Much smaller than the nearby Pernick, the Bosque makes up for its lack of size with a terrific discotheque, El Pétalo. Don't miss the floor show here. *Av. XX Aniversario,* ☎ *40 11 40. 69 cabins with bath and air-conditioning. Restaurant, bar, pool, hairdresser, shops, nightclub.*

Mayabe
DINING AND LODGING

\$ **Hotel Horizontes Mirador de Mayabe.** The hotel consists of a cluster
★ of cabins atop a hill; from several spots there are excellent views of the valley. This is a favorite Cuban honeymoon spot. One house has four bedrooms and all of the amenities. *Loma de Mayabe, La Cuaba,* ☎ *42660 and 42 21 60. 20 cabins and 1 house with bath and air-conditioning. Restaurant, bar, pool, shop, nightclub.*

Playa Blanca
DINING AND LODGING

\$\$ **Villa Don Lino.** On a small beach with the whitest sand imaginable, this spot is perfect for those who want little more than to flop on the beach. *Playa Blanca, Rafael Freyre,* ☎ *4977. 145 rooms with bath,* *half with air-conditioning. Restaurant, bar, pool, skin diving, horse-back tours, shop, game room, car rental, tourist office.*

Cayo Saetía

On this key at the end of a virgin beach, you can lay your weary head to rest at **Cayo Saetía Gaviota.** *Cayo Saetía, Mayan,* ☎ *25350,* ℻ *33 55 71.*

FROM BAYAMO TO MAREA DEL PORTILLO

Some of the most important events in the last 200 years of Cuban history—particularly those related to the 1868 revolution and to Fidel Castro—took place in Granma Province. In 1956, Castro and his guerrillas landed on Las Coloradas beach after their voyage from Mexico on the yacht *Granma,* hence the province's current name. The region's varied terrain features the broad flatlands of the Cauto River, the longest in Cuba, as well as some of the highest peaks in the Sierra Maestra. In the south, the mountains run to the sea, creating a very bold coastline.

Exploring

Bayamo

The second town founded in Cuba by the Spaniards under the command of Diego Velázquez, called San Salvador, was established beside the Yara River, but as was the case with six of his seven foundings, it was moved not long afterward. The church and the town council, the two crucial elements of colonial towns, were moved to the native village of Bayamo, which then became San Salvador de Bayamo (today it's known as Bayamo). It was from here that Velázquez set forth to capture the rest of the island.

Commercial restrictions imposed by the Spanish Crown in the 16th century led to large-scale traffic in contraband, and Bayamo was a very active center for such trade. Fabrics and manufactured goods from France and the Netherlands were exchanged for meat, leather, and indigo. By the end of the 16th century, Bayamo's brisk business and its location far enough inland to avoid pirate attacks made it a very prosperous place indeed. In 1603, when the island's governor decided to suppress trade in contraband, he discovered that most of the city's residents and local authorities were directly involved in it.

Despite its age and historical importance, there are not many old structures in Bayamo. A fire in 1869 almost completely destroyed the city. It was started by the inhabitants themselves, to prevent the town's capture by Spanish troops in the first War of Independence.

❹ There's no better way to get the feel of **Bayamo** than a **horse-drawn carriage ride.** Owing to the scarcity of gasoline, folks in Bayamo often use carriages for everyday transportation—even the police employ them. Directly descended from the trap, these carriages are typical of the area.

Begin your tour at **Plaza de la Revolución.** Surrounded by important historical buildings, museums, and traditional shops, it is a good place to take the city's pulse amid the bustle of the locals. A statue of Carlos Manuel de Céspedes, the father of the country, stands in the center of the square, as does a small bust of Perucho Figueredo, who wrote the words to the national anthem. It was at the sugar mill in La Demajagua (☞ On the Road to Marea Del Portillo, *below*), not far from Manzanillo, that Céspedes proclaimed Cuba's independence and the abolition of slavery, the event that finally sparked the 1868 revolution. One of the first acts of insurrection was the capture of Bayamo, which became the provisional capital of the defiant republic. Céspedes signed the decree abolishing slavery in the **town hall** on the Plaza de la Revolución.

Céspedes's birthplace is also on the square and, in 1968, on the 100th anniversary of his declaration at La Demajagua, it was turned into a museum. Various documents, personal effects, and mementos of his life and participation in the War of Independence are exhibited in its 12 rooms. There are also displays relating the history of Bayamo and a portion of the printing press used to put out the *Cubano Libre* (*Free Cuban*), a newspaper Céspedes established after he took the city. Several lovely pieces of period 19th-century furniture are also on view. The building is the only two-story structure to have survived the fire in 1869. ☞ *Free.* ⊙ *Tues.–Sat. 1–8, Sun. 1–5.*

When you leave Céspedes's house, turn right to reach the **Museo Provincial de Granma,** which covers the history, geography, and the natural sciences of the province. It is housed in the birthplace of Manuel Muñoz, composer of the national anthem and *La Bayamesa,* Bayamo's most popular traditional song.

The same street takes you to the **Iglesia de San Salvador.** Originally built in 1613, the church has been repeatedly destroyed and rebuilt. The oldest part is the Dolores Chapel, which was consecrated in 1740 and has a Baroque altarpiece. Tradition has it that when Céspedes entered Bayamo in triumph on October 20, 1868, the ensuing rally in the square in front of the church inspired Perucho Figueredo to write the words for the national anthem. For that reason the square has since been known as the **Plaza del Himno** (Anthem Square). Despite its small size, it is one of the most attractive spots in the city.

On one corner of the square, at No. 36, is the **Casa de la Nacionalidad Cubana.** The building is more than 100 years old and houses a center for research into the city's history and the traits that define the national character. Although it's not open to the public, a polite request may get you a quick look around. The antique furniture is interesting, as is the structure itself; its patio provides a splendid view over the Bayamo River far below.

NEED A BREAK?	In the Plaza del Himno there are two places to rest your legs and have something to drink. Next to the Casa de la Nacionalidad is the **Bodega de Atocha,** where you can sample local wine. A little farther on is **La Casona,** which offers fruit juices, tea, and coffee as well as donuts and bar snacks.

Bayamo has something of a musical tradition. In the 19th century, popular songs were composed here to be sung by ardent swains beneath the windows of their sweethearts. One of the places always included in a horse-and-carriage tour is the **Ventana de Luz Vázquez.** The story goes that it was under this window, on March 27, 1851, that *La Bayamesa,* one of Cuba's best-known songs, was sung for the very first time.

Leaving the old quarter, you cannot miss the **Plaza de la Patria,** an immense space intended for large popular rallies. It is dominated by a sculpture—the work of Jorge Delarra—that depicts key figures in Cuban history, from Céspedes and Maceo to Celia Sánchez Manduley and Frank País.

On the Road to Marea del Portillo

From Bayamo, you can explore the province along the southwest coast to the beach at Marea del Portillo, famous for its black sands. On the way you pass through one of Cuba's most traditional regions, full of sugarcane plantations in which some of the more decisive events in Cuban history took place. The road to Manzanillo passes through the town of **Yara,** where Diego Velázquez first founded San Salvador (☞ Bayamo, *above*).

OFF THE
BEATEN PATH

SIERRA MAESTRA – If you have a four-wheel-drive vehicle, make a side trip into the Sierra Maestra by way of Bartolomé Masó. The region contains some of Cuba's highest mountains and some of its most isolated countryside—the perfect place for young revolutionaries to hide out. Stop by **La Plata,** Fidel Castro's headquarters during his time in the Sierra Maestra. The long road from Bartolomé Masó goes through Providencia, El Salto, and Santo Domingo.

⑤ From Yara you can take the well-maintained main route to **Manzanillo,** the second-largest city in the province and one that owes its livelihood to its port. The city's most important monument is **La Glorieta,** in Parque Céspedes, one of the town's two main rendezvous spots. The other, Parque Bartolomé Masó, opens onto the bay and is especially active in the evening.

About 10 km (6 mi) outside Manzanillo, farther along the road to Marea del Portillo, you'll come to the turnoff for **La Parque Nacional Demajagua.** (There are few signs, so ask for directions along the way.) This former hacienda and sugar mill belonged to Céspedes, and it was here, on October 10, 1868, that this wealthy landowner first proclaimed Cuba's independence and the abolition of slavery. Among the objects displayed are the bell used to summon the slaves, a few archaeological finds, and some photographs and historical documents.

Back on the main route from Manzanillo to Marea del Portillo, the road hugs the coast, and mountains rise sharply to your left. It takes you through the town of Media Luna and then turns inland. A detour to the right goes to Niquero and the Las Coloradas beach, where the revolutionaries on the *Granma* put ashore. This is the southwesternmost point in the province—a very hot, dry area. Among the points of interest on this detour are some pre-Colombian archaeological sites, including a cave containing an idol carved from a stalagmite; the Santa Cruz lighthouse, 33 meters (108 feet) high and built in 1877; and marine terraces that rise in layers from sea level to more than 200 meters (655 feet) up. In addition, here—as along the rest of the route to Marea del Portillo—the adventures of the *Granma* expedition are commemorated at every turn.

Marea del Portillo

★ **⑥** If you continue along the main road, bypassing the detour to Niquero, you end up in the town of Pilón and, 19 km (12 mi) farther on, at **Marea del Portillo.** At Pilón the road returns to the coast, snaking its way between the mountains and the sea. At every turn, there are little coves (swimming in them is not recommended). Marea del Portillo has a 1-km-long (½-mi) beach in a small, protected bay. The black sands here create a very different feeling from that of most Caribbean beaches. Two hotels—one recently opened—can fulfill all your needs.

Dining and Lodging

For details on price categories, *see* the charts *in* On the Road with Fodor's at the front of this guide.

Bayamo
DINING AND LODGING

$$ Hotel Sierra Maestra. With its many amenities, this hotel ought to be Bayamo's best hotel. Unfortunately, though, the service here is not very good. *Carretera Central, Km 7.5,* ☎ *48 10 13. 204 rooms with bath and air-conditioning. Restaurant, bar, pool, shop, nightclub, tourist office.*

$$ Villa Bayamo. Although far from the center of town, this complex is
★ a reasonable alternative to the Sierra Maestra. The restaurant, El Tamarindo, specializes in pork roasted on a spit. *Carretera via Manzanillo and Mabay Road, Bayamo,* ☎ *42 31 02. 12 rooms and 12 cabins with bath, telephone, and air-conditioning. Restaurant, bar, pool, sports facilities, nightclub.*

Manzanillo
DINING AND LODGING

$ Guacanayabo. Right on the shore, all the Guacanayabo's rooms have bay views. *Av. Camilo Cienfuegos,* ☎ *5–4012. 104 rooms and 8 suites with bath and air-conditioning. Restaurant, bar, pool, shop.*

Marea del Portillo
DINING AND LODGING

$$ Hotel and Bungalows Marea del Portillo Commonwealth. This complex sits next to one of Cuba's warmest beaches. Its choice location makes it popular with tour groups. *Carretera a Pilón, Km 14, Pilón,* ☎ *59 42 01 to 59 42 03. 74 rooms and 56 bungalows with bath and air-conditioning. Restaurant, bar, pool, sports facilities, tourist office.*

Santo Domingo
DINING AND LODGING

$ Horizontes Villa Santo Domingo. In the heart of the Sierra Maestra, this campground is a good base for those who wish to hike to the command post at La Plata. *Parque Nacional Turquino, Municipio Barolomé Masó, Santo Domingo,* ☎ *059–5180. 20 cabins with bath and air-conditioning. Restaurant, bar, horse rental.*

Nightlife

Bayamo
Cabaret Bayam. The Bayam is one of the biggest indoor cabarets in Cuba. It offers dinner, a floor show, and dancing. Make your reservations at the tourist office in the Hotel Sierra Maestra, which is right across the way. The cover (drink included) is $44.50.

SANTIAGO DE CUBA

Santiago may be the most Caribbean city in Cuba. Because of its location, it has always been more closely linked with the other islands in the Greater Antilles than with Havana. Many of its inhabitants came from other parts of the Caribbean; indeed, the African slaves and French who fled Haiti after the revolution there have contributed a great deal to Santiago's history. Now this cosmopolitan city hosts the annual Caribbean Festival, which has participants from all the countries bathed by Caribbean waters.

With more than 400,000 inhabitants, Santiago is the second-largest city on the island. It was the capital until 1589, when—as a reflection of the growing importance of the western end of the country—Havana took its place. The city was founded in 1514 by the island's first governor, Diego Velázquez, and is thus the second-oldest city after Baracoa. At the head of a perfectly protected bay, it occupied a strategic position in the North Caribbean and was of particular importance in colonial times. Its proximity to Santo Domingo, once the capital of the West Indies, further enhanced its standing. In fact, owing to poor internal communications, it was for a long time more closely linked to the island of Hispaniola—now Haiti and the Dominican Republic—and to portions of South America than to the rest of Cuba.

Santiago is the only Cuban city that has the designation Ciudad Héroe (Heroic City), because of the role it played in the wars of independence and in the revolution. Antonio Maceo, one of the leaders of the 19th-century struggle for independence, was born here, and José Martí, the national hero, is buried here. The attack on the Moncada Barracks in 1953, even though a military failure, was one of the decisive events in Fidel Castro's rise to power.

Exploring

Tour 1: The Center of Santiago

❼ Start your walking tour at **Parque Céspedes**, a lively square where the locals run into everyone they know sooner or later. In the center there's a monument to Carlos Manuel Céspedes, the "Father of the Country," and around the square there are several interesting buildings. One side
❽ is taken up by the **cathedral**, which dates from 1523. It's crowned by two white towers, and above its central portal there is an angel of the Annunciation. Inside are the remains of Diego Velázquez and other important personages of the colonial era. The cathedral is not on the same level as the square, but is raised on a terrace below which are shops, including a bookstore; an outlet of the **Fondo de Bienes Culturales** (Cultural Assets Fund); a telephone agency where you can make international phone calls; and the **Heladerí Coppelia**, which serves *pru*—a drink made from various roots and vanilla—in addition to ice cream. The shop with the curtains is for tourists; here your dollars can buy, among other things, toothpaste and detergent.

Proceeding clockwise around the square, the next building houses
❾ **Museo de Ambiente Histórico Cubano** (Museum of Cuban History), with exhibits on the colonial era and an interesting collection of Cuban furniture (also, don't forget to look up at the glorious wooden ceilings). The structure itself was originally a private residence, and, since portions of it were built between 1516 and 1530, it is considered the oldest house in Cuba. Diego Velázquez once lived on the upper floor, and its ground floor has served as the headquarters of the Casa de Contratación (employment agency) and a gold foundry. The remainder of the building dates from the early 19th century. *Calle Félix Pena 612, at Aguilera.* ☉ *Tues.–Sun. 8–noon and 2–6.*

❿ On the next side of the square is the **Ayuntamiento** (Town Hall). The original structure was built by Hernán Cortés, Santiago's first mayor, and it was from the central balcony, on January 1, 1959, that Fidel Castro gave his first speech after Battista's escape. The recently reno-
⓫ vated **Hotel Casagranda** occupies the fourth side of the square. The bar on the second-floor terrace is a good place for a drink and some people-watching. A tourist office and the Oriente Art Gallery are on the ground floor.

At the corner, turn down the lively **Calle Heredia.** During the day there is a continuous parade of passersby and tourists, people on their way

Exploring Santiago de Cuba

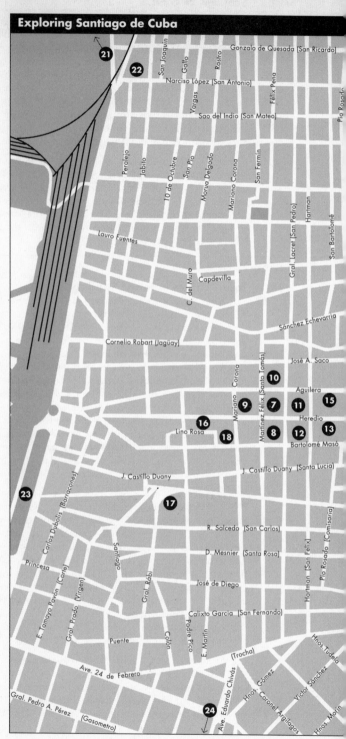

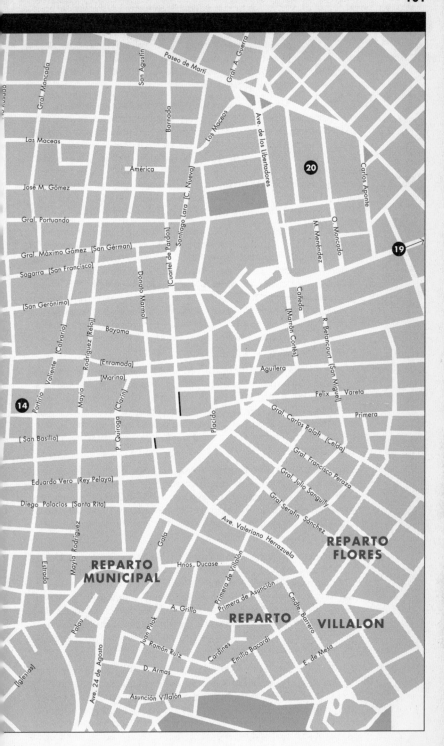

Gral. Moncada

San Agustín

Paseo de Marti

Gral. A. Guerra

Barrrada

Los Maceos

Ave. de los Libertadores

Las Maceas

América

20

José M. Gómez

Carlos Aponte

M. Menéndez

O. Moncado

Gral. Portuando

19

Gral. Máximo Gómez (San Gérman)

Cuartel de Pardos

Santiago Lara (C. Nueva)

Sagarra (San Francisco)

(San Gerónimo)

Cañeda (Marrón Cortés)

Donato Marmol

R. Betancourt (San Miguel)

Bayama

Rodríguez (Reloj)

(Enramada)

Aguilera

Felix

Vareta

(Marino)

Pórfiro Valiente (Calvario)

Mayia

Primera

14

P. Quiroga (Clarín)

Plácido

Gral. Carlos Ralaft (Celda)

(San Basilio)

Gral. Francisco Peraza

Eduardo Vero (Rey Pelayo)

Gral. Julio Sanguily

Diego Palacios (Santa Rita)

Gral. Serafín Sánchez

Ave. Valeriano Herrazuela

REPARTO FLORES

Mayia Rodríguez

Gata

Estrada

REPARTO MUNICIPAL

Hnos. Ducase

Primera de Villalón

A. Grillo

Primera de Asunción

REPARTO

VILLALON

Patau

Juan Plack

Cndte. Barrero

Ramón Ruiz

Cardines

Emilio Bacardí

E. de Mesa

D. Armas

(Iglesias)

Ave. 24 de Agosto

Asunción Villalón

to the Casa de la Trova (☞ *below*), vendors, moneychangers, strollers, and policemen. You can't go far without being asked to exchange your dollars for pesos or to buy cigars. On the weekend, this street hosts the **Noches Culturales de la Calle Heredia** (Cultural Nights of Calle Heredia), during which troubadours, actors, poets, mimes, magicians, and dancers create a vibrant spectacle.

⑫ Farther down Calle Heredia is the well-known **Casa de la Trova,** one of the most attractive places in Santiago and a veritable mecca for lovers of Cuban popular music. Groups or soloists perform here several times a day, attracting large numbers of listeners. Recitals are given on a small stage in a hall that opens directly onto the street; if the few inside seats are taken, you can watch the show from outside. A tiny bar sells drinks, cassettes of groups that have performed here, and even the odd musical instrument. *Calle Heredia 208, e/Hartmann y Lacret.* ✆ *Free. Performances Tues.–Sun. 10–1, 3–4, and 8:30–10.*

Continue along the street to **La Casa del Vino,** a restaurant formerly known as the House of Cheese (imagine what is featured on the menu). You can make reservations from 7 AM on; seatings last 45 minutes, and a doorkeeper oversees the day's reservations and the rigid timetables.
⑬ A little farther along is the **birthplace of José María Heredia,** after whom the street is named. There is a display of the poet's personal effects and a library of works by Santiago authors. A stop here gives you the chance to see a colonial home and admire its large rooms and interior courtyard. Musical events are sometimes held here. *Heredia 260, e/Hartmann y Pío Rosado.* ✆ *Free.* ☺ *Tues.–Sun. 9–5.*

At the intersection with Pío Rosado is **La Minerva,** a small antiques shop that sells furniture, pictures, desktop implements, lamps, and hats, as well as reproductions of cigar bands and tobacco-related objects.
⑭ On the opposite corner is the **Museo del Carnaval,** housing a collection of costumes and musical instruments used by masqueraders during Carnival. *Heredia 303, e/Pío Rosado y Porfirio Valiente. Closed Mon.*

Carnival in Santiago is, perhaps, the most famous of Cuba's three major festivals. For a few days in July, the streets fill with groups of costumed instrumentalists playing traditional music. The beating of drums sets the whole place vibrating, enticing everyone to dance. Conga lines made up of hundreds of people move to the rhythm of the drums and the wail of an occasional Chinese cornet.

The tradition began in colonial times, when it was known as a festival of masks or grotesques and took place on the feast days of Epiphany and Corpus Christi; it later came to be held in July. In the early days, the festival began with a procession of saints followed by groups of musicians playing catchy tunes to which the revelers danced. The music was of African origin and is the direct antecedent of the congas played in today's Carnivals. This African influence is also still apparent in the dances and costumes.

Leave Calle Heredia and turn down Calle Pío Rosado. At the inter-
⑮ section with Aguilera is the **Museo Bacardí,** which was founded in 1899 and is the oldest museum in Cuba. Its diverse collection includes one Egyptian and two Peruvian mummies as well as a number of European paintings. It also exhibits prehistoric Cuban artifacts and the personal effects of nearly all of the heroes of the War of Independence. *Pío Rosado y Aguilera.*

NEED A
BREAK? Step down Aguilera to **La Isabelica** at the intersection with Calvario. This traditional café is where the locals meet for coffee, coffee, and more coffee.

Back on Pío Rosado, continue along and make a left onto Enramada, a commercial street filled with bookstores, pizzerias, hotels, and ice-cream parlors. Walk two blocks down, then turn left on Lacret, which will lead you back to Parque Céspedes. Cut across the square and back to Calle Heredia, this time heading in the opposite direction from before. There are several examples of traditional Santiago architecture, with typical ironwork balconies. In the second block on the left, between Corona and Padre Pico, is the **Casa del Orfeón Santiago,** once the headquarters of a very prestigious choral society. In the foyer there are some lovely 19th-century furnishings. Ask to visit the colonial courtyard, where occasional evening concerts are still presented.

A little farther on, turn left on **Calle Padre Pico.** On the corner is one of the oldest balconies in the city; notice the date 1832 worked into it. With its stone steps leading up the hill, Padre Pico is Santiago's most picturesque street. Along it you will pass some buildings in very bad repair—small wonder, as some of them date from the 16th century. These houses belonged to the French settlers who started the Tívoli Festival, which is still held each year at varying times. In No. 256 there is a barbershop where customers play checkers while waiting their turn.

Climb the steps, and on the right you will see a 19th-century colonial house that is now the **Museo de la Lucha Clandestina** (Museum of the Clandestine Struggle). You may well find the building itself more interesting than the documents and photographs displayed inside. From this corner, however, there's a good view of the bay. *General Jesús Rabí 1. Closed Mon.*

Return to the stairs but don't go down; take the next street instead. In the pavement of Calle Corona you can still see the trolley tracks, unused since 1953. You'll notice some arches on the corner of Calle Bartolomé Masó. Pass through them and you will find yourself in a small open square called the **Balcón de Velázquez,** another spot with an outstanding view of the bay. At one time, authorities were stationed here to track the arrival and departure of ships. It now serves as the setting for weekend performances of the Peña del Tango (Tango Club). Continue a block down and turn right, and you're back in Parque Céspedes.

Tour 2: From the Hotel Santiago to El Morro

For this tour you'll need a car. Start across from the **Hotel Cubanacán Santiago,** the city's most luxurious hotel. If you're not staying here, at least take a peek inside; its modern design and bright colors have made it a landmark. If you follow **Avenida de las Américas**—a wide, fast street—you pass the **Bosque de los Héroes** (Forest of the Heroes), a monument commemorating Che Guevara and his Bolivian guerrillas. Farther along is the huge **Teatro Heredia,** opened in 1991. To conserve electricity, the theater presents performances only four times a month, but it organizes other events outdoors. On weekends its café has live music. Close by, in the **Plaza de la Revolución,** there is an immense **monument to Antonio Maceo,** one of the heroes of the War of Independence.

Turn left just before the monument and continue along the same street for a few minutes. You may need to ask for directions to the **Moncada Barracks,** for there are not many signs. The attack by Fidel Castro and his men on this, the country's second-most important military installation, was a crucial event in the revolution. It now houses the **Museo**

Histórico 26 de Julio, devoted to both the 19th-century War of Independence and the guerrilla fighters of the 1950s. You can still see bullet holes on the exterior. *Calle General Portuondo at Moncada. Closed Mon.*

Take Calle Moncada, then turn left on Paseo Martí and follow it all the way to the end. Along the way you'll pass the **Bacardí bottle,** a huge replica of a bottle of rum. Your goal is the **Fortín de Yarayó,** a small fort built on what was once the bank of the Yarayó River. This was the first of 116 fortifications the Spaniards built around the city. Turn ㉑ left, and follow Avenida Combret to the **Cementerio de Santa Ifigenia,** where some of Cuba's most notable historic figures are buried, among them José Martí and Carlos Manuel de Céspedes.

Retrace your route and turn right on Jesús Menéndez. There you will ㉒ see the oldest **rum distillery** in Cuba. Bacardi was originally made here, but because of patent restrictions the rum is now called "Havana Club." (Note that this spelling of Havana is not a nod to the English-speaking market but rather the original colonial form of the name; the *v* was only later changed to a *b*.) Official figures indicate that 60% of the 9 million liters (2.4 million gallons) made here each year goes to Canada and Spain; the rest is consumed in Cuba. You can visit the distillery, but taking photographs inside is not permitted. The on-site shop is the only place on the island where you can buy 15- to 20-year-old rum. *Jesús Menéndez e/San Antonio y San Ricardo.* ⊙ *Mon.–Sat. 9–6, Sun. 9–noon.*

Continuing along Jesús Menéndez you pass the **train station** (its original 19th-century tracks are still in place), the **customs building,** a **to-** ㉓ **bacco factory,** and the **Parque de la Alameda,** which overlooks the bay. Two blocks beyond the park, turn left on Avenida 24 de Febrero, also known as **La Trocha.** These streets, with their turn-of-the-century wooden houses, comprise the Old Quarter. It was here, in what is still considered the cradle of Carnival, that the slaves were permitted to hold their annual revels. Turn right on Avenida Eduardo Chivás, which becomes the road to Castillo del Morro, 8 km (5 mi) away.

NEED A BREAK?	Just before the entrance to the fortress you'll see **La Taberna del Morro,** a pleasant, airy bar-restaurant. Treat yourself to a *morro helado,* the special cocktail of the house. It is a blend of rum, ice, and lemon beaten with egg white—all seasoned with a pinch of cinnamon and a dash of Angostura bitters.

㉔ The **Castillo del Morro,** or El Morro, dominates a bluff that overlooks the entrance to the bay. The fortress was built in the 17th century, during the governorship of Pedro de la Roca, to protect the city from pirate attacks—a constant threat. The Italian architect Antonelli supplied the plans. In 1662 the fortress was besieged by the pirate Henry Morgan, and when it was rebuilt, three additional fortifications were added: La Estrella, Santa Catalina, and La Punta. El Morro is considered one of the most beautiful fortresses in the Americas and is certainly the most impressive structure in Santiago. It also houses the **Museo de la Piratería** (Piracy Museum). Only a part of the museum is devoted to the yo-ho-ho-and-a-bottle-of-rum sort of pirates that figure so prominently in Cuba's history; the rest focuses on "contemporary piracy," with an emphasis on predatory military intervention by the United States.

You enter the fortress in the most traditional of ways: along a drawbridge over the moat. There follows a series of connecting rooms with thick walls. It's difficult to get your bearings at first, as the fortress is a virtual labyrinth, however the caretakers will steer you in the right direction. Some rooms are given over to the museum, others are empty, and still others have been sealed for centuries—no one knows what they might contain. Don't forget to check out the view from the terrace. *Castillo del Morro.* ▨ *$1.* ⊘ *Weekdays 9–5, weekends 8–4.*

Tour 3: La Basilica del Cobre

La Virgen de la Caridad del Cobre (Virgin of Charity of Cobre) is Cuba's patron saint, and her basilica is an important pilgrimage site. If your stay in Santiago is brief, this short excursion is the perfect way to see a little of the city's environs. In Santiago, take either the Avenida de los Libertadores or Avenida de las Américas. Where the two intersect, turn right onto the Carretera Central in the direction of Palma Soriano and Bayamo. On the left you'll pass the Universidad de Oriente (University of the East), which has an archaeological museum with displays on the island's indigenous culture. As the road leaves the city it begins a gentle ascent into the surrounding hills. After approximately 16 km (10 mi), you will reach the turnoff to the town of El Cobre, 2 km (1 mi) away. From the distance you can see the basilica atop a small hill, with the foothills of the Sierra Maestra behind it.

㉕ El Cobre got its name from the *cobre* (copper) mining in the area, an industry that has been active here since 1550. The biggest slave rebellion in Cuba also occurred here in 1731. The **Basilica de Nuestra Señora de la Caridad del Cobre** has been the country's most important pilgrimage site since 1916, when this Virgin was named the patron saint. The story of the Virgin, however, dates from much earlier. In 1608, three mine workers went to the Bay of Nipe, on the north coast, to collect salt. One of them, only 10 at the time, later described what befell them. From their boat they spied something floating in the water. Upon investigation they found a small statue of the Virgin on a wooden base with the inscription: I AM THE VIRGIN OF CHARITY. They took the figure back with them to El Cobre. Since the altars in the town's church were already dedicated to other saints, it was decided to build a small chapel for the statue outside of town. In the years that followed, the statue disappeared three times, always reappearing atop a hill overlooking the town and the mine. During this time, the Virgin also became known for her miraculous powers, and when the old church was replaced with a new one, she was given pride of place on the main altar (replacing Santiago el Mayor or St. James the Great). She is often associated with Ochún—one of the most powerful goddesses of the Yoruba pantheon—and plays a major role in the rites of Santería, the religion brought to Cuba by African slaves.

The present church, built in 1927, is the only basilica in Cuba. A long staircase flanked by street lamps leads to it. Its central tower is topped by a red cupola, and its interior is bathed in light filtered through stained-glass windows. In a niche high up on the wall to the right of the altar stands the Virgin, and pilgrims leave their floral and votive offerings below. On the Virgin's feast day, September 8, there is a huge gathering of the faithful. The basilica is normally open from 6 to noon and from 1 to 6. Given the long lines outside of local restaurants, it's good to pack a lunch before setting out.

Tour 4: Parque Baconao

㉖ **Baconao,** the largest park in Cuba, stretches from the outskirts of Santiago to Baconao Lagoon, from the Sierra Maestra to the Caribbean. It comprises a long series of beaches with hotels and restaurants, a Mesoamerican archaeology museum, a cactus garden, an underwater aquarium, and numerous monuments. One section has been designated by UNESCO as a Natural Biosphere Preserve. The park was originally conceived as a recreation center for the people of Santiago, but it is now being developed for international tourism as well.

From the Hotel Santiago, take the Avenida de las Américas and then go straight down Avenida Pujol. As you reach the outskirts of town you will see the **Loma de San Juan** (San Juan Hill)—site of the last battle of the War of Independence—on your right. At the foot of the hill, built around a small Spanish fortress, is the Leningrad Motel. Right beside the road is an enormous **ceiba tree.** Beneath its branches, on June 16, 1898, the Spanish troops surrendered to the United States Army in a ceremony that included not a single Cuban. At the top of the hill there is a park containing a number of statues, some dedicated to the *mambises*—the soldiers who fought for Cuba's independence—and some to the American soldiers who participated in the war. The ceiba tree marks the beginning of Baconao Park.

The road continues through the countryside for several kilometers, passing small towns, cultivated fields with isolated houses, and the Oasis artist colony. At regular intervals along this route, from Santiago to Granjita Siboney, there are monuments to those who died in the assault on Moncada Barracks in July 1953. There are 26 monuments in all—20 on the right and 6 on the left—each inscribed with the names and professions of several of the fallen.

About 10 km (6 mi) from Santiago, before you reach Granjita Siboney, there is a well-marked turnoff for the **Gran Piedra,** a 1,200-meter-high (3,900-foot-high) granite outcropping from which you can see Haiti and Jamaica on a clear day. The road rises steeply, and little by little the vegetation changes. At the end of the road there is a motel; from here to the top you have to climb a long flight of stairs. Having come this far, you should visit the **Museo La Isabelica,** built in the ruins of a typical coffee plantation house, 2 km (1 mi) from the motel. This eastern region of Cuba was populated by Frenchmen who fled Haiti after the revolution there and became coffee farmers. The museum depicts life on one of these coffee plantations. Outside are the drying sheds, the bake house, and an aqueduct. *Carretera de la Gran Piedra, Km 14.* ⊗ *Tues.–Sat. 8–4, Sun. 8–noon.*

Thirteen kilometers (8 mi) from Santiago is the **Museo Histórico Granjita Siboney,** once a small farm that was used as a rendezvous point for the guerrillas who took part in the assault on Moncada Barracks. Today, the museum here displays a few arms and articles of clothing as well as photographs and newspaper clippings. *Carretera de Siboney, Km 13.5.* ⊗ *Tues.–Sun. 9–5.*

Nine kilometers (6 mi) farther on, you come to the **Damajayabo Valley,** also known as the **Valle de la Prehistória,** and its amazing life-size sculptures of animals—243 of them—from different eras. To the left are Mesozoic creatures, including a stupendous brontosaurus. To the right are animals from the Cenozoic, with one grouping depicting the evolution of the horse. A little farther along, next to the parking lot, is a Cro-Magnon man some 12 meters (39 feet) tall. Animal figures from the Paleozoic are distributed in the back. Behind the Cro-Magnon man there is a small cafeteria—where, with pesos, you can buy bottles of Havana Club—and beyond that a section devoted to the Quaternary epoch and the ancestors of Homo sapiens. On the left side of the road is a museum of natural science, with seven rooms given over to the evolution of the different species. All of the sculptures are made of reinforced concrete molded over wooden frames. The largest, diplodocus, is 27 meters (89 feet) long. *Valle de la Prehistória, Carretera de Baconao, Km 22.* ⊗ *Tues.–Sun. 8–5.*

From here on, the road closely follows the coast with its unique marine terraces rising like giant steps. On the right is the turnoff for **Playa de Daiquirí.** If you take it, you pass through fields of sugarcane and come to what remains of the railway used to transport ore from the Daiquirí mines. Tradition has it that a particularly refreshing drink was invented here to slake the thirst of the miners. Over time—and with the definite improvement of adding crushed ice—it became the cocktail that has made the name of the mine famous throughout the world. Daiquirí Beach is one of the finest in Baconao Park, and it has an attractive hotel that is the headquarters of the Centro Internacional de Buceo (International Diving Center).

Back on the main road you soon come to a fenced-in, 12-sq-km (7-sq-mi), natural animal preserve (plans are afoot to develop it into a large drive-through zoological park). On the ground just a bit farther along you'll see a picture of the *tocororo,* Cuba's national bird, created using rocks painted in the colors of the Cuban flag. Just beyond this is the entrance to the Balneario del Sol Hotel, beside a **natural pool** formed by a coral reef. Each March and April, thousands of red crabs (inedible but harmless) come down from the mountains to lay their eggs in the sea here and then return inland. By late May and early June, thousands of newborn crabs climb up the beach and make *their* way to the mountains. The migrations last no more than a week.

NEED A BREAK?	At **Playa de Sigua** are the two best restaurants in the park. On the left side of the road is **Los Corales,** specializing in shellfish, and on the right **Pedro el Cojo,** which serves Creole dishes.

The road leads on to the **Jardín de Cactus,** a park containing more than 400 different varieties of succulents. In this area the coral rock once had a number of holes through which water was forced in from below and upward at each great wave; many, however, were damaged during a cyclone. Farther on is the **Jardín Marino,** a natural aquarium. The only way to truly enjoy it is to get down in it. The next beach, **Cazonal,** with fine white sand, has grottoes at one end. The road soon ends in the **estuary of the Baconao River.** Here you see the 4-sq-km (2½-sq-mi) Baconao Lagoon. Here you'll find a crocodile farm, where you can observe the animals in their natural habitat.

Dining and Lodging

For details on price categories, *see* the charts *in* On the Road with Fodor's at the front of this guide.

Playa Baconao

DINING

$ Los Corales. This restaurant, in a house built by the man who owned the mines at Daiquirí, is atop a cliff and has good views of the coast. The house specialty is shellfish. *Playa de Sigua.*

$ Pedro el Cojo. Not far from Los Corales, right on the road and near the beach, this little eatery specializes in Creole dishes, most notably roast pig. *Playa de Sigua,* ☎ *39 81 60 and 39 81 40.* ☺ *Daily noon–midnight.*

DINING AND LODGING

$$$ Club Amigo Bucanero. The recently opened, all-inclusive Club Amigo
★ is on a small beach surrounded by cliffs—an astonishing setting. All rooms have balconies that overlook the sea. *Carretera Baconao-Arroyo-la Costa, Km 4,* ☎ *27126 and 28130. 200 rooms with bath and air-conditioning. Restaurant, bar, pool, sports facilities, shop, nightclub, car rental.*

$$ **Casa de Delta Resort Balneario del Sol.** In front of this hotel you will not find the usual beach (Playa de Sigua is a few hundred meters away) but rather an enormous saltwater pool constructed to take advantage of the reefs. *Carretera Baconao, Km 38.5, ☎ 39 81 13 and 39 81 24. 115 rooms and 24 cabins with bath, most with air-conditioning. Restaurant, 4 bars, 2 pools (1 saltwater, 1 fresh), game room, shop, tourist office.*

$$ **Cubanacán Daiquirí.** You can't beat the location—next to one of the best beaches in Baconao—or the amenities at this modern establishment. A branch of the International Diving Center has its headquarters here. *Carretera Baconao, Km 8.5, ☎ 24844 and 24735. 95 rooms and 62 cabins with bath and air-conditioning. 4 restaurants, 3 bars, 4 grills, 2 pools (1 saltwater, 1 fresh), diving school, sports facilities, shop, car rental.*

$$ **Cubanacán La Gran Piedra.** The hotel sits next to the huge rock that gives it its name. It is a refuge from the heat of summer. *Carretera La Gran Piedra, Km 14, ☎ 5913. 19 suites and 3 bungalows with bath, almost all with air-conditioning. Restaurant, bar, game room, shop, car rental, tourist office.*

$$ **LTI Carisol Resort Hotel.** At this coastal hotel, 52 of the rooms have sea views; the rest look out at the mountains. *Carretera Baconao, Km 10, Playa Cazonal, ☎ 28519 and 27601. 120 rooms with bath and air-conditioning. Restaurant, bar, pool, sports facilities, nightclub, car rental, tourist office.*

Three other affordable options in the region are: **Delta Sierra Mar Club Resort** (Carretera a Chivirico, Km 60, Guamá, ☎ 26436), **Los Galeones Delta Hotels Resort** (International Diving Center, Carretera a Chivinico, ☎ 26160), and **LTI Los Corales Resort Hotel** (Carretera Baconao, Km 10, Playa Cazonal, ☎ 27204 and 27191).

Santiago

DINING

$$ **1900.** If the setting—an old palace bedecked with crystal chandeliers
★ and antique furnishings—doesn't charm you, the outstanding Creole dishes of veal, rabbit, and turkey surely will. *Calle San Basilio 354, e/Pío Rosado y Hartmann, ☎ 23507. ⊙ 7 PM–midnight.*

$$ **Taberna de Dolores.** The Dolores is in an old colonial house with tables in the courtyard. It specializes in roasts. *Calle Aguilera y Reloj, ☎ 23913. ⊙ 7 PM–midnight.*

$ **La Casa del Vino.** This small, traditional place is popular with Cubans. Reservations are as essential as punctuality: You only have 45 minutes to feast on the offerings of wine and cheese. *Calle Heredia 254.*

DINING AND LODGING

$$$$ **Cubanacán Santiago de Cuba.** In terms of luxury and facilities, the mod-
★ ern Santiago de Cuba has no rival; in terms of service, however, you may be able to do better. The hotel's futuristic design has made it one of Santiago's landmarks. The upstairs rooms and rooftop terrace bar have splendid views of the city and beyond. Meals are served to the accompaniment of excellent musicians. *Av. de las Américas, e/4 y Av. Manduley, ☎ 42654 and 42612, FAX 41756. 270 rooms with bath, air-conditioning, and satellite TV. 2 restaurants, 5 bars, 2 cafeterias, grill, 3 pools, hairdresser, hydromassage, sauna, gymnasium, shop, discotheque, game room, solarium, child care, conference room, safe, car rental, tourist office.*

$$–$$$ **Villa Gaviota Santiago.** Built by a family who made a fortune in the
★ marble business (indeed, marble abounds here), this hotel consists of villas with three to five rooms. The place is situated on one of the city's hills, a little ways from the center. In addition to the usual excursions

offered by most hotel tourist offices, Villa Gaviota has an exclusive outing to the Altura de Malones (Malones Heights), a lookout from which you can see the American base at Guantánamo. The restaurant, Las Acacias, is possibly the best in Santiago and serves various dishes of game—antelope, wild boar, and venison—from Cayo Saetía. *Av. Manduley 502, Reparto Vista Alegre, ☎ 41368. 13 villas with 36 air-conditioned rooms, almost all with bath. Restaurant, bar, pool, shop, tourist office.*

$$ Cubanacán Versalles. The houses and cabins here provide a sense of space. This modern complex is only a few minutes from the airport. *Carretera del Morro, Km 1, Alturas de Versalles, ☎ 91504 and 91014. 46 rooms, 14 cabins, and 1 house, all with bath and air-conditioning. Restaurant, bar, pool, sports facilities, shop, nightclub, video room, safe, car rental.*

$$ Hotel Horizontes Balcón del Caribe. Although this hotel is far from the city center, it is near El Morro fortress and has lovely sea views—perhaps its best feature. *Carretera del Morro, Km 7, ☎ 91011. 96 rooms with bath and air-conditioning. Restaurant, bar, pool, shop, cabaret, tourist office.*

$$ Hotel Horizontes Las Américas. Until the Santiago opened nearby, Las
★ Américas was the only central hotel with modern facilities. The passage of time is evident, but the hotel retains an atmosphere that the Santiago lacks. The restaurant serves good Creole food and there is usually piano music. *Av. de las Américas y General Cebreiro, ☎ 42011 and 42695. 68 rooms with bath and air-conditioning. Restaurant, bar, pool, shop, nightclub, game room, tourist office.*

Another moderately priced establishment is the **Sierramar Delta Hotels Resort** (Playa Sevilla, Santiago de Cuba, ☎ 26436). For truly affordable lodgings, try **Horizonte San Juan** (Carretera a Siboney, Km 1, Santiago de Cuba, ☎ 24274).

Nightlife

Espantasueño. This discotheque in the Hotel Santiago is the most modern one in the city and has videos, light shows, and contemporary music. *Av. de las Américas y M, ☎ 42634. ☉ Daily 8 PM–3 AM.*

Tropicana. Santiago's version of a Havana cabaret offers good musical revues with large casts and the requisite lavish lighting and costumes. In addition to the show there is a dance floor, a piano bar, and a restaurant. *Autopista, Km 1.5.*

FROM GUANTÁNAMO TO BARACOA

More intrepid travelers may enjoy a trip to the province of Guantánamo, in the easternmost part of Cuba. Although the southern part of the province is flat, it becomes abruptly mountainous toward the north and east. Until only a few years ago it was very difficult to reach this area. Baracoa, on the north coast, the first of the cities the Spanish founded on the island, was accessible only by water until the 1970s. Although the area is poorly connected to the rest of the island and has limited amenities for travelers, its wonders make it worth the trek.

Exploring

㉗ Although **Guantánamo,** the eponymous provincial capital, was founded in the 18th century, it's recognized more for its contemporary history involving the nearby United States military base. Make arrangements for organized tours to the **Altura de Malones** (Malones Heights), from which you can see some of the military installations, in Santiago de

Cuba (☞ Villa Gaviota de Santiago *in* Santiago Dining and Lodging, *above*) rather than in Guantánamo itself.

The road to Baracoa is long, but the scenery is often spectacular. As you leave Guantánamo, take a detour onto the road from Puerto Boquerón to Yaretas and the unusual **Zoológico de Piedra** (Stone Zoo). The zoo's inhabitants were carved from stone by Ángel Íñigo, a local peasant, who, some years ago, suddenly decided to sculpt the nearly 100 creatures here.

Return to the road to Baracoa and the start of a long flat stretch beside the sea. This is one of the hottest regions of Cuba, and the countryside is practically desert. The beaches that follow one after another along this route are hard to resist. Among the best are Yateritas—the first one you come to—and Imías, near the town of the same name.

A little beyond Imías, the road heads inland toward mountains that completely fill the horizon. Although it seems impossible that any road could overcome such a formidable barrier, this stretch, known as **La Farola** (the Lamppost) succeeds. It snakes along the wall of mountains for 30 km (19 mi), in some places supported by columns. As you climb, the vegetation changes dramatically. Beyond the pass at Cuchillas de Baracoa you ascend into a dense forest—a striking contrast to the desert flatlands you left behind.

㉘ **Baracoa,** the first of the seven cities Diego Velázquez founded in Cuba (and the only one still sited in its original location), was briefly the country's capital. It sits beside the bay of Porto Santo, the second place Columbus visited on his first voyage to America. The landscape he praised in his diary is much the same today. Indeed, the few surviving descendants of the island's native people live in this region.

The city stretches along the shore from Bahía de la Miel—the Miel is a local river—to the inlet of Porto Santo. There is a fortress at either end, the **Matachín** and **La Punta,** and these are complemented by a third at **Seboruco** (also called Sanguily), atop a hill a short way inland. When Baracoa ceased to be the capital, it began a slow decline that left it in oblivion until the 18th century. Then suddenly, for strategic, geopolitical reasons, Baracoa came into its own. The three fortresses were constructed between 1739 and 1742, making this the island's second most fortified city (Havana holds first place). Today, Seboruco houses the Hotel El Castillo; La Punta is a restaurant; and the Matachín is the municipal museum, which has exhibits on local history from pre-Colombian times to the present. It is also one of a thriving research, documentation, and education center.

Although the majority of its buildings are not very old, Baracoa retains its colonial layout of streets and squares. Definitely worth a visit is the church of **Nuestra Señora de la Asunción de Baracoa** (Our Lady of the Assumption). Inside is the famous **Cruz de la Parra,** the cross that Columbus is supposed to have planted when he set foot in Porto Santo. Research has shown that it is made of uvilla wood, which is native to the Americas, and carbon 14 dating confirms that it is indeed old enough to be the one Columbus fashioned. Its four ends have been covered with silver-plated brass to prevent the faithful from pulling off splinters for souvenirs. Along the seafront runs the **Malecón,** which, after those of Havana and Cienfuegos, is the third-longest pier in Cuba.

Baracoa is a center for traditional arts. Whether in the **Casa de la Trova** or at a private party, you can still hear the *nengón* and the *kiribá,* two of the country's oldest traditional musical instruments. The **Centro de**

Diseño (Design Center) exhibits a collection of handicrafts made exclusively of natural fibers, coconut shells, shells, and such. In the Hotel El Castillo you are likely to find some craftsman selling his wood carvings and naïf paintings.

El Yunque, the square mountain described by Columbus, completely dominates the horizon. It is visible far out to sea, and sailors steer for it on their way into Baracoa. Its forested slopes are the home to several unusual species, and numerous archaeological finds have been made here. The tourist office organizes excursions throughout the area and to the top of the mountain.

From Baracoa there are two possible excursions along the shore. To the west, toward Moa, the pavement ends not far out of town. The road first circles the inlet of Porto Santo, where Columbus anchored. From then on, the coastline is a succession of unspoiled beaches. Some, like **Playa Duaba,** near the airport, are wide and flat, others only slivers of sand shaded by the dense foliage of white and coconut palms and wild grapes. Near the Hotel Porto Santo and the airport stands the **Duaba obelisk,** marking the spot where Antonio Maceo put ashore with 22 companions to join the War of Independence. Twenty kilometers (12 mi) farther along you come to the turnoff to **Maguana,** a small private beach. There, if you wish to escape from the world and enjoy an unspoiled paradise, you can rent the beach and a house that even comes with a cook. On your way back to Baracoa, ask for directions to the turnoff to the **Cuchillas del Toa** (Toa Ridge). The road climbs roughly 2 km (1 mi) to a perfect lookout over an exceptional landscape, with the Toa River flowing out of a distant gorge and snaking its lazy way to the sea.

You can also set out from Baracoa to the east. As soon as you leave town, the road crosses the Miel River. Superstition has it that anyone who swims in this river at midnight will find his or her ideal mate and stay in this land forever. The route continues along the shore, winding along the foot of imposing bluffs that plunge into the sea. To your left is a veritable rosary of beaches—including **Playa de Barigua,** with its spectacular gray sands—their only occupants palm trunks washed in by the waves. At one point the road passes under a natural bridge called the **Túnel de los Alemanes** (Germans' Tunnel). Twenty-five kilometers (16 mi) east of Baracoa is the little village of **Yumurí,** set in one of the region's most impressive landscapes. The Yumurí River flows down out of a canyon whose nearly vertical walls are covered with tropical vegetation. Twenty kilometers (12 mi) later, you reach **La Punta de Maisí** at the easternmost tip of Cuba. The land here is clean and unspoiled.

Dining and Lodging

For details on price categories, *see* the charts *in* On the Road with Fodor's at the front of this guide.

Baracoa

DINING

$ ★ **La Punta.** At this small restaurant in La Punta fortress, you'll find traditional food, music, and handicrafts. *Castillo de la Punta.*

DINING AND LODGING

$$$ **Villa Maguana.** For $300 a day, you can rent this four-bedroom house and have exclusive use of the private beach (☞ *above*). The villa is fully equipped and can sleep eight people. Moreover, breakfast and dinner—prepared by the resident cook—are included. *Playa Maguana.*

$$ **Hotel Horizonte El Castillo.** Its location in the Seboruco fortress makes
★ the Horizonte one of the most interesting accommodations in Cuba.
The view of Baracoa from its terraces is spectacular. *Calle Calixto Gar-
cía,* ☎ *42103,* ℻ *42115 and 42147. 24 rooms with bath and air-con-
ditioning. Restaurant, bar, pool, crafts shop, tourist office.*

$$ **Hotel Horizontes Porto Santo.** This modern hotel stands at the entrance
to the Baracoa Bay (or Porto Santo, as Columbus called it). It occu-
pies the very site where Columbus set foot on land and planted a cross
on December 1, 1492. *Carretera Aeropuerto,* ☎ *43578, 43590, and
43512. 63 rooms with bath and air-conditioning. Restaurant, bar,
pool, sports facilities, boat landing, shop, tourist office.*

 $ **El Hotel La Rusa.** Facing the sea, La Rusa was originally the property
★ of a Russian woman who came to live in this corner of Cuba. It was
completely renovated in 1992 and is a charming option for travelers
on a budget. *Calle Máximo Gómez 161,* ☎ *42102, 43011, or 43570.
13 rooms. Restaurant, bar.*

Guantánamo
DINING AND LODGING

 $ **Guantánamo.** This is a good place to rest on your way between San-
tiago and Baracoa. *Norte 13, at Ahogado, Plaza Mariana Grajales,
Caribe Development,* ☎ *36015. 124 rooms with bath and air-conditioning. Restaurant, bar, pool, shop, nightclub, tourist office.*

5 Portraits of Cuba

Chronology of Cuba

Loving Cuba

CHRONOLOGY OF CUBA

The first colonizers disembarked on the island, arriving from the European continent, 6,000 years ago. The indigenous groups were, fundamentally, three: Tainos, Siboneys and Guanahatabeys.

1492　Christopher Columbus arrives on the island during his initial voyage to the New World.

1511　Diego Velázquez and another 300 men start the conquest of the island, establishing the first permanent settlement at Baracoa.

1515　The Spanish had installed small settlements at Baracoa, Bayamo, Santiago de Cuba, and Puerto Principe (today Camagüey), Sancti Spíritus, Trinidad, and Havana [in its initial site at the southern end of the island]). These were the Siete Villas or Seven Towns founded by Diego Velázquez.

1519　Founding of Havana at its present site, on the northern coast.

1519–21　Because of its strategic position, the "key to the New World"—as the island came to be known—Cuba is used as a base. It was the point of origin for Hernán Cortés in his conquest of Mexico. This function as the supply center for the Spanish fleets on their way to and from the New World was a constant in the history of colonial Cuba.

16th century　The indigenous population—victimized by illness, mistreatment, and confrontations with the Spanish—progressively disappeared until it was practically extinct. Throughout the century, local labor was little by little replaced with black Africans brought in to work on the sugarcane plantations.

17th century　Spain maintains a monopoly on Cuban trade, violated by Cuban producers who supplied contraband to pirates and privateers. Cuba becomes the object of continual attacks from the English, French, and Dutch fleets who dispute control of the West Indies with Imperial Spain. Sugar and tobacco are the principal exports.

1762　The English, with 200 boats and more than 20,000 men, take Havana and take control of the western part of the island.

1763　The Spanish recover Havana and the rest of the occupied territory, exchanging it for Florida.

1775–83　Following the American Revolutionary War and the independence of the former British colonies, Spain authorizes direct trade between Cuba and the United States.

1795　Following the black slaves' anticolonial uprising, thousands of French flee Haiti and settle in eastern Cuba. At the end of the 18th century Cuba's population exceeds 300,000 inhabitants, the majority of them black.

1814–20　During the independence movements of the South American colonies, Cuba undergoes an epoch of economic prosperity.

1818　King Fernando VII concedes free trade, thus accentuating the wealth of Cuba's Creole or Native American aristocracy.

early 19th century　A surge of nationalist sentiment occurs. The ruling class is undecided about whether to fight for independence, to strive for reforms that increase Cuban autonomy without breaking with Imperial Spain, or to pact with the United States of America. Economic development contributes to an increased number of slaves on the island.

1837 Spain excludes Cuban senators from parliament and declares that Cuba will be governed by special laws. Arbitrariness and intolerance are the manifest characteristics of the island's political class.

1843 From this year on there are various rebellions of blacks in the sugar fields.

mid-19th century Certain groups in the United States (including presidents Franklin Pierce and James Buchanan) demonstrate a desire to purchase Cuba from Spain. Between 1850 and 1857 various schemes and subterfuges designed to separate Cuba from Spanish rule emerge, despite Spain's severity in reacting against Cubans favoring annexation.

1857 Annexationist sentiment starts to recede from the political scene. A reformist movement rises up, favoring ample administrative autonomy for the island as well as a constructive opposition party. These proposals are largely ignored.

1868–78 In October 1868, the Creoles, or native Cubans, captained by Manuel Céspedes initiate the first War of Independence in the eastern provinces. The pact of Zanjon (1878) brings the Ten Years War to a close; a period of uneasy peace follows.

1879 General Calixto Garcia and other leaders begin making contacts prior to the renewal of hostilities with Spain.

1880 Slavery is abolished by the Spanish parliament, although, in effect, the slaves continue to work for their masters in return for a minimal monthly salary.

1886 Slavery of any kind is prohibited.

1892 José Martí unifies the independent movement from exile in the United States, where he founds the Cuban Revolutionary Party.

1895 Once again in the eastern provinces, known as the Oriente, armed combat for independence is begun. This time the conflict spreads quickly through the western provinces. Spain mobilizes more than 200,000 men in an attempt to stop the rebellion.

1898 The mysterious explosion of the U.S. warship *Maine,* anchored in Havana harbor, serves as an excuse for a U.S. declaration of war. Under the Treaty of Paris, signed on December 10 with no Cuban representative in attendance, Spain cedes Cuba to the United States along with Puerto Rico and the Philippines.

1899–1902 During this period of United States occupation a constitution is drawn up. The United States imposes the so-called Platt Amendment, allowing U.S. military intervention in the event this is judged to be necessary.

1902 Tomas Estrada Palma becomes the first president of the new republic.

1903 The United States establishes its naval base at Guantánamo.

1909–25 Three presidents govern Cuba over this period, which includes three more U.S. interventions. In 1920 the price of sugar falls, thus ending the period of prosperity begun during World War I. The United States, taking advantage of the economic chaos, gradually acquires numerous tracts of Cuban real estate at low prices until it controls nearly one-fifth of the island.

1925 General Gerardo Machado, leader of the alliance between the liberal and popular parties, is elected in the presidential elections held in May.

1933 Machado, who had been reelected for a second mandate in 1928, is obliged to go into exile as a result of popular reaction to his repressive and dictatorial policies.

1934–40 Colonel Fulgencio Batista imposes and removes presidents until he himself is elected in 1940. Meanwhile, the Platt Amendment is revoked, the Communist Party is legalized, the new constitution approved, and Cuba supports the Allies during World War II.

1944 Grau San Martin, supported by the liberals and the popular socialists, is elected president, defeating the candidate sponsored by Batista.

1952 Carlos Prio Socarras, San Martin's successor, is accused of corruption and Batista takes advantage of the moment, leads a military coup, and imposes an iron-fisted dictatorship.

1953 The insurrection against the Batista dictatorship begins. The assault on the Moncada barracks occurs, directed by the youth leader of the Orthodox Party, Fidel Castro. The assault fails.

1956 Fidel Castro, exiled in Mexico, reorganizes his forces and, with Ernesto Che Guevara, returns to Cuba on the ship *Granma* with 82 men, with whom they fortify a command post in the Sierra Maestra.

1958 After the final battle at Santa Clara, Las Villas, Batista flees the country on December 31. On the following day the guerrillas take Santiago. Seven days later they enter Havana.

1959 Fidel Castro's government initiates agrarian reforms, literacy programs, and the nationalization of the country's wealth.

1961 A group of exiles, with U.S. help under the Kennedy administration, disembarks at the Bay of Pigs. The attempted invasion is a failure.

1962 Cuba is the victim of an economic blockade by the United States begun after the installation of Soviet missiles (removed that same year) on Cuban soil. Thirty-five years later, the blockade continues.

1968 The government nationalizes all private business and requires all nonmanual workers to participate in field work.

1972 Cuba becomes a full participant in the Communist bloc economy, thus further reinforcing its dependency on this group.

1976 The first congress of the Cuban Communist Party is held. The central topics are the new constitution, popular power, and the 1976–80 five-year plan.

1980 Fidel Castro offers amnesty and allows 12,000 Cubans to leave the country.

1989 Cuba signs a new 25-year aid agreement with the Soviet Union at $10 billion annually.

1990 Castro criticizes the changes in the European Eastern bloc while initiating the so-called "Embassy Crisis" with the occupation of the Spanish and Czechoslovakian diplomatic headquarters by Cuban refugees.

1991 U.S. president George Bush asks Russian president Mikhail Gorbachev to cease military aid to Cuba. In addition, the Soviet economic support is reduced. After the frustrated coup d'etat in the

U.S.S.R. and the disintegration of communism in that country, the Cuban regime announces that it will not renounce the Revolution, while asking the population to cooperate in facing the critical economic situation.

1992–93 The economic crisis worsens, especially after the approval of the Torricelli Law in the United States, which stiffens the blockade. On February 24, 1993, Cubans elect, for the first time since the Revolution, deputies to parliament via direct vote. Participation is nearly 97 percent. Economic reforms are begun. Possession of dollars is depenalized and self-employment is legalized along with certain forms of private initiative, while foreign investment and tourism are promoted.

1994 The boat-people crisis explodes in August. Some 35,000 Cubans flee to the United States in fragile seacraft in just over a month. The United States and Cuba reach an agreement in September in order to end the exodus in favor of a minimum quota of 20,000 yearly visas for Cubans who desire to emigrate to the United States. Agricultural and livestock markets subject to the laws of supply and demand are authorized.

1995 Restructuring of the central administration and a reduction of bureaucrats. The authorities, for the first time, permit the sale of real estate to foreign citizens.

1996 Demolition of the light aircraft of the humanitarian organization Hermanos al Rescate (Brothers to the Rescue) by Cuban fighter planes. This act aggravates tensions with the United States. Washington passes the Helms-Burton law, stipulating that the United States will not trade with any other country engaged in commerce with Cuba.

LOVING CUBA

SPANISH FORTUNE-SEEKERS, the so-called "indianos," would return from Cuba with gold watch chains and gold teeth, restore the village shrine to the Holy Virgin, start a school, and promenade their Creole daughters with their dark faces under the shadows of the poplar trees; later, when they were old and rich and widowed, they would marry the most beautiful girl their hometowns had to offer. Others returned defeated or dead of malaria if they were soldiers, but every Spaniard always had a hypothetical uncle in Cuba who would one day return over the rim of the horizon loaded down with wealth, and this was a hope that never faded. Cuba was also a dimension we all carried within us, though now the dream of Cuba is found on the electronic board over the waiting room of any airport where the words LA HABANA wink a green eye indicating that the time to board is now. The dream the traveler carries is to fly to this isle of plenty and to be nourished directly on the modern treasure of freedom in the tropical light while allowing no one the chance to take away that moment of immortality.

Any city whose sound is evanescent constitutes a prolonging of our interior labyrinth, and any country that we fervently desire to visit is already a part of our memory, even though we may not yet have been there. Cuba possesses all of the elements and attributes to bring this myth to life: wondrous beaches, colonial cities, ancient secret barrios thick with African legends. Throughout flows the power of a woman's body along with the din of all desires in the feel of the air, allowing the discovery of Cuba's landscapes in one's own soul and of her hot-blooded inhabitants reclining on some street corner of our bodies like one of so many forms of the pleasure of living.

All of the mystery of Cuba will be revealed if you simply allow yourself to be carried away, the first rule the traveler should follow in order to be happy here. There are very powerful forces, beyond any political or social contingency, that convert a country into an essential part of

human joy: the air, the water, the sounds, the lusty looks, the softness of the lights, the fleshlike folds of the breeze. The traveler's duty is to pass through these elements and to emerge wounded by their memory. This will happen to anyone who arrives in Cuba prepared to discover themselves through the pure forms of existence. For me, one of the most exciting moments of my life occurred in Havana during a twilight, with golden light pouring onto the facades along the Malecon. Or traveling through the sugarcane to Trinidad or Santiago. Or discovering the poetic intimacy that neglect and austerity have left in the hundred layers of scraped plaster on the decrepit mansions of El Vedado, forming squalid color scales in green, pink, yellow and the same hues that in the back streets of old Havana become inflamed when the sun slants in on them until they turn to tunnels of light extracted from a Florentine painting.

All of Cuba's cities are equipped with thousands of columns forming shady atriums under the porticoes, relief from the flaming sun or the tropical showers of midday. Let yourself go: the first obligation in Cuba. You can roll through any of the colonial cities studying expressive faces, grillworks, gestures, penthouses, balconies, ardent bodies, museums, the tumult of people within a vital density perfumed by old sweat. And later, following the itinerary of the perfect tourist awaiting only the dream of a two-week vacation, you stretch out on a beach of very white sand and accept a gift of broiled lobster, the shell reflecting a row of coconut palms and the brilliance of the turquoise sea.

Everything goes by but the genius of a people and the air around it, that light that ends up sculpting the expression of its creatures, the profile of their flesh, the power of their souls. Cuba expresses these gifts openly, and it is the longest trip around oneself to explore the island, becoming one with its peoples and their way of being, friendly souls, expressive and intelligent, enjoyers of life even in hard times, possessed by the furor of living at any cost. I see here a perfect pathway: the air is sweet, the eyes and looks are humid; you are in Cuba. Torpor and a languid weariness of the flesh invade the street corners; fortyish mulattas go by with colorful kerchiefs on their heads, dragging their own bales of guava; young people dance on their hearts in flames, and the traveler struggles under the effects of the rum, the mint and sugar, creating confusion between his own body and the atmosphere, all of which exudes a steamy vapor of humanity.

Those instants I remember of Havana are part of its aesthetic: the golden twilight of Malecon and a sunrise that surprised me sleepless on the hotel terrace. The Havana of dawn was there below, sunken in a layer of mist from which a blaze of fire was gradually emerging on the Cojimar side as the sun rose up behind the bay. From inside the haze, which was a color of mauve and rose, the cupola of the Capitolio building pushed through, the danc-ing of the Giraldilla and the profiles of El Morro fortress and of the Cabana in front of the solid mass of the Punta. The breeze caressed the senses and in the middle of the half light, gold on the Malecon and the smoky dawn was the Cuban night, its deepest treasure, that no indiano was ever able to bring home. Ascension to this paradise is within reach: it is enough to deserve it after having loved Cuba from the bottom of your soul and to fly toward her, not like those ancient indianos in search of riches, but as a novitiate trying to find in the pleasure of the dancing flesh the full and final measure of the human spirit.

— Manuel Vicent

One of Spain's most prestigious essayists and novelists, Manuel Vicent won the Alfaguara prize for the novel with Pascua y Naranjas. He writes regularly for the Madrid daily newspaper *El Pais*.

SPANISH VOCABULARY

Words and Phrases

	English	*Spanish*	*Pronunciation*

Basics

English	Spanish	Pronunciation
Yes/no	Sí/no	see/no
Please	Por favor	pore fah-**vore**
May I?	¿Me permite?	may pair-**mee**-tay
Thank you (very much)	(Muchas) gracias	**moo**-chas **grah**-see-as
You're welcome	De nada	day **nah**-dah
Excuse me	Con permiso	con pair-**mee**-so
Pardon me	¿Perdón?	pair-**dohn**
Could you tell me?	¿Podría decirme?	po-**dree**-ah deh-**seer**-meh
I'm sorry	Lo siento	lo see-**en**-to
Good morning!	¡Buenos días!	**bway**-nohs **dee**-ahs
Good afternoon!	¡Buenas tardes!	**bway**-nahs **tar**-dess
Good evening!	¡Buenas noches!	**bway**-nahs **no**-chess
Goodbye!	¡Adiós!/¡Hasta luego!	ah-dee-**ohss/ah**-stah-**lwe**-go
Mr./Mrs.	Señor/Señora	sen-**yor**/sen-**yohr**-ah
Miss	Señorita	sen-yo-**ree**-tah
Pleased to meet you	Mucho gusto	**moo**-cho **goose**-to
How are you?	¿Cómo está usted?	**ko**-mo es-**tah** oo-**sted**
Very well, thank you.	Muy bien, gracias.	**moo**-ee bee-**en**, grah-see-as
And you?	¿Y usted?	ee oos-**ted**
Hello (on the telephone)	Diga	**dee**-gah

Numbers

1	un, uno	oon, **oo**-no
2	dos	dos
3	tres	tress
4	cuatro	**kwah**-tro
5	cinco	**sink**-oh
6	seis	saice
7	siete	see-**et**-eh
8	ocho	**o**-cho
9	nueve	new-**eh**-vey
10	diez	dee-**es**
11	once	**ohn**-seh
12	doce	**doh**-seh
13	trece	**treh**-seh
14	catorce	ka-**tohr**-seh
15	quince	**keen**-seh

16	dieciséis	dee-**es**-ee-**saice**
17	diecisiete	dee-**es**-ee-see-**et**-eh
18	dieciocho	dee-**es**-ee-**o**-cho
19	diecinueve	**dee-es**-ee-new-**ev**-ah
20	veinte	**vain**-teh
21	veinte y uno/veintiuno	**vain**-te-**oo**-noh
30	treinta	**train**-tah
32	treinta y dos	train-tay-**dohs**
40	cuarenta	kwah-**ren**-tah
43	cuarenta y tres	kwah-**ren**-tay-**tress**
50	cincuenta	seen-**kwen**-tah
54	cincuenta y cuatro	seen-**kwen**-tay **kwah**-tro
60	sesenta	sess-**en**-tah
65	sesenta y cinco	sess-**en**-tay **seen**-ko
70	setenta	set-**en**-tah
76	setenta y seis	set-**en**-tay **saice**
80	ochenta	oh-**chen**-tah
87	ochenta y siete	oh-**chen**-tay see-**yet**-eh
90	noventa	no-**ven**-tah
98	noventa y ocho	no-**ven**-tah-**o**-choh
100	cien	see-**en**
101	ciento uno	see-**en**-toh **oo**-noh
200	doscientos	doh-see-**en**-tohss
500	quinientos	keen-**yen**-tohss
700	setecientos	set-eh-see-**en**-tohss
900	novecientos	no-veh-see-**en**-tohss
1,000	mil	meel
2,000	dos mil	dohs meel
1,000,000	un millón	oon meel-**yohn**

Colors

black	negro	**neh**-groh
blue	azul	ah-**sool**
brown	café	kah-**feh**
green	verde	**ver**-deh
pink	rosa	**ro**-sah
purple	morado	mo-**rah**-doh
orange	naranja	na-**rahn**-hah
red	rojo	**roh**-hoh
white	blanco	**blahn**-koh
yellow	amarillo	ah-mah-**ree**-yoh

Days of the Week

Sunday	domingo	doe-**meen**-goh
Monday	lunes	**loo**-ness
Tuesday	martes	**mahr**-tess
Wednesday	miércoles	me-**air**-koh-less
Thursday	jueves	hoo-**ev**-ess
Friday	viernes	vee-**air**-ness
Saturday	sábado	**sah**-bah-doh

Months

January	enero	eh-**neh**-roh
February	febrero	feh-**breh**-roh
March	marzo	**mahr**-soh
April	abril	ah-**breel**
May	mayo	**my**-oh
June	junio	**hoo**-nee-oh
July	julio	**hoo**-lee-oh
August	agosto	ah-**ghost**-toh
September	septiembre	sep-tee-**em**-breh
October	octubre	oak-**too**-breh
November	noviembre	no-vee-**em**-breh
December	diciembre	dee-see-**em**-breh

Useful Phrases

Do you speak English?	¿Habla usted inglés?	**ah**-blah oos-**ted** in-**glehs**
I don't speak Spanish	No hablo español	no **ah**-bloh es-pahn-**yol**
I don't understand (you)	No entiendo	no en-tee-**en**-doh
I understand (you)	Entiendo	en-tee-**en**-doh
I don't know	No sé	no seh
I am American/British	Soy americano (americana)/ inglés(a)	soy ah-meh-ree-**kah**-no (ah-meh-ree-**kah**-nah)/ in-**glehs** (ah)
What's your name?	¿Cómo se llama usted?	koh-mo seh **yah**-mah oos-**ted**
My name is . . .	Me llamo . . .	may **yah**-moh
What time is it?	¿Qué hora es?	keh **o**-rah es?
It is one, two, three . . . o'clock.	Es la una. . . . Son las dos, tres	es la **oo**-nah/sohn-lahs dohs, tress
Yes, please/No, thank you	Sí, por favor/No, gracias	**see** pohr fah-**vor**/no **grah**-see-us
How?	¿Cómo?	**koh**-mo?
When?	¿Cuándo?	**kwahn**-doh?
This/Next week	Esta semana/ la semana que entra	**es**-teh seh-**mah**-nah/ lah seh-**mah**-nah keh **en**-trah
This/Next month	Este mes/el próximo mes	**es**-teh mehs/el **proke**-see-mo mehs
This/Next year	Este año/el año que viene	**es**-teh **ahn**-yo/el **ahn**-yo keh vee-**yen**-ay
Yesterday/today/ tomorrow	Ayer/hoy/mañana	ah-**yehr**/oy/mahn-**yah**-nah
This morning/ afternoon	Esta mañana/ tarde	**es**-tah mahn-**yah**-nah/**tar**-deh
Tonight	Esta noche	**es**-tah **no**-cheh
What?	¿Qué?	keh?

What is it?	¿Qué es esto?	keh es **es**-toh
Why?	¿Por qué?	pore **keh**
Who?	¿Quién?	kee-**yen**
Where is . . . ?	¿Dónde está . . . ?	**dohn**-deh es-**tah**
the train station?	la estación del tren?	la es-tah-see-**on** del **train**
the subway station?	la estación del Tren subterráneo?	la es-ta-see-**on** del-trehn soob-tair-**ron**-a-o
the bus stop?	la parada del autobus?	la pah-**rah**-dah del oh-toh-**boos**
the post office?	la oficina de correos?	la oh-fee-**see**-nah deh koh-**reh**-os
the bank?	el banco?	el **bahn**-koh
the . . . hotel?	el hotel . . . ?	el oh-**tel**
the store?	la tienda . . . ?	la tee-**en**-dah
the cashier?	la caja?	la **kah**-hah
the . . . museum?	el museo . . . ?	el moo-**seh**-oh
the hospital?	el hospital?	el ohss-pee-**tal**
the elevator?	el ascensor?	el ah-**sen**-sohr
the bathroom?	el baño?	el **bahn**-yoh
Here/there	Aquí/allá	ah-**key**/ah-**yah**
Open/closed	Abierto/cerrado	ah-bee-**er**-toh/ ser-**ah**-doh
Left/right	Izquierda/derecha	iss-key-**er**-dah/ dare-**eh**-chah
Straight ahead	Derecho	dare-**eh**-choh
Is it near/far?	¿Está cerca/lejos?	es-**tah sehr**-kah/ **leh**-hoss
I'd like . . . room	Quisiera . . . un cuarto/una habitación	kee-see-ehr-aha oon **kwahr**-toh/ **oo**-nah ah-bee-tah-see-**on**
the key	la llave	lah **yah**-veh
a newspaper	un periódico	oon pehr-ee-**oh**-dee-koh
a stamp	un sello de correo	oon **seh**-yo deh koh-**reh**-oh
I'd like to buy . . .	Quisiera comprar . . .	kee-see-**ehr**-ah kohm-**prahr**
cigarette	cigarrillo	ce-ga-**ree**-yoh
matches	cerillos	ser-**ee**-ohs
a dictionary	un diccionario	oon deek-see-oh-**nah**-ree-oh
soap	jabón	hah-**bohn**
sunglasses	gafas de sol	**ga**-fahs deh sohl

suntan lotion	loción bronceadora	loh-see-**ohn** brohn-seh-ah-**do**-rah
a map	un mapa	oon **mah**-pah
a magazine	una revista	**oon**-ah reh-**veess**-tah
paper	papel	pah-**pel**
envelopes	sobres	**so**-brehs
a postcard	una tarjeta postal	**oon**-ah tar-**het**-ah post-**ahl**
How much is it?	¿Cuánto cuesta?	**kwahn**-toh **kwes**-tah
It's expensive/ cheap	Está caro/barato	es-**tah kah**-roh/ bah-**rah**-toh
A little/a lot	Un poquito/ mucho	oon poh-**kee**-toh/ **moo**-choh
More/less	Más/menos	mahss/**men**-ohss
Enough/too much/too little	Suficiente/ demasiado/ muy poco	soo-fee-see-**en**-teh/ deh-mah-see-**ah**-doh/ **moo**-ee poh-**koh**
Telephone	Teléfono	tel-**ef**-oh-no
Telegram	Telegrama	teh-leh-**grah**-mah
I am ill	Estoy enfermo(a)	es-**toy** en-**fehr**-moh(mah)
Please call a mehdoctor	Por favor llame a un medico	pohr fah-**vor ya**-ah oon **med**-ee-koh
Help!	¡Auxilio! ¡Ayuda! ¡Socorro!	owk-**see**-lee-oh/ ah-**yoo**-dah/ soh-**kohr**-roh
Fire!	¡Incendio!	en-**sen**-dee-oo
Caution!/Look out!	¡Cuidado!	kwee-**dah**-doh

On the Road

Avenue	Avenida	ah-ven-**ee**-dah
Broad, tree-lined boulevard	Bulevar	boo-leh-**var**
Fertile plain	Vega	**veh**-gah
Highway	Carretera	car-reh-**ter**-ah
Mountain pass, Street	Puerto Calle	poo-**ehr**-toh **cah**-yeh
Waterfront promenade	Rambla	**rahm**-blah
Wharf	Embarcadero	em-bar-cah-**deh**-ro

In Town

Cathedral	Catedral	cah-teh-**dral**
Church	Templo/Iglesia	**tem**-plo/ee-**glehs**-see-ah

City hall	Casa de gobierno	kah-sah deh go-bee-**ehr**-no
Door, gate	Puerta portón	poo-**ehr**-tah por-**ton**
Entrance/exit	Entrada/salida	en-**trah**-dah/sah-**lee**-dah
Inn, rustic bar, restaurant	Taverna	tah-**vehr**-nahor
Main square	Plaza principal	plah-thah prin-see-**pahl**
Market	Mercado	mer-**kah**-doh
Neighborhood	Barrio	**bahr**-ree-o
Traffic circle	Glorieta	glor-ee-**eh**-tah
Wine cellar, wine bar, or wine shop	Bodega	boh-**deh**-gah

Dining Out

A bottle of . . .	Una botella de . . .	**oo**-nah bo-**teh**-yah deh
A cup of . . .	Una taza de . . .	**oo**-nah **tah**-thah deh
A glass of . . .	Un vaso de . . .	oon **vah**-so deh
Ashtray	Un cenicero	oon sen-ee-**seh**-roh
Bill/check	La cuenta	lah **kwen**-tah
Bread	El pan	el pahn
Breakfast	El desayuno	el deh-sah-**yoon**-oh
Butter	La mantequilla	lah man-teh-**key**-yah
Cheers!	¡Salud!	sah-**lood**
Cocktail	Un aperitivo	oon ah-pehr-ee-**tee**-voh
Dinner	La cena	lah **seh**-nah
Dish	Un plato	oon **plah**-toh
Menu of the day	Menú del día	meh-**noo** del **dee**-ah
Enjoy!	¡Buen provecho!	bwehn pro-**veh**-cho
Fixed-price menu	Menú fijo o turistico	meh-**noo fee**-hoh oh too-**ree**-stee-coh
Fork	El tenedor	el ten-eh-**dor**
Is the tip included?	¿Está incluida la propina?	es-**tah** in-cloo-**ee**-dah lah pro-**pee**-nah
Knife	El cuchillo	el koo-**chee**-yo
Large portion of savory snacks	Raciónes	rah-see-**oh**-nehs
Lunch	La comida	lah koh-**mee**-dah
Menu	La carta, el menú	lah **cart**-ah, el meh-**noo**
Napkin	La servilleta	lah sehr-vee-**yet**-ah
Pepper	La pimienta	lah pee-me-**en**-tah

Please give me	Por favor déme	pore fah-**vor** **deh**-meh
Salt	La sal	lah sahl
Savory snacks	Tapas	**tah**-pahs
Spoon	Una cuchara	**oo**-nah koo-**chah**-rah
Sugar	El azúcar	el ah-**thu**-kar
Waiter!/Waitress!	¡Por favor Señor/Señorita!	pohr fah-**vor** sen-**yor**/sen-yor-**ee**-tah

INDEX

X = *restaurant*, 🏨 = *hotel*

128